The

Chornovil

Papers

The

Chornovil

Papers

Compiled by
Vyacheslav Chornovil

McGraw-Hill

New York   Toronto   London
Sydney   Johannesburg   Mexico
Panama

The Chornovil Papers

Copyright © Ukrainian National Federation of Canada Incorporated, 1968. All rights reserved. No part of this publication may be reproduced, stored in a retrieval system, or transmitted in any form or by any means, electronic, mechanical, photocopying, recording, or otherwise, without the prior written permission of McGraw-Hill Company of Canada Limited.

1 2 3 4 5 6 7 8 9 0   McB   4 3 2 1 0 9 8

94971

Library of Congress Catalog Card No. 68-28045

Printed and bound in Canada

Contents

v

Foreword

Few Americans realize that the Soviet Union is a multinational society. Fifty per cent of the Soviet people is non-Russian. Among these, the Ukrainians are the most numerous and potentially the most powerful. It is not inconceivable that in the next several decades the nationality problem will become politically more important in the Soviet Union than the racial issue has become in the United States.

If that happens, it will combine the current quest for freedom of the intellectual community with a greater self-assertiveness of the non-Russian peoples. While it is impossible to predict where these demands may lead, and some may merely express a desire for greater autonomy within the framework of the Soviet Union, the combination of literary ferment and national self-assertion will be a most potent one. Chornovil's manuscript is important precisely because it focuses attention on that actual as well as potential issue. It is also a deeply moving human document, and the element of human tragedy which it expresses transcends even the most important political issues.

Zbigniew Brzezinski
Director, Research Institute
on Communist Affairs
Columbia University

Introduction

BY

FREDERICK C. BARGHOORN

YALE UNIVERSITY

Although he was pleased to be asked to write an introduction
to the Chornovil papers, published in this volume, this writer
confesses that he entertained some reservations about under-
taking the task. The documents published herein relate to the
conflict over issues òf cultural freedom and civil liberties in
the last years between a number of dissenting Ukrainian intellectuals, mostly young writers, scholars and teachers, and the
government of the Ukrainian Soviet Socialist Republic, one of
the fifteen constituent republics of the Union of Soviet Socialist Republics. The dispute ultimately concerns policies for
Ukraine which are made in Moscow, capital both of the
dominant Russian republic of the Soviet Union and of the
whole of this vast multi-national state. Why, this writer asked
himself, should a scholar and citizen of a country with serious
racial and nationality problems of its own run any risk whatever of involving himself in the sensitive and infinitely complex problem of the political, social and cultural situation of
the Ukrainian people in the USSR? After he had read these
materials, assembled by Vyacheslav Chornovil, the young
Ukrainian journalist, now imprisoned because of his refusal
to aid and abet the Ukrainian authorities in what he regarded
as illegal actions, contrary to the laws and constitution both
of the Ukrainian Republic and of the USSR, this writer's
doubts were overbalanced by a feeling that a useful service to
scholarship and public information could be performed by an

objective, impartial introduction that might help to place the startling events described in this book in a relevant political and historical context.

The Ukrainian population of the Soviet Union numbers some forty million; of these about thirty million reside on the territory of the Ukrainian Soviet Socialist Republic, which according to the Constitution of the USSR is one of fifteen sovereign union republics, endowed with freedom to secede from the Soviet Union, to enter into relations with foreign states, to conclude agreements and exchange diplomatic and consular representatives, and the like. As is well known, in 1945, on the demand of Joseph Stalin, the Ukrainian and the Byelorussian Republics became members of the United Nations. Economically, Soviet Ukraine is highly developed. In terms of *per capita* production of steel, coal and other sinews of industrial power Ukraine stands roughly on a level with such advanced Western European nations as West Germany or France. The official Soviet position, undoubtedly accepted by many citizens of the Ukrainian Soviet Republic, is that Soviet policies are responsible for the economic advancement which has been achieved in what was, in 1917, a relatively backward, largely agricultural region. Like the citizens of the other Soviet republics, the people of Ukraine are guaranteed by Article 125 of the Soviet Constitution freedom of speech, press, assembly and even of street processions and demonstrations.

Obviously, however, the political authorities in Moscow and in Kiev, the capital of the Ukrainian Republic, do not fully share the perspectives on cultural and political life in Ukraine today which guide the actions of the writers, journalists, teachers, scientists and other intellectuals who have in recent years been subjected by the hundreds, apparently, to police surveillance and harassment, and by the scores to secret trials and sentences to "corrective labor camps" located, be it noted, on the territory of the Russian rather than of the Ukrainian Republic. Clearly, the charges against Chornovil and those whose cause he pleads are flimsy in terms of the rule of law as it is understood in Western democracies. They range from reading or indeed merely possessing pre-1917 Russian or recent American and Canadian Ukrainian-language publications through alleged "misuse" of the poetry of Taras Shevchenko, the great nineteenth-century Ukrainian painter and poet, to opposition to Moscow's abolition, since 1958, of compulsory instruction of the children of Ukrainian parents in the Ukrainian language. Interestingly enough, however, the dissident Ukrainian intellectuals defend their actions not in terms of "bourgeois" principles but in terms of Leninism and the Soviet Constitution. They argue that both the laws and the procedures employed against them by the KGB (Soviet security police) and the courts violate what they perceive, or at least profess to perceive, as Lenin's conception of the rights of all peoples to cultural freedom and civil liberties. It should be noted that in their defense of legality and constitutionality the Ukrainian dissident intellectuals are employing a strategy and defending principles very similar to those upheld by many distinguished Russian intellectuals, such as the writer Alexander Solzhenitsyn, who has demanded the abolition of censorship in the Soviet Union on the grounds that it is unconstitutional. Indeed, it might be argued that the most important aspect of the struggle for cultural freedom in Ukraine is not the effort of a segment of the Ukrainian Soviet intelligentsia to defend the Ukrainian national heritage, but, rather, the contribution Ukrainian intellectuals are making to the nationwide fight for freedom of expression and civil rights now being waged with increasing vigor by liberal intellectuals in many parts of the USSR. The community of interests among Soviet intellectuals of various national backgrounds needs to be emphasized. This writer ventures to suggest that although the preservation of the Ukrainian cultural heritage and language are central features of the outlook of many young Ukrainian intellectuals, the latter perceive themselves as struggling, not against the Russian nation and probably not against socialist principles, but rather against dictatorship and the police state.

Unfortunately, the rights and freedoms guaranteed by the Soviet Constitution are still nullified by some of the most basic facts of Soviet political life. Although on paper the Soviet Union is a federal state, in practice it is a rigidly centralized dictatorship, in which control is exercised by the Communist Party of the Soviet Union, a national rather than a federative organization, with headquarters in Moscow. To be sure, the party's rigid control over all aspects of policy has been increasingly challenged in recent years by liberal writers and members of other professional or even bureaucratic groups. However, the party leadership still holds and ruthlessly wields the preponderance of power in Soviet society, and applies it with particular force in the sensitive area of nationality policy and problems. Although since the death of Stalin persuasion has bulked larger and coercion smaller in the Kremlin's arsenal of political controls, the weapon of terror was never repudiated in principle or abandoned in practice even during the most liberal phases of the post-Stalin era. Since the last years of Khrushchev's leadership and even more so since Khrushchev's ouster in October, 1964, there has been a revival of the prestige and perhaps of the power of the KGB. In particular, the political authorities in Moscow appear to have instructed the KGB to suppress intellectual dissent. The decision to resort to coercion against dissenting intellectuals appears to have been made in 1965 and its most dramatic manifestation was the rigged trial of the writers Sinyavski and Daniel early in 1966. As has been the case in previous periods of heightened repression, Ukraine was a major target of the post-Khrushchev drive against dissenting intellectuals.

In order to understand why this should be the case it is necessary to review briefly the political and cultural history of Ukraine. In 1654, the elected Hetman, or leader, of the Ukrainians, Bohdan Khmelnytsky, concluded an agreement with representatives of the Russian tsar Aleksei, which could be and was subsequently interpreted either as an alliance between two independent states or as the submission of Ukraine to Moscow. Ukraine was, in practice, autonomous until the region of Peter the Great, who abolished the hetmanate in retaliation against the support given by Hetman Mazepa to the Swedish King Charles xii, in the latter's war against Peter. As a result of the partitions of Poland between Russia, Austria and Prussia in the period of the eighteenth century, most of Ukraine, with the notable exception of the important western province of Galicia, came under Russian rule. In Galicia, Austrian rule provided for considerably more political and cultural autonomy and personal freedom than was enjoyed by the Ukrainians living under Russian rule. In time, the political outlook of the Galician (Western) Ukrainians was to become somewhat different from that of the Eastern Ukrainians living in the Russian empire. The Galicians developed a more intense and aggressive national consciousness than did their Eastern co-nationals. In the development of differences between Eastern and Western Ukrainians, the fact that the majority of the Western Ukrainians belonged to the Uniate, or Greek Catholic, Rite, under the Pope, while most Eastern Ukrainians were members of the Russian Orthodox, or Synodal Church, played an important role.

Partly under influences emanating from the West in general and from Galicia in particular, the Ukrainians of the Russian Empire began in the first half of the nineteenth century to develop a national consciousness and to some extent a desire for political self-determination. As in the case of other nations, a formative role in the development of Ukrainian national consciousness was played by writers, especially by the great national poet, Taras Shevchenko. Later, especially in the Soviet period, differences over the interpretation of the Shevchenko heritage were to divide Ukrainians from Russians and in particular those Ukrainians who advocated separate national statehood for Ukraine from those who favored autonomy within a Russian state, whether it be a communist or a non-communist state. Shevchenko, who was born a serf but liberated through the efforts of a wealthy Russian patron, was severely persecuted by the tsarist government for his membership in the radical Society of Cyril and Methodius. He thus acquired a halo of martyrdom, which endeared him to members of very different political movements, including Ukrainian nationalists and Lenin's bolsheviks. To this day disputes regarding his political and cultural views rage.

Throughout the nineteenth century, and in particular after the tsarist government inaugurated reactionary policies of russification of non-Russian nationalities about 1880, increasingly vigorous Ukrainian aspirations for cultural freedom were harshly suppressed by St. Petersburg. For the most part, until the twentieth century, Russian intellectuals, especially conservative ones, were hostile to or at best indifferent toward Ukrainian aspirations. However, some Russians, such as the famous Russian radical thinker Alexander Herzen, sympathized with Ukrainian aspirations for freedom. Herzen praised the Ukrainians for their love of liberty and expressed sympathy for them in their "enslavement" at the hands of the Russians. With the growth of radical and revolutionary movements in the quarter century before the collapse of the Russian Empire in 1917, some revolutionaries, in particular Lenin, came to realize the explosive potential of national aspirations in a state in which the dominant Russians constituted slightly less than half of the total population. Lenin advocated the right of self-determination, and of political separation, for the non-Russian peoples of the tsarist empire. However, he subordinated national and cultural aspirations to the Marxist-inspired concept of the class struggle of the workers and poor peasants against capitalism. Essentially, Lenin was a centralist as far as political power in Russia was concerned and an internationalist revolutionary in world politics. Stalin, who cast himself in the role of the continuator of Lenin's role, could therefore feel justified in ruthlessly suppressing all aspirations and activities of the Western Ukrainians or of other non-Russian nationalities which he chose to regard as imcompatible with the interests of the "dictatorship of the proletariat."

When Soviet power was established in Russia in 1917-1921, Galicia was incorporated in the revived Polish state. The cultural and political aspirations of the Western Ukrainians clashed sharply with the integral nationalism of the Polish state and its ruling elite. Although most Western Ukrainians remained Catholic in religion and fiercely nationalist in politics, a considerable number were attracted to communism. Like other national conflicts in the new Poland, that between Ukrainians and Poles weakened the Polish state and helped to pave the way for the eventual sovietization of Poland. In the meantime, under Lenin and for a few years even under Stalin, relatively liberal policies were followed in the USSR toward national minorities. Realizing that extreme centralism and lack of sensitivity to national consciousness would be disruptive and would also damage the image of Soviet Russia abroad, Stalin proclaimed the seemingly liberal but highly flexible slogan, "National in Form, Socialist in Content." However, angered by the development in Ukraine of what might be termed cultural national communism, as represented, for example, by the writer Mykola Khvylovy, Stalin began about 1927 to pursue increasingly repressive policies with regard to Ukrainian aspirations for cultural autonomy. In 1930, the Soviet secret police arrested a number of Ukrainian intellectuals on false charges of having organized a separatist national liberation movement. During the period of collectivization and purges in the 1930s, Ukrainians suffered more severely than did the Russians at the hands of the police. In part, this may have been because the Ukrainian peasantry, among whom the communal and collectivist traditions which were highly developed in the Russian peasantry did not exist, resisted collectivization much more vigorously than did the Russians. The repression visited upon the Ukrainians in the 1930s, and in particular the effects of the famine which resulted from Stalin's policies and caused the deaths of several million people, left a legacy of hatred of the Soviet authority in Ukraine, but these events may also have convinced perhaps a majority of Ukrainian people that resistance to Moscow was useless. Beginning in the late 1930s, instruction in the Russian language became compulsory for all Ukrainian schoolchildren. At the same time, Stalin sought to create a new "Soviet patriotism" designed to weld all of the peoples of the USSR into a new Soviet nation, devoted to him and to the communist cause.

It is important to realize that, repressive as it was in many respects, Soviet policy in Ukraine, as elsewhere, had important positive aspects which had great appeal for many Ukrainians, especially those prepared to merge their identity into the USSR as a whole. These included very rapid industrial development, enormously increased access for all social classes, even including the peasantry, to education, and a very high degree of social mobility. Many able and ambitious Ukrainians of working class or peasant origin made brilliant careers for themselves as was indicated for example, by the prominent role of Ukrainian commanders in the Soviet armed forces during World War II.

One result of World War II was the bringing of the Ukrainians of Galicia and also of Sub-Carpathian Ukraine, formerly part of Czechoslovakia, within the Ukrainian Soviet Socialist

Republic. Like other parts of the Soviet Union, Ukraine, and especially the newly acquired Ukrainian territories, experienced severe purges in the last years of Stalin's rule. To be sure, the Ukrainians came through the war without suffering the total exile and deportation which was visited by the security police upon the Kalmyks, the Chechens, the Volga Germans, and other peoples, but it is noteworthy that Khrushchev, in his secret speech at the Twentieth Party Congress in 1956, asserted that if Stalin did not deport the Ukrainians it was only because there were too many of them and not enough territory to deport them to. In the post-Stalin era, up to about 1958, Moscow's controls over the non-Russian nationalities were relaxed. There was a resurgence of use of the native languages in education and administration. Formerly banned literary productions, such as the poem, "Love Ukraine," by the patriotic poet Sosyura, were republished. However, in 1958-59, Russification policies were again accelerated in the schools and political leaders who had apparently opposed such policies and generally sought to champion minority interests against Moscow-instituted centralizing measures were removed from office. It is widely believed that Khrushchev sacrificed his close political associate A. I. Kirichenko, an Ukrainian, to great Russian displeasure over Kirichenko's opposition to increasing Russian immigration in and economic penetration of Ukraine. The program of the Communist Party of the Soviet Union, adopted in 1961, while it promised the continued economic and cultural development of all the peoples of the Soviet Union, seemed to strike a centralist, antipluralist note, especially in its statement that the boundaries between the constituent republics were increasingly losing their former significance and in its emphasis upon the significance for all of the Soviet peoples of Russian language and culture.

Today, although Brezhnev, a Russian who began his political career in Ukraine, and Podgorny, an Ukrainian, occupy two of the three top political positions, the outlook for political and cultural freedom for Soviet Ukrainians appears weak. However, in spite of and partly because of "Leninist nationality policy," it does not appear likely that Ukrainian national consciousness will be obliterated in the foreseeable future.

WESTERN USSR

Scale of Miles
0   100   200   300   400

Boundaries

━━━ USSR
━·━ Union Republics
━━ Autonomous Soviet
      Socialist Republics

BARENTS SEA

Murmansk

Arkhangelsk

KOMI ASSR

FINLAND

Leningrad

ESTONIAN SSR

Riga

LATVIAN SSR

UDMURT ASSR

RUSSIAN SFSR

MARI ASSR

Kazan

TATAR ASSR

BASHKIR ASSR

LITHUANIAN SSR

Vilnius

Minsk

Moscow

MORDOVIAN ASSR

Kubyshev

POLAND

BYELORUSSIAN SSR

L'viv

Kiev

Saratov

CZECHOSLOVAKIA

KAZAKH SSR

HUNGARY

UKRAINIAN SSR

Stalingrad

RUMANIA

Odessa

Rostov

CRIMEA

BULGARIA

BLACK SEA

CAUCASUS

CASPIAN SEA

GEORGIAN SSR

Tbilisi

Baku

TURKEY

ARMENIAN SSR

Yerevan

AZERBAIJAN SSR

IRAN

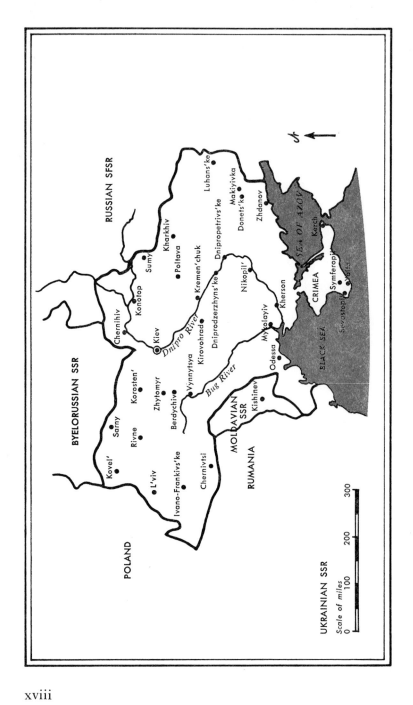

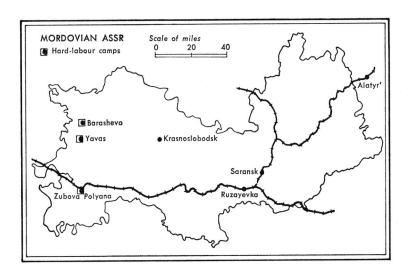

MORDOVIAN ASSR
C Hard-labour camps

Scale of miles
0   20   40

Alatyr'

C Barashevo

C Yavas   ● Krasnoslobodsk

Saransk

Zubova Polyana   Ruzayevka

About Vyacheslav Chornovil

Born in 1938, Vyacheslav Maksymovych Chornovil grew up in Cherkasy province of the Ukrainian SSR. After graduating from the Faculty of Journalism at the University of Kiev in 1960, he worked as an editor in the L'viv television studio and on the editorial staff of several publications.

When in the fall of 1965 Chornovil was assigned to cover the trials of several Ukrainian intellectuals, he was outraged by the court's disregard of Soviet law. And when he himself was summoned to appear as a witness at a secret trial, he refused, knowing that his refusal could cost him his freedom. The petition that follows testifies to Chornovil's courage and dignity in the face of certain arrest and imprisonment for his beliefs.

The Misfortune of Intellect, orginally published in Paris in the Ukrainian language, is an extraordinary collection of the letters, petitions, and diaries of twenty of those deported to Mordovian hard-labour camps. The documents, compiled by Chornovil and smuggled to the West a few pages at a time, were published on the same day that Chornovil was sentenced to one and a half years of hard labour in the Mordovian camps.

Part I

*The
Petition
of
Vyacheslav
Chornovil*

To:
Public Prosecutor of the
Ukrainian Soviet Socialist Republic,
Head of the Supreme Court of the Ukrainian SSR,
Chairman of the State Security Committee[1]
at the Council of Ministers of the Ukrainian SSR.

I am not asking you for anything. Numerous enquiries, demands, and intercessions have crashed against the cold wall of your indifference. Morose silence was your answer to Lenin prizewinner M. Stel'makh, Shevchenko prizewinners A. Malyshko and H. Mayboroda, world-renowned aircraft designer O. Antonov, motion-picture producer S. Paradzhanov, composers P. Mayboroda and V. Koreyko, and to writers L. Serpilin, L. Kostenko, and I. Drach. They asked for very little — publicity and an open trial for those arrested in Kiev, L'viv, Ivano-Frankivs'ke, and Ternopil'. You received appeals from a large group of over seventy people: writers, scientists, students, and workmen. They did not want much either: only to be present at the trials of their friends, comrades, acquaintances, and relatives. They were the ones the police ousted from the hallway of the building where secret punishment was meted out to Yaroslav Hevrych, the student of the Kiev Institute of Medicine. Many of them were also surrounded inside the L'viv regional court building by policemen and soldiers and kept under arrest, while the court, in secrecy, pronounced its sentence over the Horyn' brothers. Mothers, wives, and children spent many long months longing to at least glimpse their sons, husbands, or fathers who languished behind bars.

The orgy of searches and interrogations still makes the Ukrainian intelligentsia shudder, and makes it impossible for

---

1 The KGB, formerly MVD, NKVD, GPU, and Cheka (transl. note).

The Petition of

many of its members to do creative work in peace and quiet. You are apathetic to human tragedies, to the demoralizing effect of fear, which like a slimy serpent, creeps into the lives of many a Ukrainian family. For you, it would seem, only the law is omnipresent. So let us take a look, from the point of view of socialist legality, at what is happening nowadays in Ukraine. Today we have sufficient material for drawing conclusions. But I am not speaking out because I hope to alleviate the lot of the prisoners and convicts. You have already weaned the people from such naive expectations. But not to disclose today my own attitude towards what is taking place would mean my becoming a taciturn participant in the wanton disregard of socialist legality.

REVIVAL OF TERROR OR OF JUSTICE?

The Soviet court of law must not be engaged in the revival of terror. Its function is to mete out just punishment for crimes and to re-educate the criminals. A law student learns all about the humanity of Soviet justice in his first course — the law states: "In applying the measures of criminal punishment, the court not only punishes the offenders, but it also aims at their correction and re-education." (The Law on the Judicial System of the Ukrainian ssr, Article 3.)

During recent years it has been stated that there will be the widest possible participation of the general public in the re-education of people who violate the laws (citizens' courts, releases on bail, citizens acting as prosecutors and defenders at judicial investigations, etc.). Article 20 of the Criminal Procedure Code [cpc] of the Ukr. ssr not only guarantees the publicity of a court trial (with minor, clearly specified exceptions), but also emphasizes the necessity, for the purpose of augmenting the educational role of the court trials, of "the widespread practice of holding trials directly at enterprises, construction sites, on state and collective farms, with the participation, whenever necessary, of prosecutors and public defenders." The law guarantees a thorough, complete, and objective investigation of all the circumstances pertaining to

Vyacheslav Chornovil   3

all cases and envisages the punishments of investigators, judges, and other officials who seek convictions with the aid of violence, threats, or blackmail. The law clearly defines the procedural rules which ensure the rights of a suspect, or of the accused, guarantee respect for his dignity, and give him a chance to prove his innocence.

Finally, and this is particularly important, the law makes it obligatory for the investigative branch, the prosecutor's office, and the court "to reveal the conditions which contributed to the commission of the crime and to take measures, through the appropriate authorities, for their elimination . . . [and] to make wide use of the public's assistance in uncovering and eliminating causes and conditions which are conducive to the commission of offences . . ." (Article 23, cpc, Ukr. ssr). Let's say that the current interest in foreign Ukrainian publications and in anonymous handwritten literature is connected with acute dissatisfaction with present-day violations of Leninist nationality policy, accompanied by minor and major discriminatory measures against the national language, culture, etc. Having noticed this, the servants of Themis should not fail to question the Party and state authorities about the real grounds that breed this sort of sentiment and lead to acts that the criminal code defines as criminal.

I base my remarks about violations of the elementary principles of justice on a number of source materials, most of which I append hereto (in copies):

1. The enquiry of M. Stel'makh, A. Malyshko, and H. Mayboroda addressed to the cc cpu [Central Committee of the Communist Party of Ukraine] about the arrests.

2. The appeal for publicity and an open judicial examination, sent to the cc cpu and the Council of Ministers of the Ukr. ssr by a group of intellectuals.

3. The appeal to the Public Prosecutor of the Ukrainian ssr, and to the Chairman of the State Security Committee at the Council of Ministers of the Ukrainian ssr, for the public's admission to trials (78 signatures).

4. The appeal from a group of artists to the Supreme Court of the Ukrainian ssr motivated by the sentence passed on the teacher, Ozerny.

The Petition of

5. The appeal from writers residing in L'viv to the Regional Court, offering bail for V.[?]

6. Two complaints to the Public Prosecutor of the Ukrainian SSR from artist A. Hors'ka regarding the violation of legal procedure regulating preliminary investigation and trial.

7. The statement by V. Chornovil to the CC CPU about the spreading of provocative rumours.

8. The decision to search the living quarters of V. Chornovil, the official report on that search, two complaints to the KGB and one to the court about the illegal removal of old-edition books.

9. The letter to the First Secretary of the CC CPU from P. Skochko, literary columnist for the newspaper *Radyans'ka Ukraina* [Soviet Ukraine], and the notes taken by him at the trial of Ozerny in Ivano-Frankivs'ke.

10. The verdict recorded in the courtroom in the case of Y. Hevrych, the Kiev University student.

11. Short notes about the first day of the trial of M. Masyutko, taken at the door of the courtroom.

12. The statement of N. Svitlychna about her refusal to have a lawyer.

13. A telegram from N. Svitlychna to the Presidium of the Twenty-third Congress of the CPSU [Communist Party of the Soviet Union].

14. The materials on the case of S. Karavans'ky: his appeal to the Public Prosecutor of the Ukrainian SSR and the articles *About One Political Error* and *Trylyky* [Triple-faced] from the newspaper *Chornomors'ka komuna* [Black-Sea Commune] of the 21st of September, 1965; a copy of the document about his release from prison (dated the 19th of December, 1960); his appeal to Deputy M. Stel'makh about the illegality of the twenty-five-year term of imprisonment and his repeated imprisonment without investigation; the appeal to M. Stel'makh from Karavans'ky's wife; Karavans'ky's appeal for a libel suit against the author of the article, *Trylyky*.

15. Personal impressions from interrogations, confrontation with M. Osadchy, trials of Hevrych, Martynyuk, Rusyn, Kuznetsova, the Horyn' brothers, Osadchy, and Zvarychevs'ka.

16. Individual oral reports of eyewitnesses and trial witnesses (as an exception).

Under Article 62 of the Criminal Code of the Ukrainian SSR: "In conformity with the interests of the working people and in order to strengthen the socialist system, the citizens of the USSR are guaranteed by law: a) freedom of speech; b) freedom of the press; c) freedom of assembly, including the holding of mass meetings; d) freedom of street processions and demonstrations" (Art. 125, Constitution of the USSR). "Agitation or propaganda conducted for the purpose of undermining or weakening the Soviet rule or the commitment of individual crimes which are of particular danger to the state; the spreading, for the same purpose, of slanderous fabrications which discredit the Soviet state and social system; as well as the circulation, production, or keeping for the same purpose, of literature of similar contents — are punishable by imprisonment for a term from six months to seven years, with banishment for up to five years, or without same, or else by banishment for the term of two to five years . . ." (Article 62, Criminal Code of the Ukrainian SSR, Section "Particularly dangerous state crimes"). "It is the duty of the court, public prosecutors, and the investigation authorities, within the limits of their competence, to start criminal proceedings *in every instance* showing signs of a crime" (Article 4, CPC, Ukr. SSR). "The law is like a draught-bar, it goes to where it is pointed" (a Ukrainian popular saying).

The highly talented artist-painter, P. Zalyvakha; the art expert, B. Horyn'; the professional psychologist, M. Horyn'; the lecturers at the Luts'k Pedagogical Institute, Moroz and Ivashchenko; the teacher, Ozerny, from the Ivano-Frankivs'ke Region; the student of the Kiev Institute of Medicine, Y. Hevrych; the scientists from Kiev, Rusyn and Martynenko; the laboratory assistant of the Kiev University, Kuznetsova; the pensionary from Feodosiya, Masyutko, and others were convicted under Article 62 of the Criminal Code of the Ukr. SSR.

However, the currently popular Article 62 transgresses the Constitution. The Supreme Soviet should either annul the article or define it concretely. In its present formulation, this article completely negates the freedoms guaranteed to citizens by the Constitution of the USSR. Whenever someone criticizes the current nationality policy for its deviation from Lenin's standards (even if erroneously), he is fully entitled to do so by the Constitution of the USSR. But, on the strength of the Criminal Code of the Ukr. SSR, this person can be banished to a hard-labour camp, because his criticism may be interpreted as "propaganda for the purpose of undermining or weakening the Soviet rule" (although, in actual fact, the moral health of this very rule is at stake). If someone wanted to criticize the personality cult in Stalin's time or the reorganization mania in Khrushchev's day, could that not have been interpreted (and it was so interpreted) as "the spreading of false defamatory rumours which discredit the Soviet state and social system"? It seems that every assertion that is not in line with directives can be classified as one of these "false defamatory rumours".

The practice of recent months confirms my thoughts. Judges draw out this elastic article of the code as if it were an accordion. Everybody interprets the concept "anti-Soviet" according to his own fancy. (In the Ivano-Frankivs'ke Region, even the ancient aphorisms, the word *vatra* [bonfire], and the poetry of Shevchenko[1] were found to be anti-Soviet.) Yaroslav Hevrych was condemned to five years of hard labour for a few photocopies of books. Arkas' *History of Ukraine*, passed by the tsarist censorship, the magazine *Zhinocha Dolya* [Women's Destiny], and the apolitical book by the modernist Pachovs'kyi, *Ukrains'ka bohema* [Ukrainian Boheme] were confiscated from Ozerny, the teacher, and introduced as evidence in court. (All these books are freely available in libraries.) On the other hand, Sadovs'ky, the professional engineer and the teacher, Ivanyshyn, were let out on bail, although their colleagues were told that they had been "disseminating slanderous materials" (which was what Hevrych was imprisoned for).

1 Taras Shevchenko (1814-1861) the most famous of Ukrainian poets. He spent a large part of his life in prison for his anti-tsarist poetry (transl. note).

Mykhaylo Horyn' was sentenced to six years, Panas Zalyvakha to five years in hard-labour camps, while Svitlychny and Kosiv were freed without trial, although all of them were charged with the same crime. Where is the logic?

The law must be formulated clearly and, according to Article 4, CPC, Ukr. SSR, no crime must escape punishment. Assuming that current trials are held not merely for the purpose of intimidating the general public, but with a sincere intention to keep the letter and spirit of the law, having said "a" one must also say "b". Those who gave books to Hevrych, Martynyuk, or Ozerny must also be put in jail immediately. After spending six or seven months under the guardianship of the KGB they will tell, in their turn, where *they* got the books and will be given in due course five to six "rightful" years of hard labour, and so on. Thus "justice" will come even to the imprudent scientist, who has shown highly professional notes to somebody, or to the simpleton who "for the sake of idle curiosity" obtained a book from a tourist or a relative here on a visit from abroad. And verbal anecdotes must also have their turn. As a matter of fact, many of them are "slanderous fabrications" of the purest water which "discredit the Soviet state and the social system". Prosecution for telling anecdotes, which are so popular, will be of assistance in a radical solution of the housing crisis in larger cities. Conscientious enforcement of the 62nd article of the Criminal Code of the Ukr. SSR will make it possible to raise the population of the camps to Stalin's levels, or even to exceed them. For the article may be applied to anyone, without exception, who repeats the words of Mayakovs'ky's hero, "We have no business thinking, comrades, when the leaders are doing the thinking." The great opportunities it offers are evidenced by the following fact.

After my refusal, on the 16th of April, to give evidence at a *closed* trial in L'viv, I was informed that I was subject to prosecution under Article 179 of the Criminal Code of the Ukr. SSR (refusal to give evidence). That decision was in itself illegal, as I refused to give evidence only because it was an illegal closed trial. And in the opinion of Antonenko, the enraged public prosecutor, and of S. I. Rudyk, the judge, that decision was far from adequate; they reversed their own decision and, on the 19th of April, resolved to bring me to trial for violation of Article 62 of the Criminal Code of the Ukr. SSR. The administrators of justice were not in the least disturbed by the lack of factual evidence of my "anti-Soviet" activities (except for Osadchy's petty testimonies, confirmed neither by witnesses nor by myself); they knew very well what Article 62 was all about. But the Supreme Court of the Ukr. SSR rescinded their illegal ruling on May 17. Probably because of the simple fact that they had as yet received no signal "from above" to imprison the next batch of "anti-Soviet agitators and propagandists".

V. I. Lenin was not an all-forgiving humanitarian. Yet even during those times of tension, when the exploiting classes were still in our country, when enemies were pressing hard on all sides, Lenin was able to undertake the abolition of the death penalty in 1920. In his time Cheka agents used to spy out those who openly and aggressively opposed the Soviet rule or who were preparing for an armed uprising, but they did not persecute people for their beliefs alone. Lenin did not order a certain Sukhanov imprisoned for his anti-Marxist book, but instead entered into polemics with its author.

Even Stalin, while he was still too cautious to deviate from Lenin's standards for public life, was not afraid of anti-Soviet literature. In 1928, the Leningrad workers' publishing house, Priboy [Surf], published a large edition of the book *1919 god* [The Year 1919], written by the White[1] emigrant V. Shul'gin, which overflowed with malice towards the revolution and expressed hope for a collapse of the Soviet system. The book was reprinted from a foreign publication without the slightest abridgment. In a short foreword it was said that Shul'gin was a "nationalist and monarchist of the extreme right", an "inveterate Jew-hater", that he propagated the "zoological policy of nationalism". (We must add: he not only promoted Jewish pogroms, but was also a staunch and fierce enemy of Ukrainians.) It was mentioned that the book was of good use to a wide circle of readers because it gave them a close look at the enemy and helped them to fight chauvinism. Then, without any warn-

---

[1] Adherent of the tsarist regime (transl. note).

ings and explanations, it was Shul'gin's turn to have his say: "Of course, the Cheka must kill some people. It is dangerous for a power based on blood alone not to exercise its men in murder — they might quit the habit . . ." (p. 95). "Headquarters is the place where they devise methods for forcing 150 million people to labour indefatigably so that 150 thousand loafers, who call themselves the proletariat, can do nothing at all. This system, as is known, is called the dictatorship of the proletariat" (p. 107). "The Bolshevik mania for holding parades is not in the least smaller than in the epoch of Paul I" (p. 107). "It was said that the Cheka received from Moscow 400 absolutely trustworthy and excellently trained men. I don't know whether it was so, but their outward appearance, if not indeed frightening, then certainly aroused one's imagination . . . These men had a well fed and satisfied look. Obviously, these trusty dogs were extremely well tended and cherished . . ." (pp. 118-119). "The paltry handful of Kornilov's, Alekseyev's, and Denikin's[1] forces were able to crush countless numbers of people because they were organized on the right principles, without any committees, without conscientious discipline — organized 'in the White manner'; the Bolsheviks understood . . . and have re-established the army . . . Of course, they think that they created a socialist army that fights in the name of the Internationale — but this is nonsense . . . In actual fact, they have restored the Russian army . . ." (p. 108). "Our main, our true slogan is One Indivisible Russia . . . When Denikin went away, we did not actually forget it, we just hid it for a while. We furled our banner. And who raised it, who unfurled it? No matter how fantastic it may be, it is a fact: The banner of the one and indivisible Russia was actually raised by the Bolsheviks. They do not say so, of course . . . Naturally, Lenin and Trotsky keep on blaring the Internationale. And there is the pretense that the communist army fought for the propagation of Soviet republics. But this is merely on the surface . . ." (p. 108). "Socialism will disappear in the wash, but the frontiers will remain. In any case, it cannot be overlooked that the Russian language has occupied, to the glory of the

---

[1] Commander of the anti-Bolshevik White army (transl. note).

Internationale, one sixth of the entire land . . . surface [of the globe]. And it is obvious now that no matter who sits in Moscow, whether it is Ul'yanov[1] or Romanov[2] (please, pardon this foul comparison) . . . he must, or as the Khokhly[3] say *musyt*, continue the task of Ivan Kalita"[4] (p. 198). "It only seems to the Reds that they are fighting for the glory of the Internationale. In actual fact, although not consciously, they are shedding their blood to restore the God-protected Russian State. They can move their Red armies, made up in the White manner, in all directions only until they reach solid border-lines, where they encounter the firm resistance of other state organisms — in other words, the natural boundaries of the future Russia. The Internationale will vanish in the wash, but frontiers will remain . . ." (p. 207).

When I wrote excerpts from this book, I added "Leningrad 1926" at the end of every quotation. I was afraid that my comrades from the KGB might appear to make another search and, after tearing out these excerpts, accuse me, in accordance with Article 62 of the Criminal Code of the Ukr. SSR, of malicious defamation of the Soviet system, of Lenin, and perhaps, even of imperialistic chauvinism. My apprehensions are not without foundation. Certainly somewhere in the Kiev regional KGB office there is a file on me, containing various quotations from the works of our writers and a bibliography of foreign Ukrainian publications. It does not contain a single sentence which could have been written by myself. As I was making marginal notes, I did not know when, or in what context, I would make use of that material (or whether I would use it at all), but the KGB firmly believes that all of it has the purpose of "anti-Soviet propaganda and agitation", of "undermining", of "weakening", and of "spreading slanderous fabrications". Otherwise, they would not have kept that file for half a year, along with fifty-five old-edition books, among which there is even a complete run of a Ukrainian journal for the year 1900.

---

1 Lenin (transl. note).
2 Tsar's family name (transl. note).
3 A derogatory Russian term for Ukrainians (transl. note).
4 Ivan I of Moscow (d. 1340) who started consolidation of the Grand Duchy of Moscow (transl. note).

Vyacheslav Chornovil 11

In 1926 Stalin was not afraid that anyone who had read Shul'gin's book would turn into a staunch monarchist and overthrow the Soviet rule. Ten years later he suspected treason and had many of his closest collaborators shot; but twenty years later this was called the cult of personality. Another decade has passed since then, and suddenly old notes begin to jingle in the speeches of certain leaders. Comrade Shulzhenko, deputy chairman of the KGB, addressing the Academy of Sciences of the Ukr. SSR, spoke quite cleverly about foreign intelligence services until he came to "ideological diversions". According to him all oppositional tendencies and acts within our country are exclusively the results of the influence of bourgeois propaganda and intelligence services. So if by a wave of a magic wand the bourgeois world suddenly ceased to exist, "contentment" would rule supreme. Everyone would be satisfied with the fate of villagers without passports, who are assigned for life to their collective farms. In towns all Ukrainians would be proud of the fact that they had become renegades without kith or kin — nobodies, with merely a family-name determined in the regional or district committee's office. The well-known critic, Ivan Svitlychny, would not have had to spend eight months in jail; Bohdan Horyn', the art expert, and Zalyvakha, the artist, would not have found themselves behind barbed wire. Instead, they would have accepted the russification policy of internationalism and been serenely happy about the success of such "internationalism".

The deputy chairman of the KGB made one more revelation to the scientists in Kiev. It seems that a person whose ideological foundations are weak will immediately develop anti-Soviet feelings upon reading a book with a "hidden text" which contains a valid criticism of our system. The most obvious solution is to erect a fence between such people and subversive books in order to protect them in every possible way, even to the point of putting them in jail or in a hard-labour camp.

But then what about the Marxist thesis that the social reality (and not hostile books) determines one's direction? For ten years I was educated in a Soviet school. In the last paragraph of every composition I invariably endeavoured to mention the

Party and Stalin, even if I had to write about the *Tale of the Host of Ihor*.[1] For five years I faithfully studied Marxism-Leninism at the university. All other subjects were also invariably based on the Marxist foundation. Finally, just recently I passed the master's examination in Marxist-Leninist philosophy. Then all of a sudden, quite by accident, I laid my hands on a book in Ukrainian, published abroad, and I immediately became a "bourgeois nationalist" Some time later I read a leaflet from Peking about the "opportunism of the cpsu" — would that make me a follower of Mao Tse-tung? Later still I listened on the radio to a speech by the Pope of Rome (by the way, it was brought up in the indictment of the teacher Ozerny) — was I then a Jesuit?

Could it be that Article 62 of the Criminal Code of the Ukr. ssr was devised expressly to protect Soviet citizens against such kaleidoscopic changes in their ideological outlook? Without a doubt, Marxism-Leninism is stronger than the bourgeois ideology. But in our country anyone who reads a book published in the West is subject to prosecution, whereas *our* books and newspapers, containing all kinds of criticism of capitalism, of bourgeois nationalism, and of the current policies of capitalist powers, can be easily obtained (even by mail) in the usa, Canada, and in many other foreign countries. The newspaper *Visti z Ukrainy* [News from Ukraine] is published in Kiev especially for Ukrainian emigrés, but it is impossible to read that paper here in Ukraine, because it contains specialized truths — for export only.

Is it possible that non-Marxists have absorbed better than our leaders the Marxist-Leninist thesis that revolutions and social-economic changes are not exported, that an idea can be implanted on new soil only when all the social, economic, and political prerequisites are completely ripe for it, and that to forbid the spreading of ideas is to increase their strength and attractiveness? This last reason is why those who inspire and execute the arrests and trials that roll like an ominous wave across Ukraine may find *themselves* punishable under Article Criminal Code of the Ukr. ssr?

---

1 A famous twelfth-century work of the old Ukrainian literature (transl. note).

What lesson do our citizens learn from Article 62 of the Criminal Code of the Ukr. ssr? They are taught to follow blindly and accurately the tracks of the latest trends published by the press; they learn the petty-bourgeois morals — to fear and to look behind.

II. HOW ARE THE "ESPECIALLY DANGEROUS STATE CRIMINALS" DISCOVERED?

"The inviolability of the homes of citizens and privacy of correspondence are protected by law" (Article 128, Constitution of the USSR). "Illegal search, illegal eviction, or other acts which violate the inviolability of the homes of citizens, committed by an official, are punishable by imprisonment . . ." (Article 130 of the Criminal Code of the Ukr. ssr). "Violation of the privacy of correspondence, committed by an official, is punishable by corrective labour . . ." (Article 131 of the cc of the Ukr. ssr). The Party holds that the moral code of the builders of communism includes the following norms: ". . . humane relations and mutual respect between individuals — man is a friend, comrade, and brother to other men . . ." (Program of the cpsu). "In an age when the whistles of rockets on Mars have awakened its inhabitants, who would have thought that in a city one would be followed by spectres . . ." (M. Kholodny).

The work of KGB agents is easier than that of the militia. A thief or a murderer is in hiding, but the "particularly dangerous state criminal" is quite the opposite. Often he ascends the platform at a jubilee celebration (for example, Shevchenko's) and speaks. Afterwards he walks with his friends in the street, calmly and without looking around. A secret agent can walk almost beside him and listen to his every word. Whenever a "particularly dangerous" person is dismissed from work on a signal from the KGB, he does not complain, because the KGB is justice personified. Their word is final. If he remains tearless, does not confess, and continues his "dangerous talks", he must be given more serious attention. The most modern techniques are used as helpful means. It is not difficult to persuade the postal, telegraph, and telephone people. Just enquire among

The Petition of

the postal and telephone employees, and you will easily find one who will tell you in confidence how correspondence and conversations are checked upon. They even use a common term — eavesdropping. (This is how they refer to a certain floor of a building, which I think is on Khreshchatyk Street [in Kiev], where Article 128 of the Constitution of the USSR is implemented.) If the "particularly dangerous" person lives on an upper floor (and this is most often the case), he may suddenly observe that the attic door previously open is now tightly locked, and he is not even allowed to get his belongings stored there. Or he may be given a new apartment, and at night hear a clatter behind a wall where nobody lives. Or he may find under his bed in the students' residence a kind of metallic "feelers" attached to a masked lead wire outside his window. (Such a device was found beneath the window of M. Plakhotnyuk, the student at the Kiev Institute of Medicine.)

Or one day a new lodger appears in your apartment. He hears everything: to whom and about what you talk, what you whisper into your wife's ear. As soon as you guess the true identity of the "unregistered lodger", your life becomes hell. You weigh every word, you become taciturn and irritable. You acquire the habit of speaking in whispers, you look around you in the street, you stick out your tongue at the man who brazenly photographs you with your friends. At times you make a mistake and insult a respectable citizen, taking him for a secret agent. Meanwhile your newly opened file is swelling. You may say that all this is pure invention, that there is some purpose in the existence of Article 128 of the Constitution of the USSR and of the corresponding article of the Criminal Code. That finally, the humiliating watching, eavesdropping, and spying on Soviet citizens, who are perhaps guilty only of their desire to have unconventional thoughts, is foreign to the spirit of our system.

In the summer of 1965, two or three months before the arrests, friends of the writer, Yevhen Kontsevych, arrived from Kiev to visit him. They came to Zhytomyr not to perform "particularly dangerous crimes", but to wish a happy birthday to a friend, bedridden because he was paralyzed. Close on their heels, completely uninvited, came the local "poet", Oksentiy

Mel'nychuk, barely known to Kontsevych. By the way, the KGB officials in Zhytomyr even failed to inform their messenger that it was Kontsevych's birthday. And so the newly arrived Sherlock Holmes had to mumble nonsensical rubbish. "I stopped," he said, "to enquire about the state of your health," (it was at eleven o'clock at night, in rainy weather, in the outskirts of the city) "and brought you a small album of exotic postcards." Later, after Yevhen had had a good look at them, he would take it away. Having said that, he sat down on a chair, chewed and swallowed jokes hinting at his sideline profession, and strained his ears. The next day, late in the evening, Yehven's family happened to remember Mel'nychuk's "gift", and upon close inspection they found inside the album's covers a miniature communication device — either a tape-recorder or a radio transmitter. The whole Kontsevych family was stunned; they didn't expect that kind of gift.

Early next morning Mel'nychuk called for the album. After getting an earful of everything he deserved and a few well-placed blows, he made a headlong dash to his bosses. Soon a car full of KGB agents with a lieutenant-colonel in charge drove up to the house. When they made excuses and begged tearfully for the return of the birthday gift, Kontsevych took pity on them and gave it back. Too bad! He could have had something to illustrate his story for the scientists of the Academy of Sciences of the Ukr. SSR.

How can one explain this incident in Zhytomyr? What did the KGB agents expect to hear at a birthday table, where some of the people gathered did not even know each other? How can the revolting act of smuggling an eavesdropping device into the bed of a very sick man be reconciled with the exalted principles of a builder of communism? This is a man who writes bright and gallant stories, who never gave any cause for suspicion of criminal activities, whom the press was comparing with Korchagin.

There are no more brazen agents than those in Zhytomyr. Mel'nychuk should have taken a course of lectures from the spy Yaroslav Korotnyts'ky (also a "poet") who operates in L'viv. Once he appeared in Feodosiya where his countrymen, the Horyn' brothers, were vacationing. He met them "purely by accident" at the beach and, while talking about this and that, he also told them the sad story of his life. It appears that he suffered agonies in Stalin's camps but wrote verses about Ukraine there. Poor fellow, he was so lonely there because he did not hear even a word of his beloved native tongue. Later on, he visited his countrymen, bringing a bottle of good wine with him, and talked about the unfortunate Ukraine. When the Horyn' brothers left for home, it was, of course, Korotnyts'ky who saw them off at the station, and when they found at the ticket office that there were no vacancies on the train, Korotnyts'ky managed to quietly talk the woman train conductor into taking two more passengers. Somehow he made such an impression on her that she personally ran to the ticket office in Dzhankoy to get the tickets. At the last station before L'viv the Horyn' brothers were arrested. Long before that the "poet" had flown off to L'viv to start a new assignment.

There is no end to facts of this kind. The metamorphoses in the attic of the scientist Mykhaylo Horyn', about which he spoke with bitter irony shortly before his arrest. Something of the same kind in the apartment of the critic, Ivan Svitlychny. The phantoms who appear suddenly at a literary evening, or "promenade" below the windows of Ivan Franko's sons or grandsons, or dart through the street behind some of the young poets or critics, and cause poets to joke sadly, "Well, I don't mind having to wipe off sweat with my deathly pale hand. He's the first person who ever became a follower of mine."

III. PRELIMINARY INVESTIGATION, or [?[1]] "CRIME".

a) Search and Arrests

"When issuing an arrest warrant, it is the duty of public prosecutors to personally examine the material of the case and, whenever necessary, to question the accused (suspect) both as to the substance of charges pressed against him and the circumstances connected with the application of preventive measures" (Article 157, CPC, Ukr. SSR). *"The investigator's duty is*

---

1 One word illegible in the original (transl. note).

to inform the wife (husband) or another relative about the arrest of a suspect, or the accused, and of his whereabouts; he must also notify his [the arrestee's] place of employment" (Article 161, CPC, Ukr. SSR). "During a search or sequestration, it is permissible to remove only those items and documents which *have a bearing on the case . . .*" (Article 186, CPC, Ukr. SSR). "Acts and resolutions of the investigation offices may be appealed to the public prosecutor, whose duty it is to examine the appeal *in the course of three days. The appellor must be notified of the public prosecutor's decision concerning his appeal*" (Article 110, CPC, Ukr. SSR). "Ravens do not peck out other ravens' eyes" (a popular Ukrainian saying).

At last the file is complete. The man has spoken of russification, criticized the authorities, upheld human dignity and the right of independent thinking. There are no doubts — this is a "criminal particularly dangerous to the state". He must be given such a lesson that others will be discouraged. However, for appearance's sake, it is advisable to preserve the semblance of due process and obtain a search and arrest warrant from the public prosecutor. Secret agents are always on the lookout for a Ukrainian book published abroad or a handwritten article about the situation in Ukraine in the hands of "particularly dangerous" persons. In conformity with the thoroughly unconstitutional Article 62, CC, Ukr. SSR, this would definitely constitute "material evidence".

When guardians of state security appear in your apartment to conduct a search, you must wait with your hands up, just like a prisoner of war, while your "friend, comrade, and brother" ransacks your pockets. Sometimes, to scare the wits out of your wife or your neighbours, you will be asked to surrender your weapons. (The Kiev KGB agents demanded weapons from the electrician Peredenko, who was in bed at the time.) Later they will show you the warrant, which says that the search is conducted for the purpose of "discovering and removing anti-Soviet documents circulated by the suspect". However, when the guardians of security take along the man of the house and lock up the apartment, seven to nine hours later, they carry with them big bundles of old books (some of which used to be "circulated" seventy years ago, in the days of Emperor Franz Josef), letters, daily newspapers, and notes for scientific work. Don't even think of writing a protest or of referring to Article 186, of swearing that letters to your beloved were not written for the sake of anti-Soviet agitation, and that some authors of the anti-Soviet books taken away from you died long before the revolution. You will not get an answer, either from the investigator, CPC, or from the public prosecutor. It will be exactly the same later, when you complain about the falsification of the interrogation reports, about threats, and so forth (although Articles 110, 129, 189 and 234-236, CPC, Ukr. SSR, prescribe precise time-limits for answering complaints and intercessions).

Now and then KGB officials forget about such boring formalities. As a matter of fact, without any warrant whatever authorizing search and sequestration, they confiscated from Masyutko's brother, an artist in L'viv, three books mortally dangerous to the Soviet system: a collection of Bohdan Lepky's[1] poems, an old edition of a first-grade reader, and a tattered geography book (in the Russian language). If, in the course of searching, the guardians of security should spot a book or a photocopy of a so-called "anti-Soviet" book published abroad, prison doors will assuredly close behind you for many long months. Then the initial investigation will begin. The schedule outlined earlier is not dogmatic. Sometimes arrests are made in trains, en route from vacations (as in the case of the student Hevrych), or on a day of rest (critic Svitlychny, the brothers Horyn', the teacher Ozerny). At that time their quarters were literally turned upside down; at Svitlychny's home they took away such books as *Transactions of the Shevchenko Scientific Society*, *Literaturno-Naukovy Visnyk* [Literary-Scientific Herald], *Geography of Ukraine*, *Kobza and kobzari*, as well as other "anti-Soviet" literature, but not a single word was said to his wife about her husband's arrest. She was not told about it on the next or even the third day. At long last, out of pity they assured her that her husband did not fall under a train or drown in the sea, but was finishing his rest period in the jail of the Kiev KGB.

---

1 Ukrainian scholar, writer, and poet (1872-1941) (transl. note).

They were even more close-mouthed with Hevrych's father. For two weeks he haunted the thresholds of the police, then of the KGB in Kosiv, Ivan-Frankivs'ke and Kiev, before he could discover what had happened to his son. Apparently the public prosecutors did not give much thought to the matter when they issued the search and arrest warrant. They were not required to "personally examine" the material of the case, or to interrogate the suspect "regarding the substance of the charges pressed against him" (see Article 157, CPC, Ukr. SSR). Otherwise, the watchful eye of the public prosecutor would have noticed at once the white threads of fabrication with which the charges were stitched together.

Undoubtedly the arrests were carried out upon centralized orders "from above". This is made convincingly evident by the mere fact that, in various regions of Ukraine, there were arrests of a large group of people, the majority of whom were not acquainted with one another and were not in any way associated. (They are being tried now either separately, or in groups of two to three persons.)

b) Interrogation of the Accused and of Witnesses. Confrontations.

". . . Courts, public prosecutors, and investigators have no right to shift the burden of proof onto the accused. It is forbidden to extort testimony from the accused by *violence, threats, or by other* illegal means" (Article 22, CPC, Ukr. SSR). "Upon his request, the accused must be given the opportunity to present his testimony in his own handwriting . . ." (Article 146, CPC, Ukr. SSR). "Upon request from relatives and close friends of the arrested person, the investigator or the public prosecutor may permit them to *visit the prisoner* . . ." (Article 162, CPC, Ukr. SSR). "The publication of testimonies given by persons who attended the confrontation during preliminary hearings is permissible only after such testimonies have been given at the confrontation and have been recorded in the minutes. The interrogated persons have the right to demand that the minutes be supplemented and amendments made in them. Such supplements or amendments are subject to obligatory entry into the minutes" (Article 173, CPC, Ukr. SSR). "The use of coercion to obtain testimony at an interrogation by means of illegal action on the part of the person conducting the investigation, or the preliminary investigation, is punishable by imprisonment for a term of up to three years. Similar action, combined with the use of violence on or mockery of the person under interrogation, is punishable by imprisonment for a term of two to eight years" (Article 175, Criminal Code of the Ukr. SSR). "Why do you try to find fault with me, a peasant, and when you do not find any, still bear me a grudge?" (S. Zalygin).

It is not obligatory to slam doors on fingers, to stick needles under fingernails, or to strike someone's face in order to force him to denounce his deeds as terrible crimes, or to confess everything that the investigator needs to complete the evidence he has contrived beforehand. All that is needed is to lock the man inside a stone sack with bars, a privy, to forbid him any contact with close relatives for a half a year, to hammer into his head day after day, for several hours at a time, the feeling of great guilt and, finally, to drive that man to such a state of mind that he would not at first recognize his wife if she came to visit him. As a result of moral terrorization, threats, and promises (which are usually forgotten at the trial), they squeeze the required testimony from the man. At a confrontation with Y. Hevrych, early in December of last year, the witness Hors'ka asked him, "Yaroslav, tell me what forced you to tell lies about me?" and she heard the typical answer, "In a hundred and five days here you can be taught to lie." Of course, this phrase, despite Hors'ka's insistence, was not entered into the minutes of the confrontation.

This is the dialogue between the judge and the teacher Ozerny at the trial in Ivano-Frankivs'ke:

Q: You have told the witness that you read it. (This concerns the manuscript of an article dealing with the burning of the library of the Academy of Sciences of the Ukr. SSR in Kiev[1]

---

[1] The manuscript entitled *The Trial of Pohruzhal'sky* accuses the Soviet authorities of organizing the burning of an important section of the Academy's Library, containing invaluable "withdrawn" documents on modern Ukrainian history. The manuscript was published in the Munich monthly, *Suchasnist'*, No. 2(50), February 1965, pp. 78-84 (transl. note).

— V. Ch.) You said at the interrogation that you took the article out of your briefcase and gave it to the witness. Did you give it, do you remember? Which testimony is true?

A: This one here at the trial.

Q: Why didn't you say so during the investigation?

A: I was so tired at the interrogations that at times I signed things I didn't agree with. I was questioned for eleven hours and then for ten hours more.

Q: Weren't you given a break?

A: For dinner. (Eleven plus ten, plus dinner time, makes twenty-two hours. And what about Article 143 of the Criminal Procedure Code of the Ukr. ssr?)

Q: Were you tired? (A naive question . . . the judge should have been submitted to an interrogation without sleep and rest. Perhaps then he would admit that the trial he was conducting was anti-Soviet.)

A: Yes, I told the investigator that I gave no documents to Malyarchyn. I was dead tired and signed whatever was written. I was called for questioning forty-six times. That time I was questioned six hours and forty-six minutes. My present testimony here is true. I told this to the investigator, also. He tired me out so much that I said, write whatever you want. And I signed it.

At that same trial, witness A. Matviyenko stated that, in accordance with Article 234, cpc, Ukr. ssr, she protested against the terroristic methods of interrogation used by Captain Rudy. Then the following conversation took place:

Public prosecutor: What kind of terroristic method did Rudy use on you?

A: It was moral terror. Sorry, but I shouldn't quote his obscene words here.

Q: How did he threaten you?

A: He said that he would deprive me of absolutely everything I have.

Q: So what?

A: That is enough.

Q: You spoke about a woman's pride?

A: Yes, it was insulted.

Q: You said during the first interrogation . . .

A: During the first interrogation you were examining my letters.

Q: Why didn't you give truthful testimonies, then?

A: I was bullied.

Q: How many times were you interrogated by Rudy?

A: For four days. From nine o'clock in the morning till seven at night.

A. Matviyenko's protest was suppressed; Captain Rudy is somewhere questioning a new victim, while master of philology [M.A.] A. Matviyenko, in accordance with the court's verdict, has joined the ranks of unemployed "seditious" intellectuals. We do not know what kind of obscene words Captain Rudy used to demoralize Matviyenko, but it seems that in L'viv Captains Klymenko and Rybal'chenko and Colonel Sergadeyev browbeat witness Lyuba Maksymiv, shouting the most dreadful obscenities at her. When they saw that their "eloquence" was making quite an impression on the terrified girl, they added more strength to their attack by shouting, "You pig! We'll make your life and your family's life unbearable, both here in L'viv and in Drohobych!"

Do you think that Sergadeyev, Klymenko, and Rybal'chenko were tried under Article 175 of the Criminal Code of the Ukr. SSR and banished to Mordovia, or to some other autonomous republic, to develop the national economy there? Nothing of the sort! Colonel Sergadeyev will have many more opportunities to send others there, because he is the chief of the investigation branch of the L'viv KGB. There are articles in the Criminal Prosecution Code that assure the accused of the right to submit their testimonies in their own handwriting. Why, then, was no one ever given the opportunity to take advantage of this right? Investigators often produced such an embroiled version of testimonies that everything was turned upside down.

After reading the minutes of her interrogation in Donets'k, Ivan Svitlychny's sister refused point-blank to sign "her own" testimonies in the form they were written. "The investigator did not always write down what I wanted," complained Ozerny at the trial. During the confrontation between the accused Osadchy and the witness Chornovil in L'viv, Captain Klymenko, in violation of article 173, told how it all "was", and

Osadchy just parroted him. When Osadchy said that, perhaps after all, he did not take the text of Eisenhower's speech at the unveiling of Shevchenko's monument in Washington (a terribly anti-Soviet document from the witness), Klymenko pounced on him. "Then why did you say earlier, at the interrogation, that you did take it?" Osadchy's doubts vanished as if by magic. The witness Chornovil asked that the doubt be recorded in the minutes just the same, but he was told that he had no business interfering with Osadchy's testimonies, that all he had to do was to read and sign his own. (Article 15, CPC, Ukr. SSR reads that prior to the court's verdict, "no one may be considered guilty of the crime committed".)

When this same Osadchy was visited by his pregnant wife, even before the end of the investigation, he told her exactly where his future detention would be — the political prisoners' camps in the Mordovian ASSR. I know very well that prior to his arrest Osadchy, a lecturer at L'viv University, knew nothing about the camps in Mordovia. Bohdan Horyn' received identical information about his future from the investigator, and long before the trial he shared the news with his fiancée. The investigator Malykhin erred by only one year when, in December of last year, he told Ol'ha Horyn' how many years her husband would get. If the fate of prisoners is decided by the KGB, then why the comedy of trials (what is more, closed trials)? Would it not be simpler to make up a list of "particularly dangerous" people and to mark against each name: this one seven years, that one five, another four. By the way, the KGB agents who "guarded" Hevrych's closed trial were more frank than usual when they told the sympathizers they chased from the hallway, "You will all be there." And the civilian "guardians" of that trial pointed at the black van, the Black Raven[1], and with epic nonchalance informed them, "We have many cars like that one. Quite enough for all of you."

Besides using a whip an investigator makes use of the carrot; admit that you have committed a dreadful crime, expose all those who also read the books — and you will be pardoned, thanks to your open-hearted confession. Ozerny appeared in

---

[1] Black Maria.

court with great assurance. His assurance was further strengthened by a meeting with the Chairman of the KGB at the Council of Ministers of the Ukr. SSR, about which Ozerny told the court, "On the 20th of November, 1965, on the premises of the Ivano-Frankivs'ke KGB, I had a meeting with Nikitchenko, the Chairman of the KGB. After our talk, I was informed the other day that, on the advice of the KGB, Nikitchenko took my confession into consideration."

In view of this, Ozerny conducted himself at the trial with dignity, rejected the public prosecutor's groundless accusations and the nonsensical testimonies of such witnesses as the illiterate teachers, Mel'nychenko and Khats'ko. He even joked to the prisoner Hereta, who had been summoned from Ternopil', "Our case is finished. I'll be paying you a visit soon."

The judge then interjected ominously, "Keep on laughing, Ozerny. Who knows who will laugh last?" The last one to laugh was the judge.

The state charge made by the public prosecutor, Paraskevych, and the inhumanly cruel demand for a six-year imprisonment, were like a bolt from the blue to Ozerny. Stunned, completely bewildered, he repented, wept, implored, and appealed to the "great justice" of the Soviet court. It seems that this was exactly what they expected from him, and to be logical, his punishment should have been reduced so that all others who are caught reading books will "confess", not five to six months after their imprisonment, but at once, in the hope of being pardoned. But, alas! The court complied with the cruel demand of the public prosecutor, perhaps because it was too late to ignore orders received beforehand "from above". (It was not expected there that Ozerny would make such a strong confession.) Even when the comedy in Ivano-Frankivs'ke became a matter of public knowledge, the Supreme Court did not set Ozerny free, but reduced his sentence to three years.

All subsequent trials were out of bounds, even to specially selected people. Probably many more acts of moral terror (and, possibly, not only moral? How can one find out? The trials are closed.), fraud, and deception were revealed there. At a rendezvous with his brother after the trial, Yaroslav Hevrych complained bitterly about the cruel KGB investigator, Koval, who deceived him after promising him golden mountains[1] for an "open-hearted" confession of his "crime". The golden mountains turned out to be five years in hard-labour camps.

The following facts show some of the methods used during the preliminary investigation:

a) Use was made at inquests of evidence obtained in an illegal and inhuman way by eavesdropping with the aid of special devices installed in apartments. Because of this Mykhaylo Horyn' warned one of the witnesses at a confrontation, "Don't hold back — they know everything. My whole apartment was wired." The incident at Kontsevych's birthday was already mentioned. Investigators are not very secretive about it. At one of M. Kosiv's interrogations, when he was quite unable to recall a certain conversation, he was asked, "Do you want us to play it back to you right now?"

In order to shock and embarrass the defendant and to extract the suggested confession, investigators are not averse to rummaging in the intimate lives of defendants and witnesses, although they may have no bearing whatsoever on the case. That happened in the case of Ozerny. Slimy insinuations about allegedly intimate relations between the witness and the defendant trickled through to the trial: "So, you know Ozerny well? — I have met him twice and at the time I was fully convinced of his respectability. — Was that when you were with him in a boat and in a restaurant?" This is irrelevant to the case. The investigators Rybal'chenko and Rapota tried to persuade L. Horbach that she and Osadchy used to kiss each other in doorways, although she knew him only very slightly. This method of the KGB investigators is not a Ukrainian national achievement. As can be seen from the complaint to the Public Prosecutor General of the USSR from Yuli Daniel's wife, Moscow investigators also blackmail witnesses in the same way.

b) Ol'ha Vorbut, a student at the Kiev University who was held in custody for several days at the beginning of September, was subjected to the humiliating procedure of a personal search and had to undress completely. Nothing was found, nor did

---

1 In English, "promising the moon" (transl. note).

they expect to find anything, but they managed to obtain her "confession" and to inflict irreparable injury to her soul. Identical procedure was periodically applied to all prisoners in their cells.

c) Thanks to a "good-hearted" guard and a "sympathetic" woman in the adjoining cell, M. Zvarychevs'ka received three notes from Mykhaylo Horyn' and even one from the outside, from Horyn's wife, Ol'ha. All the notes said more or less the same thing: "Mykhaylo is telling everything. So are the witnesses. You must tell everything too and wriggle out of it(!)" It came out later that neither Mykhaylo nor Ol'ha Horyn' had ever sent notes to Zvarychevs'ka. They were concoted by a handwriting expert in one of the offices of the KGB.

d) In my capacity as a witness in the case of Osadchy, I had to listen to threats and insults, starting with the plaintive "sympathy" of Captain Koval' in Kiev — "Think of your little children. You will end up in jail." — and culminating in the cynical rudeness of Captain Klymenko in L'viv — "Why are you lying and trying to wriggle out of it? We can easily just keep you here."

Similar facts could be cited endlessly. And as a result of these techniques and the effect of long imprisonment, people with weak will-power lose control of themselves. I do not want to believe the rumours that prisoners are given drugs in their food to weaken will-power and induce apathy. (Apropos of that, these rumours grow and spread because the trials are closed.) Even Horyn's lawyer used to spread his hands helplessly because his client was confessing everything, putting the blame on himself for things that had or had not happened; he even refused to have a private conference with his lawyer, although the law guarantees that privilege. He kept on saying that he had no secrets from the investigator. You can see the kind of close friendship that developed after seven months behind bars.

In Makiyivka of the Donets'k Region, teacher Petlyak, scared out of his wits by an unexpected and intense interrogation, wrote a ten-page confession. Since he had no criminal facts to report, Petlyak filled ten pages with an analysis of thoughts and moods of his acquaintances and comrades, as well

as of his own. He went so far that he started to look for subversive "undercurrents" in his own collection of short stories.
Donbas Publishers had a lot of trouble later trying to prove
that "undercurrents" should be looked for in the stories but
not in the confession of the terrified Petlyak. This tragicomedy
came to an end when his acquaintances were threatened with
prosecution and thrown out of work.

c) Imprisonment, Time Limits for Preliminary Investigation.

"Preliminary investigation in criminal cases must be completed within two months. *In particularly complicated cases*
the regional public prosecutor has the right to extend the investigation period, on the strength of a motivated decision of
the investigator, *for one more month.* Further extension of
the time limits of preliminary investigations may be granted
in exceptional cases only by the public prosecutor of the Ukr.
ssr, or by the chief military prosecutor" (Article 120, cpc,
Ukr. ssr).

"Whenever there are sufficient reasons to assume that the
accused, who retains freedom of movement, might hide from
investigation and trial, or interfere with the establishment of
truth in a criminal case, or become engaged in criminal activities . . . the investigator and the public prosecutor have the
right to apply to the accused one of the preventive measures"
(Article 148, cpc, Ukr. ssr).

"Detention in custody during the investigation of the case
may not last more than two months. This time limit may be
extended only due to the *extraordinary complexity of the case*
by the regional public prosecutor, or by the military prosecut-
ing officer of a district or fleet, *for not more than three months,*
or by the public prosecutor of the Ukr. ssr or the chief military
prosecutor, *for not over six months* from the day of arrest.
Further extensions of detention in custody . . . may be granted
in *exceptional cases only* by the public prosecutor general of
the ussr for an additional term of *not more than three months*"
(Article 156, cpc, Ukr. ssr).

Let's assume that a person who has read a book and given
it to others to read can be considered such a serious criminal

that it is necessary to apply the so-called preventive measures to him during the investigation period. But why must people invariably be put in jail and isolated completely? If a written promise not to leave his place of residence had been taken from Hevrych, who made photocopies of several books, or if he had been let out on bail, could this possibly have prevented the investigators from finding out that Hevrych made these copies in the house of his acquaintance, Morhun, and that he told his fiancée, Sendurs'ka, and her brother about them?

The law says that a person may be kept in jail more than three months "due to the extraordinary complexity of the case", and for over six months in "exceptional cases" only. Are a photocopy of a book and a reprint of an anonymous article really an "extraordinary complexity" and an "exceptional case"? How should one then qualify rape, murder, or embezzlement of state property? Is it possible that we are regressing to Stalin's time, when murderers were called "socially congenial", while writers and artists were considered dangerous enemies? The whole purpose of detention is to break the prisoner's will-power and to force him to say memorized words at his trial. The longer a man sits behind bars, the longer he has only one person he can talk to, one person who substitutes for his former intellectual companions, and that one person is the KGB investigator, with his monotonous little song about the terrible crime and confession. The longer the lock clicks on the door of his cell and the guard looks through the peephole now and then, the more certain it is that the prisoner will turn into soft clay that can be moulded into anything one may desire. The malicious protraction of investigations is aimed at the total destruction of human dignity and of social impulses. Everything that is human in a person is systematically suppressed and replaced by animal instincts of fear and self-preservation.

Let us take the case of Osadchy, which as a witness I know best. Osadchy was arrested on the 28th of August, 1965. In the very first days he fully satisfied the searching curiosity of the KGB officials in L'viv. The charges against him were so insignificant that the investigation could have been completed in one week. But a whole month had passed until, on the 30th of September, they searched my apartment in Kiev and began to interrogate me as one of the few witnesses in the case. One more month later I was summoned to L'viv for questioning and confrontation. I repeated what I said on the 21st of September, and Osadchy reiterated his testimonies of the end of August. This was followed by a lull of a few more months. Osadchy got so sick and tired of sitting behind bars that at the last rendezvous with his wife he spoke earnestly of wishing to leave his prison cell, even if it meant being sent to a camp. Osadchy's crime (as I learned during the interrogations and from tales of other witnesses) was so insignificant, his confession and docility so boundless, and his past so bright (a television studio editor, instructor in the ideological department of the regional Party committee, lecturer at L'viv University), that a week after his arrest he could have been let out on bail, bearing in mind that the "crime and the man who committed it were of no great danger to society" and that the "culprit's activities did not cause any grave consequences and that the offender made a frank confession" (Article 10, CPC, Ukr. SSR). Nothing of the kind! Osadchy sat awaiting his trial for almost eight months, dreaming no longer of a candidate's degree in science[1] (he defended his dissertation shortly prior to his arrest) but of camp.

Dreams nowadays have the habit of coming true. On the 19th of April, 1966, the regional court in L'viv sentenced Osadchy, for nothing at all, to two years in a hard-labour camp. But 1966 is not 1930; it is not easy these days to fabricate another SVU[2]. Two attempts to hold "open" trials of prisoners ended in the utter defeat of those who tried them.

The defendant Moroz spoke in Luts'k about russification and the unequal status of our "sovereign" republic; he declared that he is in no way a bourgeois nationalist, that he does not subscribe to any bourgeoisie or to nationalism; he merely wants Ukraine to have the same rights as her socialist sisters — Russia, Poland, Czechoslovakia. Ozerny in Ivano-Frankivs'ke, on the other hand, despite his admission of guilt, proved him-

---

[1] Equivalent to a Ph.D. degree in North America (transl. note).

[2] This abbreviation stands for *Soyuz Vyzvolennya Ukrainy*, Union for the Liberation of Ukraine (transl. note).

The Petition of

self to be morally and intellectually a head higher than his judges and some of the witnesses. His students at the Luts'k Pedagogical Institute spoke with enthusiasm of their lecturer. And so when the trials ended in a fiasco, the pillars of justice resorted to the ultra-legal measure of closed trials.

IV. COURT

a) VIOLATION OF LEGAL PROCEDURES IN COURT. "A copy of the bill of indictment and summons to appear in court shall be handed to the defendant and a signed receipt obtained from him not later than *three days* before the trial. *All other persons* shall be informed about the date of consideration of the case *within the same time limit*" (Article 254, CPC, Ukr. SSR).

"Documents which figure as evidence in the case *shall be examined or read at the trial.* This can be done either on the initiative of the court, or upon the *request of persons taking part in the trial* at any time during the consideration of the case in court" (Article 315, CPC, Ukr. SSR).

"*A verdict of guilty* cannot be based on suppositions" (Article 327, CPC, Ukr. SSR).

"An interrogation, a preliminary or judicial investigations are in any case considered to be one-sided and incomplete: (1) whenever persons whose testimony has a material bearing on the case have not been interrogated . . ." (Article 368, CPC, Ukr. SSR).

"Verdicts are considered to be in variance with the factual circumstances of the case: . . . (3) whenever, despite the contradictory nature of evidence which has a material bearing on the court's conclusions, *it is not stated in the verdict* for what reason certain evidence was taken into consideration and other rejected by the court" (Article 369, CPC, Ukr. SSR).

It takes the squeaky wagon of the preliminary investigation five to eight months to creep up to the trial. It creeps up despite the numerous violations of investigation procedures that have been described earlier. No attention whatever is paid to these violations by the public prosecutor. The "defence" attorney does not object to them, and the protests of witnesses (and, probably, of the defendants) are voices crying in the wilderness. One would think that there is no reason to fear justice. On the contrary, it is recommended in the Code to raise the "educational role of the court trials" by giving them the widest possible publicity (Article 20, cpc, Ukr. ssr). Moreover, it is recommended that the judge presiding at the trial "assure the proper educational level of the court trial" (Article 260, cpc, Ukr. ssr).

Perhaps you may think that the trial of lecturers of the Luts'k Pedagogical Institute was held in its largest auditorium, filled to capacity by students and lecturers? Only some of them were lucky enough to hear what Ivashchenko and Moroz were accused of. Even more carefully chosen was the audience at Ozerny's trial in Ivano-Frankivs'ke; the courtroom was mainly filled by selected "guests" with admission passes who had no connection with the defendant. Besides, there was nothing to listen to; not even one citation was produced from the allegedly "anti-Soviet" documents. Do you think that, in the creative organizations and institutions of Kiev, L'viv, and Ivano-Frankivs'ke, posters were billed: Go to the trial, listen, convince yourself of the rectitude of those who judge; do not make the same mistakes as Horyn', Zalyvakha, Hevrych, Martynenko, Masyutko? Why no, because all the trials following Ozerny's were closed. And to avoid unwanted guests, sometimes even the nearest relatives were not notified. Rusyn's mother and Hevrych's father found out about the trial of their sons only accidentally from witnesses. As a rule witnesses were invited on the second day of the trial, so that on the first day no one disturbed the controllers of justice. It would seem that there is nothing to fear if only judges, the defence, and the defendants are in the courtroom. Why, then, were all the witnesses not called before the court?

How is it possible to manage without the witness who, according to the findings of the kgb investigators and according to the verdict, was one of the two who supplied "anti-Soviet" literature to Hevrych? Perhaps the judges were afraid that A. Hors'ka, a resolute and uncompromising woman, might declare her attitude towards closed trials, as did another witness, the university student M. Plakhotnyuk. A person who is not as well-shod legally as Mats'ko, the head of the Kiev regional court, and the public prosecutor, Komalenko, would surely be surprised by the following sentence in the verdict of Yaroslav Hevrych: "The testimonies of witnesses Pronyuk and Hors'ka, denying that they ever gave anti-Soviet materials to Hevrych, do not merit consideration, because they are disproved by the testimony of the defendant Hevrych and by the material evidence."

A person who has been in the care of the KGB for several months, and who after a long silence says "yes", is believed. Another person is free to come and go; his "no" is, therefore, of a doubtful value. It is not clear why the "material evidence" taken away from Hevrych should testify against Hors'ka and not against somebody else. If this were reviewed by legal experts, they would insist that appropriate reference, required by law, should be made in the verdict. Thus, under Article 369, CPC, the verdict "is at variance with the factual circumstances of the case" because it is not stated therein "for what reason certain evidence was taken into consideration and other evidence rejected by the court."

The rude and mocking tone in which the judge and the public prosecutor accosted the defendants and witnesses should also be regarded as a direct violation of legal procedures. Here are samples of the erudition and culture of the court in Ivano-Frankivs'ke.

This is how the public prosecutor, a man with a higher legal education, talked to the candidate of philology and docent[1] of the Kiev State University, A. Matviyenko, who had the misfortune of obtaining a copy of Eisenhower's speech at the unveiling of Shevchenko's monument: "There are no mistakes. (The speech had been copied by hand—V. Ch.) Commas and periods are in the proper places. You were, of course, educated in a Soviet school." "Why are you writing for the entire city of Kiev? I also often visit Kiev, and I have dealings with people just like you . . ." "Why are you so concerned about the Ukrainian language, when you're willing to teach German or Turkish or whatever?" Matviyenko was teaching

---

[1] Roughly equivalent to an assistant professor in North American universities (transl. note).

Vyacheslav Chornovil   33

Polish at the university; she is the author of a popular book about the language. *(Zhyve slovo* [The Living Word] — V. Ch.) "Nemyrovych, sit down beside the candidate of sciences." *Nemyrovych* (with reference to Ozerny's work — V. Ch.): "Worthless scribbling." *Public prosecutor*: "Is the candidate of sciences of a different opinion?" *Matviyenko*: "I object. I have a family name," etc.

*

Prosecutor: Is your son married?

Hereta (witness): No.

Prosecutor: Well, they'll soon marry him there. (The witness' son was in jail in Ternopil' — V. Ch.)

Prosecutor (to witness G. Mel'nychenko): Where do your foolish thoughts come from? Ukraine, as a vassal of some capitalist country?

Judge: How did Ozerny approach you? Cunningly?(!)

Mel'nychenko: We saw that he was a clever and competent man.

Judge: I don't know this word. *(vatra* [bonfire] — V. Ch.) What kind of a word is it? I couldn't find it in a twelve-volume dictionary.

Ozerny: The word *vatra* has existed in the Ukrainian language for six hundred years. It was used by Kotsyubyns'ky and Franko. I have not heard of a twelve-volume dictionary of the Ukrainian language. But excuse me, perhaps it was compiled during my absence. (Poor judges and public prosecutors! Into what areas, so foreign to a jurist, does Article 62 of the Criminal Code of the Ukr. ssr lead them, and into what disgraceful mire are they frequently seated by it!)

Prosecutor (to witness Kosiv): Wasn't there some other word added to *vatra*?

Kosiv: No. (One might think that Ozerny was given six years just for this word *vatra*.)

Judge: You are an atheist, and yet you say, *day bozhe* [to your health; literally, may God give you health].

Ozerny: The first secretary also used these words.

*

The Petition of

The witness Khats'ko (a woman teacher): In my opinion, there is no point in misusing Shevchenko. He was a lonesome and unfortunate man and therefore wrote sad verses.
Judge: Was this (misuse of Shevchenko — V. Ch.) done on the initiative of Ozerny?
Khats'ko: Yes.

*

Prosecutor (to the witness Malyarchyk): Have you known Ozerny long? Did you treat him to wine or vodka? Do you often drive a motorcycle while drunk?

*

Prosecutor (in the state's indictment): Nationalists have sold themselves for a piece of rotten sausage, and a canned sausage at that. . . . Mel'nychenko's question, why Belgium enjoys independence, when we do not, could not but force his father to get in touch with the KGB. There were certain scientists and writers making statements here, but Mel'nychenko's father, as far as his cultural and political development is concerned, stands far above them. (Perhaps, if denouncements to the KGB can be regarded as signs of culture. More detailed information on Mel'nychenko Senior's "culture" may be derived from his testimonies. It seems that the public prosecutor, Karaskevych, is at the same level as Mel'nychenko Senior — V. Ch.) There is no organized plot against these people. No such organization can exist in this day and age. The cases of Ozerny, Hereta, and so forth are isolated instances."

One can only guess at the behaviour of judges and prosecutors at the other eight trials when they found themselves eye-to-eye with their victims. It is true, however, that witnesses related some instances of prosecutors' courtesy in closed trials. Personally, I had a chance at the trial of the Horyn' brothers, Ozerny, and Zvarychevs'ka to get acquainted with the public prosecutor of the L'viv region, Antonenko. (He is also a writer and the author of a book about the valiant Cheka agents and the supreme justice of our courts.) I declared that I would not give any evidence at a *closed trial* because I did not wish to participate in a flagrant violation of Soviet law and, at the same time, presented flowers from their friends to the people unlawfully condemned. Then the prosecutor jumped up and in a high-pitched voice called me an *enemy* who had no right to speak of socialist legality. Soldiers were ordered to remove me from the courtroom, and they performed their offensive operation with such lightning speed that I did not have enough time to open my mouth. But I had a great desire to ask the prosecutor, a writer, why it is that I, who was protesting against the revival of lawlessness similar to the cult-of-personality days — the closed tribunal — am branded an enemy, while he, who in his capacity as the regional public prosecutor sanctioned this gross violation of the letter and spirit of our laws, claims to be a friend of the Soviet system.

In his concluding remarks the public prosecutor, writer Antonenko, gave one more proof that in literary erudition he was not inferior to his colleague in Ivano-Frankivs'ke. He adopted Markiyan Shashkevych as a fellow fighter against "particularly dangerous" (state crimes) by using the famous words of the rouser of the Galicians,[1] "The Rus' language has borne us, the Rus' language has swaddled us, so why is that language not dear to us? Why must we be ashamed of it, and cherish a foreign one?" as proof of the Galicians age-old yearning to be merged with the "older" brother, Russia. Prosecutor Antonenko, who more than a year or two ago was posted to L'viv to instruct the Galicians in socialist legality, still does not even know that *rus'kyy*[2] in the past did not mean "Russian" at all. I feel sorry for Markiyan Shashkevych. The writer-prosecutor made him appear to march in step with a Black-Hundred[3] member, Shul'gin. But the violations of articles of the CPC, Ukr. SSR, mentioned above pale in comparison to the ordeal of a closed trial of those who criticize the state. This is a crime against humanity.

---

1 Inhabitants of Galicia (Western Ukraine), which was part of the Austrian Empire (to 1918), Poland (to 1939) and of USSR since (transl. note).
2 "Rus' " being the ancient name of Ukraine (transl. note).
3 Member of the extreme monarchists' group in pre-revolutionary Russia (transl. note).

b) CLOSED TRIALS. *"In all courts of the* USSR *cases are heard in public,* unless otherwise provided for by law, and the accused is guaranteed the right to defence" (Constitution of the USSR, Article 111).

"In accordance with Article 91 of the Constitution of the Ukrainian SSR, in all courts of the Ukrainian SSR cases are heard in public unless otherwise provided for by law" (Law on the Judicial System of the Ukrainian SSR, Article 11).

Public court trials. "All cases shall be tried in open courts, with the exception of cases when this is contrary to the interests of *preservation of state secrets.* Closed court trials may be authorized in other cases by a substantiated court resolution in respect to crimes committed by *individuals under the age of 16 years,* in cases of *sexual crimes,* as well as in other cases where it is necessary to prevent leakage of information *about intimate aspects of life of persons* who take part in the trial. *Court verdicts in all cases shall be announced publicly.* For the purpose of raising the educational role of the court trials and of crime prevention, courts shall duly inform the workers . . . about the court proceedings which are scheduled to take place. . . . The courts are obliged to *practice widely the holding of judicial proceedings directly at enterprises,* construction sites, state and collective farms, with participation, whenever necessary, of citizens' prosecutors and citizens' defenders" (Article 20, CPC, Ukr. SSR). "Verdicts shall be rescinded in every case . . . where the provisions of this Code which call for an open court trial have been violated by the court." (Article 370, CPC, Ukr. SSR). "All persons accused of committing a crime have the right to be considered innocent until their guilt is established legally *by way of a public court examination,* during which they shall be given every opportunity for defence." (The Universal Declaration of Human Rights adopted by the United Nations, Article 11.)

Article 20, CPC, Ukr. SSR, is quite understandable even to junior-grade students. It does not contain any reference to the existence of some other laws or instructions which would broaden the circumstances under which closed trials could be held. Why then were Zalyvakha, Hevrych, Hereta, Hel', Menkush, Kuznetsova, Martynenko, Masyutko, Rusyn, and others tried in a closed court? They were all of age, they committed no sexual crimes, and there was no necessity to touch upon the intimate aspects of their lives in court. None of them passed any military or technological secrets to foreign intelligence (provided, of course, that data on the number of Ukrainian and Russian schools in the republic, on the language of instruction in the institutions of higher learning, or on the volumes of literature published in the Ukrainian ssr in the Russian and Ukrainian languages are not classified as state secrets).

However, the trial of Penkovs'ky, the spy, was given the widest publicity; the stenographic court record was published in a very large edition. The matter in question there was the passing of secret materials abroad, but here were books which are freely accessible to everybody beyond our borders. Yet in our country they turned out to be that super-bomb so feared by those who advocate closed court sessions.

Explanations of the defendant, testimonies of witnesses, the defence of "lawyers", the last words of the defendant, and the fiery indictment by the prosecutor were heard in the course of several days by the prosecutor himself, by judges, by the "defence lawyer", by the defendant, and by several rows of empty seats in the courtroom. The public was represented by soldiers in full battle dress. (Naturally, for it is not a murderer on trial, but an artist or a teacher. He is certainly likely to attack the High Court!) It is not necessary to have a highly penetrating mind in order to understand that people were brought to court only because they tried to have thoughts of their own and their own convictions; the trials were closed to keep the absence of evidence hidden within four empty walls.

Even though the audiences were screened before they were admitted to the trials, the judges were afraid that Zalyvakha, Horyn', Martynenko, Rusyn, and others might tell the *truth* in public, as did Moroz in Luts'k. The defendants might have begun to talk about the shameful violations of the Leninist nationality policy. They were bound to say that they were interested, not so much in the thoughts and conclusions of the authors of those books and anonymous articles from abroad, as in factual materials (particularly about the terrible years of the personality cult). For some reason these facts do not appear on the pages of our newspapers, magazines, and books. The judges were afraid that the insignificance of the charges and the unspeakable methods of conducting investigations and of psychological terror would come to light.

"The law rules supreme here," the newspapers announced in large letters at the trial of Synyavs'ky and Daniel. And the fact that it was an open trial (at least, officially) was regarded as the main argument in proof of its legality. Why, then, does this kind of law not "rule supreme' 'in Ukraine today? Not a single newspaper published even an inkling about the secret trials. Not only the "crime", but even the very fact that there have been political arrests is concealed from the people. We have only scant information (it is rumoured that Zalyvakha categorically denied his guilt) about the closed trials in Ternopil' and Ivano-Frankivis'ke. I will, therefore, relate in greater detail how justice was meted out in Kiev and in L'viv.

The trial of Yaroslav Hevrych, from the 9th to the 11th of March (?), was conducted by Mats'ko, the Head of the Kiev Regional Court, assessors Yarko and Zahorodniy, and public prosecutor Komashchenko. (I had no time to write down the name of the "defence lawyer", but after all, he had no role to play.)

The illegality began when nobody, not even any of the relatives, was notified about the trial. And so on the first day comrade Mats'ko had peace and quiet in court. Witnesses were summoned for the 10th of March, with the result that a few people found out about the trial. (Perhaps they should try to hold a closed trial *without* witnesses? Then nobody need know.) Buttonholing Mats'ko, Hevrych's friends and colleagues from the institute tried to question him about the law that allowed a closed trial for Hevrych. To prevent them from impeding the administration of justice, police and plainclothesmen ousted these exceedingly inquisitive citizens from the court hallway, pulling this one's sleeve, pushing another's shoulder. In vain, however. People did not go away; they ignored the plainclothesmen and without the required respect, started to speak of lawlessness. To get rid of them it was then announced that the sentence would be passed the next day at two o'clock (for according to the law sentences must be read openly).

As might have been expected, the high court lied; the sentence was announced at about eleven o'clock in the morning. "Don't you really understand why it was done?" asked the "lawyer", astonished at the naïveté of the disappointed people. Unfortunately comrade Mats'ko made a slight error in his calculations, and at eleven o'clock several scores of people had already gathered at the court building. So a new tactical decision was made. A large group of people, almost in march formation, filed into the courtroom past Hevrych's astonished friends. Police and civilian door guards respectfully admitted them. When the sentence was announced minutes later, only a few of those who were anxious to get in had managed to do so. There was "no room left" for the rest. All seats, except the last row, were taken by the unexpected "friends" of the defendant who were led inside in formation. There is no need for detailed commentaries on the sentence. It speaks for itself.

Only comrade Mats'ko's mistake merits special attention. Instead of "court in a closed judicial session has considered the case," he for some reason read, "in an open judicial session". The Head of the Regional Court is not supposed to make such mistakes, because for all we know some of those present (we do not refer to the organized company of "friends" of the defendant) might think that comrade Mats'ko wanted to whitewash himself before history by falsifying documents. And when after the trial three men from the audience broke through the police and the KGB officials to comrade Mats'ko, they asked him three questions:

1. Under what article of which code was the trial held in closed court? 2. Why did the court deceive the defendant's friends when it proclaimed the time of the announcement of sentence? 3. Why were those who wanted to come in not admitted and who were the people who were led inside in formation?

The chairman of the provincial court could not (or did not want to) answer two of these questions. As an answer to the third, he simply said, "*Your people* also walk in groups."

Kuznetsova, Martynenko, and Rusyn were tried by Mats'ko

"and comrades" after they had learned from their mistakes of the previous trial. Larger details of police and plainclothesmen were called. This time the "public" planted for the reading of sentences were brought in surreptitiously, either through the window or through the back entrance (because the main entrance was blocked by a crowd of people who wanted to be present at the trial). And this time comrade Mats'ko tried to avoid being seen. A person with a membership card from the Writers Union of Ukraine, who wanted explanations from other officials of the provincial court, was escorted inside by the police.

For the actual reading of the verdict only three "outsiders" were let in, and even they were tightly surrounded by the "public" present there. But even those three outsiders managed to distress those who administer the law. Probably knowing that the verdict would not be secret, because "in all cases it is pronounced publicly" (Article 20 of the Code of Criminal Procedure), poetess Lina Kostenko and Lyubov Zabashta decided to make a note of it. The "public" forcibly took those notes away from them. And when Miss Kostenko threw flowers to the convicted after the verdict was passed, those flowers were, of course, immediately seized. Lina Kostenko herself was bullied and interrogated intensively in the court building, but the grand finale of the closed trial of "especially dangerous state criminals" had already been completely ruined. And the already ruffled composure of comrades Mats'ko and Komashchenko was completely unbalanced by those ignorant citizens who waited for hours for the Black Raven, then tried to keep up the convicts' morale by shouting encouragement and throwing flowers under the wheels of the van.

However, the Kieven KGB officials and those who administer the law there are veritable angels with wings in comparison with their colleagues in L'viv. No matter how many procedural standards they violated, no matter how cruel their sentences for the crime of reading books, the Kievans were still unable to stage anything to equal the case of Masyutko. (I shall write later about that case, which rivals anything that happened in the thirties.)

The judges in Kiev at least took partially into account the

law which demands that verdicts of the judges be made public in all cases. They also allowed the relatives of the accused and a few acquaintances, besides the "public", to be present at the reading of the verdict. In L'viv they looked at the matter more soberly.

If Article 20 of the Code of Criminal Procedure of the Ukrainian ssr, concerning the open nature of the court investigation, could be flagrantly violated, then why should they not bypass the public reading of the verdict? And so no one was admitted to the reading of the verdict in all three trials in L'viv. There is no evidence that even the "public" was present there, apart, of course, from the soldiers of the guard. Masyutko's verdict was passed without any outsiders present. Evidently the court officials thought that nobody would find out about the absurd charges and that nobody need know the names of the lying "experts" who were witnesses. The "crimes" of the Horyn' brothers, Hel', Menkush, Zvarychevs'ka, and Osadchy were also concealed from the people. If the verdict was passed in secret, then perhaps those people were not guilty at all?

The officials of the L'viv KGB also distinguished themselves by keeping "order" in the court, especially during the trial of the Horyn' brothers. In fact they behaved as though L'viv were an occupied territory and not Soviet land. How else can one explain why the police openly threatened the people who gathered in front of the court? How else can one justify the cynical behaviour of a KGB major (in civilian clothes) who tried to close Ol'ha Horyn's mouth with his hand when she wanted to point out to her two-year old daughter her father as he was led from the Black Raven? How should one evaluate the behaviour of another major (in uniform) who brutally cursed the witness while escorting him from the court chamber?

By what moral standards of our society can one justify the cynical deceit used by Lieutenant-Colonel Kherosnyuk (at least he called himself that) to "clear" the floor during the trial of the Horyn's and others? Chasing the people downstairs, he gave his word of honour that he would inform the relatives about the verdict and would admit to the reading of the verdict some of those who wished to hear it. When everybody reached the first floor, they realized they were trapped. The police would not let them go upstairs and armed soldiers would not let them outside. They were kept under arrest until the secret verdict was passed and the convicted were led out through the back door. The guardians of the law were afraid of a repetition of the incidents of previous days, when the citizens of L'viv showered one Black Raven with flowers and chanted, "Glory!"

When the people detained in the hall were let out into the street, they saw that the adjoining streets were blocked off by militia. The crowd chanted, "Shame!" The lieutenant-colonel of the militia, Kherosnyuk, the major who was closing people's mouths, and other KGB officials laughed brazenly, as if to say, "We fooled you. We prevented you from being present at the reading of the verdict and from seeing the convicted leave!" Ironically the L'viv guardians of "state security", who were the cause of the protest demonstration, later used motor vehicles to force the people back from the street adjacent to the court or dispersed the crowd with water hoses. (Next to come, probably, would be policemen's truncheons and tear gas.)

As a member of the United Nations the Ukrainian SSR delegation voted for the Universal Declaration of Human Rights, which was adopted by the General Assembly. More than that, the Soviet delegation considered that "the absence of specific instructions about the compulsory observance by the countries of the declared rights and freedoms of man represents a shortcoming of the Declaration." To supplement that deficiency, the Soviet Union proposed to include in the Declaration the following article: "The rights and basic freedoms of man and citizens, enumerated in this Declaration, are guaranteed by state laws. Any violations or restrictions of these rights, direct or indirect, constitute violation of this Declaration and are incompatible with the high principles proclaimed in the Statute of the United Nations." (Journal *Mezhdunarod-naya Zhizn* [International Affairs], 1955, No. 12, page 145.)

It is clearly written in this Declaration, however, that every accused person has the right to defence and to a "public trial" (Art. 11 of the Declaration)!

Either we are the greatest hypocrites in the world, or we have such short memories that we forget today what we so passionately defended yesterday. When it was announced that the Leninist standards of legality, previously trampled in the mud, were to be restored, it seemed that *troykas*[1] and secret trials of those whose only crime was their ability to think were gone forever. Is it possible that we were so terribly mistaken in our expectations?

b) THE RIGHT TO DEFENCE. THE "ATTORNEY". "The defence attorney is under obligation to make the most of all legal means and ways in order to establish the circumstances which would acquit the defendant or would lessen his responsibility and should render the necessary legal assistance to the defendant" (Art. 48, CPC, Ukr. SSR).

"The defence attorney assists the defendant in the realization of his rights and in the defence of his legal interests. The defence attorney has the right to meet with the accused, takes part in the examination of evidence, brings before the court the request for the utilization or the addition to the case of new evidence which would acquit the defendant or would lessen his responsibility. He also submits to the court other requests, and expresses his opinion about the requests of other participants of the court trial. The defence attorney takes part in court debates, expressing his opinion about the evidence examined in the case, about the presence of circumstances which would acquit the defendant or would lessen his responsibility, as well as his observations concerning the application of the criminal law and the imposed penalty" (Art. 266, Criminal Procedure Code, Ukrainian SSR).

"The defence attorney may be invited from the persons mentioned in Art. 41, Section 4, of this Code, by the defendant himself, his legal representative, his relatives or by other persons at the instruction or request of the defendant" (Art. 47, Criminal Procedure Code, Ukr. SSR).

"The defendant or the accused has the right to decline a

---

[1] Closed police courts employed from December, 1934, against certain categories of political offenders; abolished after the death of Stalin (transl. note).

defence attorney at any time during the proceedings of his case" (Art. 46, Criminal Procedure Code, Ukr. ssr).

In a closed trial the right for defence, which the accused supposedly possesses, becomes an empty fiction. But when there are members of the public present in the court, even the most prejudiced judge must take their presence and conscience into account and he must also find answers to the arguments of the defendant. A closed trial resembles the closed cage of a boa-constrictor who is given a small rabbit for his breakfast; before the rabbit is devoured he is allowed to present before the hungry predator all the arguments of his innocence. The most ridiculous figure of our court, especially during the trial of "especially dangerous crimes", is the defence attorney.

The defence attorney is forbidden to speak about the special circumstances which led the accused to the action which was elevated to the rank of "crime". Any venture into this realm is a mortal taboo for the attorney. Neither in Luts'k nor in Ivano-Frankivs'ke did the "attorney" *once contest the judge or the prosecutor*, even when they spoke the most ridiculous nonsense (about the "bonfire" or about Shevchenko's works, etc.), although he had full right to do so in accordance with Art. 261 of the Criminal Procedure Code of the Ukr. ssr ("the equality of rights of the participants in the court hearing".)

At the trial in Ivano-Frankivs'ke, during the questioning of numerous witnesses, the attorney was silent as a fish. He did not ask the students their opinion of Ozerny as a pedagogue — the students themselves volunteered praise of their teacher. The attorney, who has "equal rights" with the prosecutor, did not protest when the prosecutor insulted his client and the witnesses — they had to protest for *themselves*. The attorney did not critize the court for deviating from the line when it dealt with the meetings of teachers and launched into a long and boring investigation of how many verses of Shevchenko pupils were required to memorize; the name of the school club; the shortcomings of Ozerny's lecture on Shevchenko; and how frequently Ozerny attended political lectures. The attorney did not resent it when the accused was charged with employing archaic language. (Or maybe the attorney thought that such expressions as "healthy spirit in healthy body" and "the enemies of your people are your enemies" were invented by the *banderivtsi*?[1]) He also remained silent when the proof of Ozerny's crime was presented in the form of the *History of Ukraine* by Arkas,[2] a poem by Chubynsky, *Ukraine Is Not Yet Dead*,[3] written one hundred years ago and which today has only a historical-literary interest (although somebody is apparently still afraid of it!), and Shevchenko's poem, *The Ransacked Grave*.

The only question that the attorney forced himself to ask was one that a prosecutor might ask: Why Ozerny was not punished by the teaching staff for the "crimes" mentioned above! Ozerny's "attorney" did not resent the fact that during the examination of witnesses, as well as in the state indictment, the prosecutor brought up a table talk during a drinking party at Hereta's place. Neither the defendant nor the witnesses could fully reconstruct this conversation, and their testimonies had to be brought to a common denominator with the help of data obtained by the KGB in a more "sober" way (perhaps something à la Zhytomyr "album"). Furthermore, the attorney did not demand that the supposedly anti-Soviet documents, which were mentioned in court by names only, be read into the transcript. According to the law, he had every right to demand that the content of those documents be revealed, or at least that more information be given about them. (Perhaps then the passages taken at random from Eisenhower's and Pope Paul's speeches would not be described as terrible documents.) The attorney could, finally, have given "his opinion about the significance of examined documents . . ." The attorney broke his silence, which lasted for several hours, with a defence speech by which he proved that when the legal profession completely dies out in our country, he will be a candidate at least for the position of assistant to the public prosecutor.

Here is an extract from a speech which was supposed to be

---

1 Members of the Bandera movement. Bandera, one of the leaders of the Organization of Ukrainian Nationalists, was murdered by the Soviet agent Stashynsky in Munich in 1959 (transl. note).

2 A popular pre-revolutionary text in Ukrainian history (transl. note).

3 *Shche ne vmerla Ukraina*: the text of the Ukrainian national anthem, banned in Ukraine (transl. note).

"favourable to the defendant in the realization of his rights and in defence of his legal interests" (Art. 266, Criminal Procedure Code of the Ukr. ssr): "At the present time, the life of people living in the western provinces of Ukraine has improved considerably. If we compare our present village with that of the landlord's Poland of yesterday, we must admit that it is a huge step forward. It is strange that such a phenomenon as a manifestation of nationalism still exists. (Hasn't he been helpful! — V. Ch.) It would be easier to understand if it were right after the war! These are the isolated dark spots on our white body. The present case showed that the highest principles were defiled. (He even helped to mitigate the punishment . . . V. Ch.) We heard here about some kind of humiliation of the Ukrainian language, about russification. Older people remember the times when it was an event when a Ukrainian found a job. Now we are all guaranteed work and to talk about some kind of russification is an absurdity and stupefication of youth. (Are unemployment and russification one and the same thing? — V. Ch.) I will not contest that the offence was proved. I agree." (What else! — V. Ch.)

Having started, the attorney decided to "defend" not only his client, but also the witnesses: "Let's consider Hereta, senior scientist of the Ternopil' Museum. He is supposed to glorify the past (?). But how can he perform his duties well when he is the son of a clergyman?"[1] (How aromatic is this breeze of the humanity of the 1930's. — V. Ch.) It is true that the "attorney" did not completely copy the prosecutor. He named the mitigating circumstances, noting that the defendant acknowledged his "crime"; that he had two children; that he and his wife were in ill health. But his main point was that letters of reference written about Ozerny in 1959-1961 characterized him as a very "positive" person. Lack of logic played a dirty trick with the "attorney": How did it happen that the very positive Ozerny suddenly became very negative, even to the point of being an "especially dangerous state criminal"?

Could the casual meeting with the woman lecturer of Kiev

---

[1] In the thirties the clergy and everyone else not of peasant or worker stock were condemned as members of the exploiting class. There is still a tendency to condemn children for the "sins" of the fathers (transl. note).

University be the reason? If positive people become criminals so easily, it must be that either their crime is not a crime at all or that there are some social conditions that encourage people to commit that "crime". In that case, one cannot brush off the situation as "dark spots on a white body". A ludicrous figure like the attorney is not usually taken seriously. It was natural, then, that his timid remark that "in my opinion, six years is too much" made no impression on the court. The prosecutor's demand was fully satisfied. Ozerny received the full treatment from the regional court.

More ridiculous, even disgraceful, is the role of the attorney at a closed hearing. Essentially, he has nothing to do. When somebody hires an attorney he hopes that the attorney will at least report on the health and well-being of his imprisoned relatives. (After the investigation is completed the attorney has the right to see the imprisoned person in private.) But no such luck here. The "attorneys" were mute as fish. What's more, contrary to all laws, the "attorneys" sometimes did not even notify the defendant's relatives about the trial. For instance, Yaroslav Hevrych's "attorney" notified neither the parents of the defendant nor his friend, student M. Plakhotnyuk, who actually *hired the "attorney"*.

The witness for the defence, M. Plakhotnyuk, was right when he voiced his indignation at the court session about the conduct of the "attorney", together with his protest against a closed trial. (It would be interesting to know whether this protest and his indignation were recorded in the transcript of the trial. Or did comrade Mats'ko restrict himself only to immediately notifying the Medical Institute about the "improper" conduct of the student Plakhotnyuk?) During the closed trial of the Horyn' brothers, Osadchy, and Zvary-chevs'ka, it was unpleasant to watch the attorneys trying to avoid the defendants' relatives. And while they muttered meaningless phrases to those relatives, their eyes darted watchfully to and fro. The value of their defence can be seen from these comparisons: The prosecutor demanded a six-year prison term for M. Horyn', a four-year term for B. Horyn', three years for M. Osadchy, and a conditional year-and-half term for M.

Zvarychevs'ka. The court decided accordingly on six, four, two-year, and eight-month terms respectively.

Perhaps the relatives of the condemned men simply had no luck with the attorneys? Perhaps they engaged the services of defence attorneys who were not qualified to handle those cases and whose ability to think logically and to look at the problem more broadly was poorly developed? That's the way it goes! You may not engage the attorney you want, but the one you are *given*, the one who has a *special pass* to handle "exceptionally important cases". Ozerny's "attorney" had such a pass, while the brilliant attorney of the poet-translator Brodsky, who was tried in Leningrad for "parasitism" (What luck! — V. Ch.), probably did not have it. Once they have gained possession of those passes by their faithful service, it is understandable why these attorneys become so silent.

If you inspect all basic legal acts — The Fundamental Principles of Criminal Procedure of the USSR and Union Republics, the law on the Court Organization of the Ukr. SSR, the Criminal Procedure Code of the Ukr. SSR, and finally the Regulations of the Legal Profession of the Ukr. SSR — you will not find anywhere even a hint of any special passes. On the contrary, Art. 44, par. 4, of the Criminal Procedure Code of the Ukr. SSR says, in effect, take any attorney you like. But in the office of the bar you are told, "No, Petrenko cannot defend you because he has no special pass. We recommend that you take Pawlyuk." Then during the trial one of those attorneys with "special passes" will tell you, "You are all nationalists and anti-Soviet individuals. (This is how the woman attorney who "defended" Hevrych answered the demands made by his friends.) All of you deserve the same treatment as Hevrych."

It is true that even among those who have "special passes" there are some human beings whose consciences are not completely extinguished. Such was Masyutko's attorney, Serhyenko. The accusation was completely absurd and not supported by any evidence, and the deductions of the learned committee of experts were quite ridiculous. Acting on the dictates of his conscience, Serhyenko refused to agree that the defendant was guilty of the crimes attributed to him. Of course he was ignored, and during the intermission the prosecutor drew the attention (of the "equal participant in the court hearings") to the fact that he, as a communist, was acting contrary to his convictions. After that Serhyenko complained that he might be expelled from the Party and as a consequence forfeit his pension rights.

Knowing who is allowed to defend "state criminals", and in what situation the attorneys are placed, some of the defendants prefer to forgo their rights to an attorney and to defend themselves. However, this is not always possible. Contrary to Art. 46, CPC of the Ukr. SSR, and despite his refusal, Mykhaylo Horyn' had an attorney imposed on him by the court. Why? In order to increase the number of participants in this farce that took place behind closed doors, and in order to deduct from Horyn's meagre salary a substantial fee for the "attorney's services". It looks as though Ol'ha Horyn' will have to do without food for her child for a while in order to pay for the "defence" of her husband. It appears that those "dollars", about which so much was said by the Party officials right after the arrests, were probably detained on their way.

V. THE ABSURDITY AND SENSELESSNESS OF ACCUSATIONS AND THE
CRUELTY OF SENTENCES

"The punishment imposed by the court shall not be considered as corresponding to the seriousness of the crime and the personality of the convicted if the punishment is manifestly unjust either by its softness or by its severity, even if it does not exceed the limits imposed by the applicable article of the Criminal Code" (Art. 372, Criminal Procedure Code of the Ukr. SSR).

"The sentence of the court should be *based on law and substantiated*" (Art. 323, Criminal Procedure Code of the Ukr. SSR).

"During the court session the defendant has the right . . . to request the court to make public the evidence which is pertinent to the case" (Art. 263, Criminal Procedure Code of the Ukr. SSR).

"In the application of the measures of criminal punishment, the court not only punishes criminals, it aims also at correcting and reforming them" (Art. 320, Principles of the Judicial Structure of the Ukr. SSR).

"Sentences of the Court of Special Sittings, which was an obedient instrument in the hands of the government, were hideously cruel. People were sentenced to ten, twelve, fifteen years of hard labour for a few revolutionary talks with small groups of workers or for reading or circulating a forbidden book. Thus, the same thing which is done completely freely in any West European country, in our country is punished in the same way as a murder" (Stepnyak-Kravchinsky, *Popdol'naya Rossiya* [Underground Russia], London, 1883, pp. 20-21).

*

Famusov: It's teaching is the plague, it's learning is the reason
That now, far worse than e'er before,
You see all 'round mad folks, mad acts, mad speculations.
Skalozub: I've got good news for you: if all reports are true,
They're going to reform schools, colleges, gymnasiums.
In future we shall teach in Russian style: One, Two!
And books they'll only keep, well, just for great occasions.
Famusov: Sergey Sergeich, no! From evil ways to turn them,
You'll have to take all books and burn them.
(Griboyedov, *Wit Works Woe*[1])

*

Now let us see the output of the machine of "justice" in Ukraine over the last few months:
Sentenced to various terms of imprisonment in severe hard-labour camps — sixteen people:

---

[1] Cited in translation by Sir Bernard Pares in Noyes, G. R. (ed.), *Masterpieces of the Russian Drama.* (New York: Dover Publications, 1960), Vol. 1, pp. 135, 136. The title of this play can also be translated as *The Misfortune of Intellect,* and is the source of the title of Chornovil's collection of the documents of the convicted which comprises Part II of this book (transl. note).

1. Ivashchenko — lecturer in Ukrainian literature at the Luts'k Pedagogical Institute — two years;
2. Moroz — lecturer in history in the same Institute — four years;
3. Ozerny — teacher of Ukrainian and German languages in the Ripkivs'ka Secondary School in the Province of Ivano-Frankivs'ke — six years (the Supreme Court reduced this term to three years);
4. Hevrych — fifth-year student of the Kiev Medical Institute — five years (the Supreme Court reduced this term to three years);
5. Kuznetsova — laboratory worker at the Kiev University — four years;
6. Martynenko — engineer (Kiev) — three years;
7. Rusyn—scientist at the Scientific Research Institute (Kiev) — one year;
8. Masyutko — pensioner (Feodosia) — six years, out of which three years in isolation;
9. Zalyvakha — artist (Ivano-Frankivs'ke) — five years;
10. Hel' — labourer, an evening school student (L'viv) — three years;
11. Menkush — designer in a fashion house (L'viv) — two and a half years;
12. Horyn', Mykhaylo — scientist at the Laboratory of Industrial Psychology (L'viv)—six years, out of which three years in special camps;
13. Horyn', Bohdan — art expert, employee of the Museum of Ukrainian Art (L'viv) — four years;
14. Osadchy — lecturer at the University of L'viv — two years;
15. Zvarychevs'ka—employee of the Regional Archives (L'viv) —eight months;
16. Hryn' — candidate of science, scientist in the Geophysical Institute of the Academy of Sciences of the Ukrainian SSR (Kiev) — two years;

Sentenced conditionally:
1. Hereta — research worker in the Ternopil' Museum of Local Lore — ?
2. Chubaty — teacher in the School of Music in the village of Velyki Hayi district of Terebovlya, Region of Ternopil'—?

(There are still unverified data on other arrests).

Exiled without investigation and without trial to the camps for political offenders (Mordovian A.S.S.R.) — Karavans'ky — writer and journalist (Odessa).

Released after five months of imprisonment in the jail of the KGB — five persons:

1. Ivanyshyn — teacher of physical education in the village of Duba, district Rozhnyatyn, Region of Ivano-Frankivs'ke;
2. Baturyn — bookkeeper of the L'viv Regional Consumers' Co-operative;
3. Kosiv — Head of the Institute for the Study of Franko and lecturer at the L'viv University. During imprisonment he was seriously afflicted with a heart ailment. After his release he became unemployed;
4. Sadovs'ka — engineer in the Project Institute (L'viv);
5. Morhun — artist of the Theatre of I. Franko in Kiev.

Ivan Svitlychny, a literary critic, was released after eight months of imprisonment. Several persons — for instance, electrician Perediyenko, a university student Vorbst (Kiev), Ol'ha Horyn' (L'viv), and others — were released after short-term detentions (lasting several days). Scores of people were subjected to searches and confiscation of books, letters, memoirs, and notebooks. Hundreds of people were questioned (the interrogations still continue).

Under the influence of the KGB (at least indirectly), many people were dismissed from their jobs and were subjected to administrative fines.

A very colourful picture! It makes it fully possible to speak about the systematic, deliberate, and purposeful nature of the "pacification".

WHAT WERE THE ACCUSATIONS?

So far, we have mainly discussed the violations of procedural standards for trials and investigations. I am going to dwell upon this subject in detail, relying primarily upon the materials supplied by the trials of Hevrych, Ozerny, and Masyutko. I have less information about other trials. As it is known, it was forbidden to make notes on the sentences passed on Kuznetsova, Rusyn, and Martynenko. The sentences of Hel', Menkush and the brothers Horyn', Osadchy, and Zvarychevs'ka were passed in secret. As it became known later, the brothers Horyn', Zalyvakha, and others did not completely acknowledge their guilt and did not repent. However, the regional court imposed upon them the same punishment (or less, in the case of B. Horyn') as that received by Ozerny and Hevrych. Thus, the KGB managed to press such serious charges against Hevrych and Osadchy that their confessions did not help them. (After all, the sentence remained quite severe even after it was reviewed by the Supreme Court of the Ukr. SSR.)

What do those charges consist of? Let us consider all the things that were said in court in Ivano-Frankivs'ke during those several days of the trial, "absence from political lectures", "misuse of Shevchenko", "the bonfire", strong emotions,[1] the irrelevant conversation about an "anthem" at a drinking party at Hereta's, etc. (if the KGB could overhear all the drunken conversations, half of the population of Ukraine would be in prison), as well as the so-called "catch phrases",[2] at least those cited at the trial. (If there were any others, they should have been mentioned.)

By the way, during the trial who gave the right to interpret the phrase about obedience to national leaders as if it referred to the *Banderivtsi?* Those are purely subjective presumptions. Why could Shevchenko and Franko not be mentioned in the past, Shelest and Shcherbyts'ky in the present, and why did they have to drag out Bandera, who was killed five years ago? If we reject all these and similar "crimes", which took up most of the discussion at the trial, all that is left are several articles which were mentioned or read to close friends by Ozerny: *The Trial of Pohruzhal'sky; Ukrainian Education in a Chauvinistic Stranglehold*; the speech of Pope Paul VI; Eisenhower's speech at the unveiling of Shevchenko's monument in Washington; the reply of Canadian and American cultural workers to the cultural workers of Ukraine; as well a short work by Ozerny himself, which he did not circulate, and an anecdote

---

1 In original, "football emotions" (transl. note).
2 In original, "winged terms" (transl. note).

or account written by him about the shortage of food supplies during the time of Khrushchev. While the "bonfire", the "anthem", and the pupil's letter to the teacher absorbed God knows how much time, these other items were mentioned *by names only*. Can the name alone (for instance, *The Trial of Pohruzhal'sky*) indicate that the work is anti-Soviet? Unless there were closed court sessions (and they were not mentioned!) how did the assessors find out that this or that handwritten article was anti-Soviet? Did they simply take the prosecutor's words for granted? If so, then why did they sit in those august chairs for several days? Was it just to listen to anecdotes about the "bonfire" and the non-existent twelve-volume dictionary of the Ukrainian language? Can people be tried for reading official speeches (of Pope Paul VI or of the president of a foreign country), even if they are ideologically foreign to us? Such speeches (or summaries of them) ought to be printed in newspapers and refuted with arguments, as is sometimes done on the pages of *Pravda*.

An especially shameful incident occurred with the letter from the overseas Ukrainians. Two years ago, a group of Ukrainian literary and cultural workers addressed, through *Literaturna Ukraina*,[1] a message to Ukrainian emigrés overseas, in which they wrote in quite a restrained manner about the unveiling of the Shevchenko monument in Washington. Our cultural leaders did not protest against the very fact of the unveiling of the monument, but asked their overseas kinsmen (without this time calling them "mercenaries", and without mentioning the "piece of rotten sausage" which had usually figured in the conversation between the two sides) not to permit the transformation of this event into a distortion of Shevchenko's creative legacy. This open letter was *reprinted* abroad and the answer to it was given. Of course, the reply was never read by those to whom it was addressed. And the one who did manage to read it was brought before the court.

At the trial in Ivano-Frankivs'ke it was not proved that Ozerny actively multiplied and disseminated those materials. The only incident that was mentioned was when Ozerny asked

---

[1] *Literary Ukraine*, organ of the Union of Writers of Ukraine (transl. note).

his friend to re-type for him the article, *The Trial of Pohruz-hal'sky*, and the Pope's speech (which incidentally could have been heard by thousands of people when it was broadcast on the Vatican radio station, which is not "jammed" here). The circle to whom Ozerny "disseminated" the seized materials was restricted to two or three close friends, with whom he shared those items of "news" that he possessed (sometimes during social drinking, as was the case with the Malyarchyks). So even if we accept that Art. 62 of the Code of Criminal Procedure of the Ukr. ssr conforms with the spirit of Soviet legality, then we must admit that the treatment of Ozerny was extreme.

The cited "catch phrases" and drunken conversations do not yet, of course, constitute "agitation or propaganda, carried on for the purpose of subverting or weakening the Soviet rule or of committing particular, especially dangerous crimes against the state"; and as for the articles, one cannot seriously talk about "circulating or preparing . . . literature of such content". The only charge that remains is the "keeping" of such literature. Then why such severe punishment as six (or even three) years in hard-labour camps?

Two films were confiscated from Yaroslav Hevrych during the search of his place. (It was never revealed during the trial what kind of photographs they were. They might have been photographs of his relatives!) There were also two photographic copies of books. During the six months of interrogation, Hevrych confessed to the charge that he had allegedly taken other films from Pronyuk, which he later returned together with prints, and to the accusation that he had supposedly taken a photocopy of a book from Hors'ka; but the confession was not corroborated (by any witness or by the experts), and only Hevrych's admission appears in the verdict.

It is possible that during the secret trial the materials confiscated from Hevrych were analyzed — we do not know about that. However, in the verdict it is said only that there were films and copies. (For instance, Hevrych's brother told Yaroslav's friends that among the confiscated materials there was a film of the poems of Vasyl' Symonenko.[1]) Only two book titles

---

[1] A young Ukrainian writer (1935-1963) who openly spoke in opposition to the Soviet nationality policy in Ukraine (transl. note).

are mentioned: *Ukraine and the Ukrainian Policy of Moscow* and *The Deduction of Ukraine's Rights*. (The latter, judging by its title, was probably the work of Mazepa's associate, Orlyk, written in the 18th century).[1] Thus, it is a question of two or three photocopies of books (not even of several copies of the same book) that Hevrych prepared. And how did he disseminate them? If we reject the assertion about Pronyuk, which was not proven by the court, then Hevrych read (or re-told) some passages from the above-named material to his fiancée Sandurs'ka (again, the only basis here is Hevrych's testimony, because Sandurs'ka testified that she hardly remembered what it was all about) and *promised to give* something to Sandurs'ka's brother to read. This is all the "dissemination" that took place and which the investigators of the KGB have blown out of proportion within the last six months. It all amounted to Hevrych's reading the "forbidden" literature himself and giving an offhanded account about it to one of his acquaintances. Therefore, there could be no question of a deliberate and systematic dissemination — at least, not on the basis of the information contained in the verdict. Rather, we have here a case of an understandable curiosity about "forbidden fruit".

If for such a crime Hevrych was sentenced to *six years in a severe hard-labour camp*, despite his repentance, then what was the offence of Rusyn, who was sentenced to only one year? Perhaps he just read some book or told an anecdote? (Try to find out: The trial was secret; no one was allowed to be present at the reading of the verdict; and notes were torn out of the hands of those who wanted to record the proceedings.)

No matter how baseless or senseless the accusations were, someone is bound to say, they must after all be based on some real grounds. The convicted did read something that was forbidden and they did pass it on to others. Perhaps they were given too severe a punishment for their offence, and perhaps those offences were not punishable at all. Perhaps some norms

---

[1] Chornovil is probably wrong. The seized publication bearing this title apparently was a collection of documents relating to Ukraine's struggle for independence, which was published abroad in the 1960's under the editorship of B. Kravtsiv (transl. note).

of investigation and of trial were violated — but there still must have been something to it. Such a skeptic-optimist would conclude that one certainly cannot compare these practices with the times of Stalin's lawlessness. After all, during those times people were punished on the basis of completely fabricated accusations.

THE CASE OF MASYUTKO

In the middle of March [1966], several days before the commencement of the Twenty-Third Congress of the Communist Party of the Soviet Union, a retired teacher, Mykhaylo Savych Masyutko, was secretly tried in L'viv. Not a single witness was called from outside; no one was allowed to be present while the verdict was passed. The defendant's wife found out only from the defence attorney that her husband was sentenced to six years and that he was supposed to serve the first three years in prison in conditions of complete isolation. No one else would have found out anything about Masyutko's offence if it were not for a few accidents. On the first day of trial, it appeared that nobody knew about it, and so the security measures were relaxed; thus some people managed to listen at the doors of the court and to write down part of the state's accusation and part of the defendant's defence. The defence attorney also involuntarily revealed some details. Masyutko himself managed to pass a note to his wife during a meeting with her following his conviction. Thus a picture of the trial was obtained, a picture that reminds one of those good times when a rabbit could be forced to admit that he was a camel.

Masyutko was arrested in Feodosiya on September 1, 1965. During the search of his home, reprints of the poems of Sosyura, Franko, Pluzhnyk, Symonenko, Kostenko, Drach, Vinhranovsky, Letyuk, Yevtushenko, and Slutsky were confiscated. Also taken were transcripts of folk songs, Masyutko's diary, old-edition books, several copies of the so-called "anonymous anti-Soviet" articles, and many works by Masyutko himself (some of them about the times of Stalin's abuse of power). It was not proven during the interrogation that Masyutko disseminated anonymous articles (no witness was present at the trial); he did not even give his own works to anyone to read. It followed that he should have been released from detention, or, if he were to be tried, then only for the offence of keeping several copies of those terrible articles. Then why was he sentenced to six years, especially of severe hard labour?

A diligent organization [the KGB], which is supposed to track down poets and writers, was helpless in trying to identify the authors of the anonymous articles about the situation in Ukraine. In order to keep up their reputation — that of contemporary "Chekisty", glorified in dozens of novels and films — the KGB, having failed to find the author, made Masyutko the author, just as forty years ago, the GPU created the SVU (Union for the Liberation of Ukraine). They considered Masyutko a suitable candidate. He was little known; in the thirties he spent some time in Kolyma[1] (though he had been rehabilitated, one could hint at a "relapse"); he was also the author of many poems and short stories, though he had not published anything.

Thus, by the will of the KGB (and later by decree of the prosecutor and the court) Masyutko was suddenly made the author of at least ten so-called "anti-Soviet" articles and materials, namely: 1. *The Trial of Pohruzhal'sky*; 2. *The Present and Future of Ukrainian People*; 3. A letter to Vasyl Symonenko's mother; 4. *Literature and Pseudo-literature in Ukraine* (later this article was exempted from the "anti-Soviet" list); 5. *Twenty Questions to the Students of Social Sciences*; 6. *The Program of the Ukrainian Liberation Movement*; 7. *Contemporary Imperialism*; 8. *Ukrainian Education in a Chauvinistic Stranglehold*, and others.

The absence of proofs and witnesses did not bother the fighters for legality. Because the trial was held behind closed doors and even the sentence was passed secretly, Masyutko could have been convicted for causing the earthquake in Tashkent. To prevent Masyutko's uncompromising position from making an undesirable impression on other defendants, and in order to hide the falsification from the public, Masyutko,

---

1 Concentration camp in the far north (transl. note).

despite his protest, was tried separately (although he was tried in the same case as the Horyn' brothers, Osadchy, and Zvarychevs'ka). Having failed to extract a "confession" from Masyutko, the court called "experts", people with scientific degrees but quiet consciences, who agreed for a substantial fee to substantiate the authorship proposed by the KGB. These men of science did not aspire to fame on account of their scientific discovery; on the contrary they were guaranteed a good honorarium and complete secrecy. But sooner or later such secrets become public.

Here are the names of members of two such "panels of experts":

1. I. Shakhovsky, Professor of the L'viv State University;
2. Neboryachok, Head of the Department of Ukrainian Literature at the L.S.U.
3. Matviychuk, Doctor of Philology, Institute of Social Sciences in L'viv;
4. Hrytsyutenko, Candidate of Philology, the L.S.U.;
5. Zdoroveha, Candidate of Sciences, Faculty of Journalism of the L.S.U.;
6. Kybal'chych, lecturer in the Faculty of Journalism, L.S.U.;
7. Yashchuk, Candidate of Philology, L.S.U.;
8. Khudysh (L'viv);
9. Kobylyansky, Doctor of Philology (L'viv);
10. Babyshkin, Doctor of Philology (Kiev).

There were some individuals who declined to make a shameful profit from the misfortune of other people, among them the following scholars: 1. Kovalyk, Doctor of Philology, Head of the Department of Ukrainian Language, L'viv State University; 2. Shablyovs'ky, Doctor of Philology, Institute of Literature, the Academy of Sciences of the Ukrainian SSR in Kiev; 3. Volyns'ky, Professor, Head of the Department of Ukrainian Literature, Pedagogical Institute of Kiev; 4. Zozulya, expert on Ukrainian literature, Moscow; 5. Shchurat, Institute of Social Sciences in L'viv.

The "experts", as behooves their status, started with a classification. They divided the above-mentioned seditious articles into three groups;

1. Those that were absolutely certainly written by Masyutko;
2. Those that were certainly written by him;
3. Those that were less certainly authored by Masyutko.

This classificatory certainty was established by the scholars on the basis of lexical-stylistic "peculiarities", most of which were heard by the people listening outside the courtroom door. (We cite them along with the refutations offered by Masyutko.)

1. In all the anonymous articles there is a similar method of employing the *antithesis*, which is also used by Masyutko in his own works.

Masyutko: There is probably no polemical work published anywhere in which antithesis is not employed. (Here he cites several examples from the now unquoted works of Lenin concerning the nationality question.)

2. The usage in some of the anonymous articles and in Masyutko's original works of verbs in the *pluperfect tense*.

3. In all anonymous articles the words *chauvinism* and *imperialism* are infused with a hostile content are used in a specifically hostile context.

Masyutko: Can the words "chauvinism" and "imperialism" have both a positive and a negative meaning? In whatever context they were used, their meaning and implication is always negative (examples from Lenin's works). This is the way those words are and one cannot change their meaning.

4. In many articles the *colon* is used to reveal the content and to emphasize the importance of a particular passage.

Masyutko: The colon is used by anyone who has at least a few years of formal education, let alone by people with a secondary or a university education. It is also quite frequently used in the works of Lenin (example).

5. The usage of the word *total* (and some others).

Masyutko: But those are widely used international words (gives examples).

6. The usage of the *verbal form "na" — "no"*.

Masyutko: This form is frequently used by every newspaper (Let's add: a despicable journalese — V. Ch.) (gives examples from the press).

7. The usage of *rhetorical questions*. Masyutko: it would

be hard to find even a single polemical work without such questions (examples from Lenin's works).

8. In the original works of Masyutko there occasionally occurs an orthographic mistake; for instance, he writes *ne* [not] *together with an adverb*. Such a mistake was also found in the anonymous articles.

Masyutko: Such a mistake could be made by anyone, in particular when a person transcribes a text in a hurry.

9. The usage of *iya* instead of *ia* (in the word *sotsiyalizm* and others).

Masyutko: This is an orthoepic form which used to be orthographic. I am not the only one who uses it. Anyone could have committed such an error.

10. The usage of *zalya* instead of *zal* [hall].

Masyutko: This is the normal form of the Ukrainian literary language.

11. The usage of dialecticisms in Masyutko's original works and in the anonymous articles.

Masyutko: I use dialecticisms, especially Galicisms, in my works deliberately, putting them in my heroes' mouths. (Masyutko himself was born in the region of Kherson—V. Ch.) In the articles the author or authors use them themselves. It is evident to everyone that those are completely different things.

The twelfth "peculiarity" could not be heard. The people who were eavesdropping were finally chased away from the door. Perhaps it was an observation by the experts that in both Masyutko's works and the anonymous articles periods were placed at the ends of sentences. The paid scholars failed to take into account that with manuscripts which deeply agitate men, authors are liable to get lost as they get lost in folklore. Everyone who transcribes or retypes an article changes its style, and sometimes its content, depending on his likes or dislikes. The fact that Masyutko, or someone else, wrote *imperiyalizm* during the transcription does not mean that such spelling was used by the original author. Professor Shakhovsky or Dr. Babyshkin, if they subscribe to the literary journal, *Radyans'ke Literaturoznavstvo* [Soviet Literary Science], should have noticed the article recently published there about transcripts of Shevchenko's works. If the *poems of a national poet* were changed so much, then what may be said about the anonymous articles!

Refuting the hypocrisy of the "panel of experts", Masyutko pointed out that certain "indications" occur in only one or in a few articles. There are articles completely without the indicated "peculiarities", but the authorship of all of them was basically attributed to Masyutko. After the first expert examination had "proved" Masyutko's authorship beyond any doubt, the real author of one of "Masyutko's" articles suddenly confessed to being the author of that article, and the second expert examination had one less article to examine.

Clearly, such scholars should be well fed. The court decreed to bill Masyutko 1,000 rubles to pay for their work, in addition to other court expenses. Later, the attorney explained to the family of the convicted that the reason for such a high payment was that the members of the panel were professors and doctors, who usually demand high pay. The amount of money that a farmer on a collective farm earns over a year, a learned "expert" gets in a day.

I dwell on Masyutko's "case" at such length because this is the most brutal retribution out of the whole series of arrests and trials in the last few months. In pure cynicism perhaps only the case of Karavans'ky can be compared to it. Masyutko's trial showed that, as in the past, it is possible now to settle accounts with any disagreeable person by charging him with the most absurd offences. For instance, could I be guaranteed that I will not be punished for writing this petition? After all, looking through my article I found in it almost all the "peculiarities" of the anonymous articles, except, perhaps, only the spelling of the word *imperiyalizm* and the dialecticisms. If the KGB gets hold of one more anonymous article, it might not be very difficult to find its "author" among those who at the present time are actively protesting against arrests and closed trials. Even a person who is only partially unbiased must draw a conclusion from the above-given facts: The trials and the inhumanly cruel verdicts are not a reaction to accomplished acts, but the means to frighten both the defendants and all others who try to think independently and who try to understand the complex contradictions of life.

"The imprisonment shall be prescribed for a term of three months to ten years; or for exceptionally grave crimes, as well as for exceptionally dangerous recidivists, in instances provided for by the laws of the U.S.S.R. and the present Code, for a term not exceeding fifteen years" (Art. 25, Criminal Code of the Ukr. SSR).

"A *law* which eliminates the *punishability* of an act or reduces the punishment for it has a retroactive force, that is, it *extends also to acts committed before its enactment*" (Art. 6, Criminal Code of the Ukr. SSR).

"Punishment does not have the purpose of causing physical suffering or the degradation of human dignity" (Art. 22, Criminal Code of the Ukr. SSR).

On November 13, 1965, on a street in Odessa, several men in civilian clothes approached the poet and translator Svyatoslav Karavans'ky and told him, "Come along." In a few days Karavans'ky found himself in a camp for political prisoners in the Mordovian ASSR. It all happened without an investigation or an interrogation, without any confrontation, "defence attorney", or witnesses, and without a public prosecutor.

Don't you consider this to be a strange illegality? Do you think perhaps that the Republican Prosecutor or the Prosecutor-General of the USSR, having learned about this incredible fact, will immediately order the release of Karavans'ky? And perhaps the people who were guilty of such an abuse of power will be sent to a camp in the Mordovian ASSR? Not so! The order to send Karavans'ky to a camp outside his own country was given by the Assistant Prosecutor-General of the USSR himself!

You will look in vain, both in the Constitution of the USSR and in the Principles of Legislation or in the Code, for an article granting the right to deport a person to a severe hard-labour camp without any trial and investigation. Nor is there any clause which declares that a person who has been released from jail after many years of imprisonment can be sent there again (without a new investigation and without another trial) for the same offence. Instead, there is a Decree of April 10, 1960, which allows the deportation of a person who was released before the end of his twenty-five-year term of imprisonment, without any proof of guilt, at any time, to serve the remainder of the term. Thus the released person lives in constant fear of what might happen to him if someone from the KGB finds some fault in his behaviour. Stalin's barbaric law of 1929, providing for the twenty-five-year term of imprisonment, was revoked after the cult of Stalin was exposed; fifteen years became the maximum term of imprisonment. According to Art. 6 of the Criminal Code of the Ukr. SSR, any mitigation of legislation has, without fail, a retroactive force — it extends to the previously committed offences. Then why was this law nullified by the Decree of April 10, 1960? (For more details about the twenty-five-year term of imprisonment, see S. Karavans'ky's letters from the Mordovian camp.)

Let us return to Karavans'ky. In 1944, the military tribunal in Odessa sentenced him to a twenty-five-year term in prison. It is difficult to judge today the gravity of Karavans'ky's crime, committed in his youth. The article *Trylyky* [Triple-faced], published in the *Chornomors'ka komuna* [Black Sea Commune] (21.XI.1965), tells a detective story about a border crossing and a capture, as well as about the recruiting of supporters during the German occupation of Odessa. Let us assume that, as far as wartime was concerned, Karavans'ky was punished justly. The authorities were concerned both with what he had already done and, even more, with what he could do. Karavans'ky spent sixteen years in the Stalin and post-Stalin camps. It seems that this was enough time to reform a person who did something wrong at the age of twenty, and in 1960 he was released by the camp administration, which applied the Decree of August 17, 1955. His prison term was reduced to twelve and a half years.

According to the Decree of April 10, 1960, the Prosecutor-General of the USSR has the right to revoke the decision of the camp administration as groundless. But this was not done either in 1960 or in the next four years. Karavans'ky returned to Odessa and began to live the life of a Soviet citizen. He married, enrolled in evening courses at the university, translated Shakespeare and other English poets, lectured on the culture of language. His name was often seen on the pages of national and local magazines and newspapers (*Literary Ukraine*, magazine *Ukraine, Reader's Friend,* etc). Karavans'ky prepared for publication and submitted to the publishers a dictionary of rhymes in the Ukrainian language — a muchneeded work which demanded intense effort.

It is natural that Karavans'ky, being a poet, translator, journalist, and finally a person who became a Soviet citizen with full rights, was disturbed by the state of the Ukrainian language in the Ukr. SSR (as it worries many others!). He was amazed by the fact that the *Vuzy* [institutions of higher learning] in the Ukr. SSR were for the most part russified. Finally, he came face to face with the fact that graduates of secondary schools were required to pass their entrance examinations in some Ukrainian *Vuzy* only in Russian. As a result, graduates of Russian schools had a considerable advantage and the percentage of Ukrainians who entered universities was considerably lower than their percentage as graduates of secondary schools. Not being able to write about this fact in the press, Karavans'ky petitioned the Prosecutor General of the Ukr. SSR, asking him to indict the Minister of Higher and Specialized Education, Dadenkov, for national discrimination (Art. 74, Criminal Code of the Ukr. SSR). In addition, Karavans'ky sent an article to the party press, under the title *About One Political Error*, in which he properly criticized Khrushchev's law authorizing the parents of children living *on the territory of a sovereign national republic* to decide themselves whether their children are to learn the language of that republic. Karavans'ky's petition, as well as his article, were both supported by references to Lenin, especially by references to Lenin's last works, which are known in history as the *Political Testament of Ilyich.*

When the arrests in Ukraine began, the Karavans'kys' home was visited by KGB officials, who made a search of their apartment. Nothing was found, but Karavans'ky was taken for questioning. The only charge was that his petition to the prosecutor somehow found its way into the hands of a Canadian communist. Subsequently, permission was received from Moscow, and Karavans'ky was deported for having forgotten his past and trying to defend the Leninist nationality policy. How else can it be explained? Why then did they not send the former top leaders of the Bandera movement, who were also released before the expiry of their sentences, to serve the remainder of their twenty-five-year terms? Yet in comparison with them, Karavans'ky was an innocent lamb during the war. Will they now meet the fate of Karavans'ky? Or maybe they are left alone only because they do not write about the culture of language and do not read the works of Lenin but are quietly mining sulphur at the Rozdol Combine [in the L'viv region]?

If the petition and the article written by Karavans'ky are anti-Soviet, then why was he not tried before an open court as an example to others? Is the concept of the criminality of some action dependent on the person who committed that action? What if Karavans'ky's petition had been written by me, the author of this petition? At the time when Karavans'ky was taming the North, I was the chairman of a Pioneer[1] Team Council, later the Secretary of a Komsomol[2] organization, a member of district and city committees of the Komsomol, and was involved in carrying out two Komsomol blitz construction projects. Would there be sufficient grounds to try me? How can we reconcile the profoundly humanitarian commandments inscribed in the Program of the CPSU with the fact that a man must suffer for his past offence *throughout his whole life until his death*, even after he had been punished for it?

CONCLUDING REFLECTIONS: WHERE ARE WE HEADING?

"The Party solemnly proclaims that the present generation of the Soviet people will live under communism" (Program of the CPSU).

"The end justifies the means" (Ignatius Loyola).

"If all the people in the world held the same views and only

---

1 Young Pioneers, the official Soviet organization for children (transl. note).
2 The Leninist Communist Youth League, the Party's affiliated organization for teenagers and young adults (transl. note).

a single person professed different ones, humanity would have no right to silence him, just as he would have no right to silence the rest of humanity" (John Stuart Mill). "Not to state the truth means to let it serve the counter-revolution" (Peter Karvash). "Communism represents the highest development of the spiritual world of every individual."

Man is not a soulless computer living in accordance with an established program. Man examines each program with his brain and with his heart. The meeting of thoughts, the contest of opinions, the crossing of ideas constitute a powerful lever which always has and always will continue to move humanity forward. The highest material saturation, without free thought and will, does not constitute communism. It constitutes a great prison, in which the food rations for prisoners have been increased. Even under communism people will suffer — the sufferings of the ever-striving intellect. Even under communism there will be contradictions, occasionally tragic ones — the contradictions of spirit and action; but they will not be solved by coercion and violence, but by a common awareness of individuality and identity. The great minds of mankind have always dreamt of a society like this. It has been declared in our country today that communism is being transformed from dream to reality, that "the present generation of the Soviet people will live under communism". (Program of the CPSU).

Under communism, then, they would live together: student Yaroslav Hevrych, after returning from the camp — and judge Mats'ko who put him in that camp for reading books; translator Karavans'ky (if he survives the camps)—and that prosecutor who sent him there to complete the twenty-five-year term; the sister of the critic Svitlychny and that investigator of the KGB from Donets'k who told her during the interrogation, "We haven't shot enough of you in the past!"; Masyutko and the "experts", as well as the prosecutor Sadovs'ky, who were shamelessly slandering him. Perhaps, under such communism, the camps for non-conformists will remain, along with the secret trials and the KGB — the highest Synod in matters of nonconformity. Perhaps our generation will live under a *declared* communism, in the same way as we are living presently in a *declared* socialist legality? History has more than once refuted the Jesuit principle, "The end justifies the means." The most equitable society cannot be built by terror and by suppression of people's civic impulses. The dialectics of history are implacable; improper means distort the end, and the result that is achieved becomes only a rachitic shadow of the intended.

It is quite possible that, as individuals, comrade Mats'ko of the Kiev Regional Court and comrade Koval' of the Kiev KGB are not predatory and bloodthirsty men (which cannot be said about the KGB officials in L'viv). Perhaps somewhere deep in their hearts they are not too happy to deal with such unpopular cases. Comrade Mats'ko would probably preside with greater satisfaction over the trial of some bureaucrat-embezzler or bribe-taker in a courtroom filled with spectators who would applaud his just verdict. And comrade Koval' would probably be much happier to interrogate an apprehended foreign spy. However, such unpleasant feelings (of course, if they exist in those individuals) are superseded by categorical directives from "above" and by a soldier's readiness to be severe in the interests of the state. They do not stop to think that by upholding the order by means of prisons and camps, by violating the laws, they undermine the foundations of the Soviet system and defame the people's dream of the most equitable society in the world. By their indifferent obedience they do a hundred times more harm than any book or article, because the further the articles are from the truth, the less influence they will have.

KGB officials today do not like to have their actions compared with the activities of their predecessors during the thirties. Then, they say, people were charged with absurd and unsubstantiated offences; they were tortured and tried by the *troyka* without proper investigation, and so on. We do not wish to argue that physical terror and moral terror are closely related phenomena, that Stalin's *troykas* and the present secret trials are like twins, and that today's curses and foul language may easily turn into brutal beatings and broken bones tomorrow. But, for instance, the judgement of the "experts" in the case of

Masyutko and the accusations against Ostap Vyshnya, who was charged with the preparation of an attempt on Postyshev's[1] life, are phenomena of the same order.

Somehow, many people associate the beginning of the Stalin terror with the year 1937, when renowned Party leaders were sent to jail. In fact, it all began much earlier, though at first glance the earlier suppressions might have appeared more respectable. In Ukraine, at least, we find that the tendencies toward gross violation of socialist legality appeared by the end of the twenties. At first, with the expansion of collectivization, they arrested a part of the intelligentsia (predominantly from the villages), those who had supported the UNR [Ukrainian National Republic[2]] during the revolution but who later became absolutely loyal to the Soviet regime and who enthusiastically welcomed the ukrainization[3] announced by the Party. It was not too difficult to convince the public of their guilt by referring to their old sympathies.

At the same time, a group of well-known Ukrainian scholars was also eliminated (Yefremov, Hermayze, and others). Although they did not conceal their opposition sentiments, they did not engage in any organized struggle against the Soviet regime, and contributed greatly to the development of Ukrainian culture. The NKVD[4] fabricated the SVU [Union for the Liberation of Ukraine] and by means of promises and threats, extracted confessions from the scholars arrested (though not from all of them) and staged an *open show trial* of leaders of the non-existent Union. Subsequently, the non-Party intelligentsia who stood firmly on Soviet positions (Vyshnya, Kurbas, Yalovy, and others) became the object of persecution. Those people were accused of the most senseless offences, invented by the NKVD officials themselves. By that time no one could even dream of such a luxury as an open trial.

---

1 Party plenipotentiary sent from Moscow to Ukraine in the thirties. Postyshev launched a vigorous campaign of terror against Ukrainian cultural, literary, and learned institutions (transl. note).
2 An independent government (transl. note).
3 The policy of some concessions to the Ukrainian language and culture, which had been suppressed during most of the 1920's in the Ukr. SSR (transl. note).
4 Should be the GPU, as it was replaced by the NKVD only by 1934 (transl. note).

After the tragic day of December 1, 1934, the terror was intensified. Arrests increased among the creative intelligentsia who were members of the Party. By 1937, Ukrainian science and culture had been bled white. After the provocative murder of Kirov, arrests began among Party officials, even among those who several years earlier had openly praised the work of the NKVD. The climax was reached in 1937, when one could find in the same prison cell the informer, the former defendant, and the interrogator. Initially, the NKVD applied tortures only amateurishly and sporadically. At first they tormented people by not letting them sleep, by hunger, by inhuman conditions in prisons, and by threats. But in the middle of 1937, when torture of the "enemies of the people" was officially sanctioned, the bloody slaughter began. The machine finally caught up with those who started the whole process; the followers of Yezhov were exterminating the followers of Yagoda, and the followers of Beria were exterminating the followers of Yezhov. A look into the past shows to what extremes lawlessness, and the lack of principles in the activities of the investigating bodies and courts, lead once they are permitted.

Today someone might be subjected to a search without a warrant, might have pre-revolutionary editions of books confiscated as "anti-Soviet", or might have his complaint ignored; tomorrow, with the help of highly paid "experts", the authorship of an article might be attributed to someone who has never seen that article. The day after tomorrow, they might fabricate an "organization" and might start punishing completely innocent people.

We would like to believe that the series of arrests and secret trials in Ukraine represents an ominous interim of error in history, caused by the vagueness of the Party line during the period between the October 1964 Plenum of the Central Committee of the CPSU and the Twenty-third Congress of the Party, and not a new, even more twisted course in nationality policy.

Some Party leaders took a suspicious stand. Instead of intervening in the unlawful actions of the KGB and stopping the abuse of power, they joined the KGB's secret informers in trying to shape public opinion by the most unscrupulous methods. Soon after the arrests, we began to hear statements from high and middle-echelon officials about nationalist organizations, American dollars, printing shops, and even weapons. The lies became too obvious and then came, for a change, stories about massive anti-Soviet agitation and propaganda. All this was done when the investigations were not yet completed and when, according to Soviet law, the defendants could not be considered guilty. In November of last year, the First Secretary of the Central Committee of the CPU, P. Shelest, promised Rusyn's wife, who managed to secure an interview with him, that no one would be unjustly punished, that the defendants would be tried in an open court with the fullest attendance of the public, and that the press would write about their offences. Then, at the end of March, 1966, on the eve of the opening of the Twenty-third Congress of the CPSU, Rusyn, Kuznetsova, and Martynenko were tried behind closed doors and in complete secrecy from the public.

In his report to the Twenty-third Congress of the Communist Party of Ukraine, Shelest called poet Ivan Drach one of the best young poets of Ukraine. Soon afterwards, a major of the KGB who kept "order" during the secret trials in L'viv came out with a somewhat different evaluation of the poet's work. He said, "Are you Drach? Why do you write all sorts of literary garbage instead of educating people? In addition, you defend anti-Soviet individuals. They all should be hanged, the scum!"

Which should we believe today, the words of the First Secretary of the Central Committee of the CPU or the actions of writer-prosecutors and majors of the KGB in the role of literary critics?

Who is put behind bars in Ukraine today? The authorities are trying mostly young people who grew up under the Soviet regime, who were educated in Soviet schools, Soviet universities, and in the Komsomol. Tried as bourgeois nationalists are people who do not remember the bourgeois system, whose grandfathers or fathers suffered privation in their rich native land. And no one even thought of looking for a deeper reason, instead of talking idly about the influence of the bourgeois ideology and bourgeois nationalism.

Who needs all these "bourgeois" labels, comrades, if not

yourselves, for the stereotyped formula which is supposed to replace honest thinking and a brave search for roads to justice. Brainwashing by police will remain powerless if we continue to close our eyes to unsolved problems, especially the nationality problem. Again and again it will be necessary to imprison those who persistently refuse to call what is black — white. It will be necessary to trample on human consciences, instead of trying to depend on people with a developed sense of honour and conscience. It will be necessary to undercut the roots of the tree instead of encouraging the new shoots that are so badly needed after the devastating storms. And later on it will be necessary anyway to rehabilitate people and recognize that truth for which they sacrificed their youth.

History always brings everything into clear waters. At this point in time, when the condemnation of Stalin's despotism and violence is final and irretrievable (although some not too clever and hopelessly cruel people would like very much to turn back the clock), experiments with the undercutting of roots, experiments with silencing and intimidation, are unfit and historically irresponsible. I will say, with full conviction, that this is essentially an anti-Soviet affair. That is why I write about it.

Vyacheslav Chornovil
Kiev Region,
Vyshhorod,
Berizky, 1/17.

To the First Secretary of the CC of the CPU, Comrade P. Iu. Shelest

Esteemed Pyotr Iukhmovych, I am writing to you not as a rank-and-file journalist to the First Secretary of the CC of the CPU. I turn to you as one Soviet citizen to another Soviet citizen, as one Ukrainian to another. I address to you a question that pains each individual who has not fallen into the mire of petty bourgeois heartlessness. The arrests and closed court trials that have rolled across Ukraine during the past nine months were not a mass phenomenon, and to nearsighted people they may seem too minute an episode in the life of a republic to merit serious attention. But illegality and high-handedness allowed as an experiment today may become a frightening, all-encompassing epidemic tomorrow. The KGB and the prosecutor's office evidently inform you of their activities. But this information is one-sided, as evidenced by the secret letter of the CC of the CPU, which is now being circulated among creative organizations. In it, separate phrases are plucked from the testimonies of Ivan Svitlychny. Taken out of context, these phrases attest to Svitlychny's profound repentance and discredit our creative youth, who long for the just Leninist solution of painful questions (especially the nationality question). The letter of the CC of the CPU deals with the repentance of the arrested. But why is it not mentioned how Mykhaylo Horyn', Valentyn Moroz, Mykhaylo Masyutko, Panas Zalyvakha handled themselves at the trial (rather than in the "isolators" of the KGB)? After all, does repentance gained by means of threats, blackmail, and long imprisonment, by means of anti-popular and illegal closed trials, reflect the real feelings of the condemned? Ostap Vyshnya once "confessed" in similar conditions that he prepared an attempt on Postyshev's life; Bukharin "confessed" that he was a participant in an anti-Soviet underground; thousands upon thousands of the murdered, who are today rehabilitated, "confessed". Having been informed of the contents of the secret letter of the CC of the CPU, I decided to send you my comments on the gross violation of socialist legality, which I had sent two weeks ago to the Head of the KGB at the Council of Ministers of the Ukr. SSR, Comrade Nikitchenko, and to the Prosecutor of the Ukr. SSR, Comrade Hlukhov. If so many gross violations of the letter and spirit of the Soviet laws have become known, despite the fact that these were secret investigations and secret trials, one can imagine how many of them there really were.

I could not but take up my pen when I myself experienced how the lieutenants and captains of the KGB, the judges, and the prosecutors understand legality. When I made notes of the

The Petition of

court proceedings, I had only one goal in view: to prevent a repetition (under different labels) of the terror of the thirties, which bled the Ukrainian people white and reduced Ukrainian Soviet statehood to a fiction. At the same time, I appeal to you with a personal matter. On April 19, the L'viv Regional Court decided to arraign me under Article 62 of the Criminal Code of the Ukr. SSR (anti-Soviet propaganda and agitation), although the court did not have nor could have had any evidence of such "propaganda and agitation". This was their revenge against me for my refusal to give evidence at an illegal closed trial. On May 17 the Supreme Court of the Ukr. SSR cancelled the verdict of the L'viv Regional Court as unfounded, and I did not find myself behind bars.

But knowing what wide opportunities the notorious Article 62 offers to the KGB and to the court, can I and my family be guaranteed that they will not soon settle the score with me because I dared to write about this high-handedness and illegality? That is why I am asking you and, in your person, the CC of the CPU, to offer me protection from possible repressions.

Respectfully,
Vyacheslav Chornovil
May 22, 1966

P.S.: I implore the official of the apparatus of the CC CPU, who will be the first to read this letter, to pass it on directly to Comrade Shelest and not to give it to that Secretary of the CC CPU[1] whom a part of the public considers the initiator and [illegible word] of repressions against the Ukrainian intelligentsia.

*

In September of 1965, Vyacheslav Chornovil was dismissed from his position as a newspaper editor, and for the next year he worked at a number of jobs. His first conviction and the

---

[1] The writer obviously refers to Andriy Danylovych Skaba, ideological secretary of the CPU Central Committee (previously, in 1959-61, minister of higher and specialized secondary education), who has long been considered the chief "russifier" and neo-Stalinist in the Soviet Ukrainian leadership (transl. note).

subsequent reversal mentioned in the petition occurred in April and May of 1966. In March of 1967, Chornovil's Kiev residence permit expired, and he moved to L'viv. There, on August 3, 1967, KGB agents entered his apartment, conducted a lengthy search, and confiscated a number of old books and manuscripts. That evening Chornovil was arrested.

At a closed trial on November 15, 1967, he was sentenced to three years of hard labour. The three months he spent in prison during the investigation were deducted from the sentence, and a further year and a half was deducted due to the general amnesty on the fiftieth of Soviet rule.

Part II

The
Misfortune
of
Intellect

Portraits of Twenty "Criminals"

Materials compiled by
Vyacheslav Chornovil

Nothing seemed to disturb the ordinary rhythm of life in Ukraine in the days of August and September, 1965. Newspapers carried stories about the successive victories on the labour front; a *Pravda* editorial called for the strengthening of friendship among nations and warned that the Party would permit no interference with that aim. In the Ivan Franko Theatre in Kiev, M. Stelmakh's play, *The Right and the Wrong*, was being performed, and the audience applauded the fearless hero who defeated the insincere members of the NKVD with but a single word of truth.

In the meantime, for some reason the literary critic, Ivan Svitlychny, the scientist-psychologist, Mykhaylo Horyn', the teacher, Mykhaylo Ozerny, and the student, Yaroslav Hevrych, failed to return from their vacations. The research worker of the L'viv Museum of Ukrainian Art, Bohdan Horyn', the lecturers of the L'viv University, Mykhaylo Osadchy and Mykhaylo Kosiv, the engineers from Kiev, Olexandr Martynenko and Ivan Rusyn, failed for unexplained reasons to show up at work.

Gradually the news spread that some thirty lecturers, artists, and scientists were suddenly transferred from their classrooms, desks, and laboratories to quarters with double bars on the windows. Some Ukrainian families were visited by sombre-faced individuals who turned their apartments upside down, taking away old editions of books, letters, and manuscripts. Messengers delivered notes on grey paper with categorical demands: "You must report to the interrogator N. as a witness." Hundreds were drawn into this ominous game.

But not everyone paid attention to the rumours. There were no official announcements, and the names of those arrested continued for a while, owing to inertia, to be mentioned publicly as if nothing had happened. A discussion of Mykhaylo Kosiv's review continued in periodicals. The newspaper,

The Misfortune

Literaturna Ukraina, published Mykhaylo Masyutko's article about the distortion of geographical names; the October issue of the magazine, *Mystetstvo,* included a reproduction of Panas Zalyvakha's painting, *The Girl from Poltava Region,* and books illustrated by the same artist were on sale in bookstores. Responses and comments on Svyatoslav Karavansky's *Dictionary of Rhymes in the Ukrainian Language* continued to arrive at his address in Odessa. In the spring of 1966, at a seminar for members of the press, linguists of the Academy of Sciences of the Ukr. SSR analyzed Ozerny's and Karavans'ky's newspaper and magazine notes about language. In village clubs they still screened newsreels showing Mykhaylo Horyn' at work in the laboratory of the L'viv truck factory. All this was unknown to the authors of the articles and the heroes of the filmstrips, who were isolated from the outside world by thick stone walls.

Considerable factual material has been collected about the methods of interrogation and about the way the indictments were pieced together. Leading Party and state officials and individual representatives of the Ukrainian public are acquainted with this material. Within five to eight months . . . .[1] twenty persons were put on trial, accused of anti-Soviet nationalistic propaganda and agitation and some of them, additionally, of "organizational activity". But even those whose confessions were extracted after long months of imprisonment refused to admit in court that they had read the "forbidden" book or article with the intention of "undermining or weakening the Soviet regime". (This is the offence for which the arrested were indicted and is punishable by Article 62 of the Criminal Code of the Ukr. SSR.)

To convict a person for reading some book or article, without investigating his beliefs and intentions, is unheard of in the judicial practice of the vast majority of the world's countries, and it is totally incompatible with the Declaration of Human Rights, which was ratified by the Soviet Union. But let us look at the case more soberly. Was it for reading those few foreign books and for giving them to some of his closest friends, predominantly scientists, that scientist Mykhaylo

---

1 Two words were illegible in the original manuscript.

Horyn' was sentenced to six years (not months, but *years*) in severe hard-labour camps? Or perhaps this charge was only a pretext — though of doubtful legality — to settle accounts with him for expressing opinions at variance with the state's views? And is this not why they secretly tried fifteen individuals out of nineteen and exiled the twentieth without any trial or investigation, making a mockery of the law?

The Ukrainian intelligentsia, accustomed to periodic pogroms over the last few decades, reacted rather meekly to this latest bloodletting. But the lesson of the 1930s was not entirely wasted. Influential people signed enquiries and sent them to the highest authorities. Young people used every available means to demonstrate their solidarity with the accused. During the trials in Kiev and L'viv there were spontaneous demonstrations of protest. To neutralize this reaction, officials read a document to a small group of intellectuals. This paper contained some phrases, freely extracted from the interrogation minutes, which were supposed to confirm that the accused had accepted their punishment as a just consequence of their deeds; a high-ranking official declared that there was no organized action directed against Ukrainian intellectuals and that only a few criminals, who had no relationship to creative societies, were arrested.

Indeed, the names of the majority of the convicted do not mean anything to most Ukrainians, even to those who would sincerely like to raise their voices in their defence and to demand their rehabilitation or at least amnesty on this fiftieth anniversary of Soviet rule.

*

If it were possible to compile a typical biography of the average person convicted in 1966 for "anti-Soviet nationalistic propaganda and agitation", it would look as follows: The convicted N. was twenty-eight to thirty years old at the time of his arrest. He came from a peasant's or worker's family, graduated with honours from secondary school, entered university (perhaps after serving in the army), where he actively participated in scientific discussion groups. Being an excellent student he obtained a good position, wrote a postgraduate dissertation (or succeeded in defending one), and his articles were published in periodicals (or he even published a book). Even if his profession was a technical one, he took an interest in literature and art and grieved for the state of his native language and culture. He is still unmarried or was married shortly before his arrest and has a small child.

Almost all the convicted fall into this category. Only the following are conspicuously different: P. Zalyvakha, E. Kuznetsova, D. Ivashchenko, M. Masyutko, and S. Karavans'ky. The first two happened to live outside Ukraine during their youth, and their decision to return to their homeland was the result of great spiritual turmoil. D. Ivashchenko and M. Masyutko fought in the last war, and Masyutko tasted the terror of the thirties and the "diligence" of the early fifties. But fate prepared the worst trials for S. Karavans'ky, a man of exceptional talent, who paid a heavy price for the error of his youth.[1] He spent seventeen years in the Stalin and post-Stalin camps. Then, after a period of five years of active literary work, he was sent back, without any investigation and without a trial, to complete the inhuman twenty-five year term.

Most of the "draftees of 1965" found themselves behind bars at the time when their creative abilities were showing a definite upward trend. In this respect, a letter from the camp written by the able scientist-psychologist, Mykhaylo Horyn', is very revealing. He wrote:

"Just at the time when my head was full of new ideas, my progress was cut short and I was assigned the trade of a lathe-turner. It is as if fate itself were tearing me away from that time and place where everything was ready for the realization of my ideas. It is as if fate were unwilling to let me consolidate my accomplishments and would not wait for me for even a year. After all, if I were arrested in 1966, I could have accomplished a lot . . ."

It is a bitter situation when the dream of a nationally conscious Ukrainian intellectual is to have been arrested at least one year later.

---

1 Karavans'ky was a member of the Organization of Ukrainian Nationalists, a group dedicated to Ukrainian independence.

A lecturer at the L'viv University, Mykhaylo Osadchy, was given even less time than Horyn'. There were only a few months left before he was to receive the confirmation of his candidate's degree from Moscow, a few weeks before his first collection of poems was to be published, a few days before his marriage.

Similar misfortunes ruined the rising hopes of the young prose writer, Anatoly Shevchuk, the translator, Svyatoslav Karavans'ky, the historian, Moroz, and especially of the artist, Zalyvakha.

Even in his early works Panas Zalyvakha displayed a painting technique of the highest calibre. He refused to take the well-trodden path and to follow traditional patterns, but instead searched for other methods of artistic self-expression. This search brought him through impressionism and post-impressionism to the modern trends of the West.

Because of his deep attachment to his native land, Zalyvakha absorbed the forms of Ukrainian folk art but was in no hurry to use them in his own work. He looked for a creative synthesis. Perhaps as a result his colours became brighter, his lines lighter, and in place of a somewhat superficial external approach he evolved a deeply philosophical one. While the composition of Zalyvakha's earlier works was sometimes not completely organized, and while the paintings contained spaces that appeared to be empty, he had finally achieved full understanding of compositional integrity.

Zalyvakha's creative work was interrupted at the time when he had attained artistic maturity. We say "interrupted" because while in camp Zalyvakha managed to paint only one portrait, that of Ivan Rusyn. After that his paints were confiscated. He was forbidden to paint and was given the explanation, "You came here to be reformed, not to paint." — reminiscent of the notorious directive of Nicolas I:[1] "With the prohibition to write and to paint". History is indeed repeating itself.

*

---

[1] Against Shevchenko in prison (transl. note).

The first poems of Mykhaylo Osadchy, published in L'viv periodicals, failed to capture the reader's imagination. It seemed that they were written somewhat too intellectually. In addition, the poet was easily subjected to the influence of others. Osadchy did not completely succeed in eliminating these shortcomings even in his first collection, *Misyachne pole* [Moonlit Field], which failed to reach any readers anyway. It appeared that the poet needed a shock, some incentive to have his verse become real poetry. Paradoxically as it sounds, prison and the camp have made a poet out of him.

Osadchy was even less guilty than the others of the offences attributed to him. Actually, he was completely innocent and his conviction was an absolute misunderstanding. Because of someone's senseless whim, yesterday's instructor of the Regional Party Committee, lecturer at the university, and candidate of sciences was forced to walk the bitter path of humiliation and suffer the complete destruction of human dignity, a path of abuse and obscenities delivered by the interrogators and of predatory prejudices of the judges. The chasm between yesterday and today was so great that it should have completely broken the man. He was probably saved by his strong peasant nature, being an "intellectual of the first generation". It is worth comparing the poems cited below from his destroyed book with those written in the hard-labour camp. We can see the abyss which exists between the seemingly perfect verse of the former and the poems of the latter, full of sincerity, though less perfect in form. (The poet himself looks upon his camp poetry as raw material which he will publish later, when he is freed.) Probably the most revealing in this respect is the poem, *Elehiya druhoi zym* [Elegy of the Second Winter], perhaps one of the most masterful of the poems known to us from the camp period and the one most remote from the poetry of the former Osadchy.

It is interesting to observe the formation of Osadchy as a poet on such a difficult subject (because it has been over-exploited) — the subject of the Fatherland.[1] His poems about

1 In original, *bat'kivshchyna*. In Ukrainian this word has the connotation of "native land" rather than the literal "Fatherland" (transl. note).

Ukraine in his collection, *Moonlit Field,* were the best poems in the whole collection. Although even there he proclaimed, "With the warmth of kindness, I shall reduce the vampires into ashes and fall as a free man on the soil of the Cossacks," it was felt that all this was just a declaration. In the camp poetry, his love of Ukraine is much closer to that intense state where there is the right to hate through love:

Where are you, where are you, stray gipsy,
Where are you, my tender Fatherland?

It sounds like the famous line of Sosyura's:[1] "I love you, my Ukraine, so much that I don't know what I am saying."

A definite interest is aroused by such of Osadchy's poems about prison and camp as *Elegy of Stone Solitude, Sonnets to the Fatherland,* and others, as well as the sketches of camp and prison life:

There was everything: foul language,
Fists flying about one's ears,
Stomachs demanding a piece of stale bread . . .
Getting curses instead!
In the distance is the mighty Volodymyr's route,
Where covered craters creep in the shadows of the night . . . ,
. . . . . .[2] one's place in a historical perspective:
Am I alone? There were millions of us who marched
To Kos-Aral[3], behind the walls of Solovky[4] . . .

The poet tries to comprehend this situation from the point of view of the future:

And as I shared the fate of Taras[5] . . . ,
This life I gave a drop of Taras's blood . . .
All Solovs, all central prisons, all Yavases[6]
Will be remembered in his thoughts, Ukraine, my land.

It is difficult to say how Osadchy's talent will develop after his return from Mordovia. Unless his poetical maturing is

---

[1] A prominent Ukrainian lyrical poet who died in 1966 (transl. note).
[2] The first words of this line are illegible in the original.
[3] Place of Shevchenko's exile (transl. note).
[4] Infamous concentration camp in the North (transl. note).
[5] Taras Shevchenko (transl. note).
[6] Yavas: village in Mordovian Autonomous SSR (part of the Russian Federal SSR), site of the hard-labour camp where Osadchy is imprisoned (transl. note).

The Misfortune

arrested, we believe that Osadchy will take his place among the better poets who entered Ukrainian literature in the sixties. But then, evaluating the contribution of Osadchy, searching for the sources of his growing skill, a future critic has no right to ignore the name of the interrogator from the L'viv KGB, Klymenko, of whom the poet writes:

I cannot guess without the cards
Whether there still exists respect among people,
Because too many curses and obscenities
Were heaped upon me
By my freckled instructor
Who came from a gang worthy of him.

*

A mere list of publications authored by Bohdan Horyn' shows him to be an expert on art and a frequent literary critic. Anyone who even once listened to his talks at the Union of Writers of Ukraine or during discussions of art exhibitions may realize that Ukrainian art criticism, which hitherto had been limping on both legs, has suffered a significant loss. Although on some occasions during polemical discussions Horyn' expressed thoughts which were not quite fully mature, and although his appraisals may have appeared to be too subjective (after all, is it possible to have absolutely objective appraisals?), his artistic taste and his ability to distinguish the first flash of talent from a fake were undeniable. He was one of the first who wrote about the mastery of sculptor F. Biryzh; he gave a thorough analysis of S. Karaffa-Korbut's graphic arts and introduced to the Ukrainian reader an interesting female artist, H. Sevruk.

When we compare Horyn's brilliant public lectures with his printed articles, we find a certain academic dryness in the latter, probably because of the necessity to fit his artistic opinions, which were far from orthodox, into the officially sanctified Procrustean bed. After all, scores of Ukrainian writers and critics are familiar with the torment caused by

insincerity with themselves and with their readers, as well as
the necessity to use Esojnan language.[1]

*

Mykhaylo Horyn' is a very talented scientist and psychologist. He is both an experimentalist and practician who at
the same time seeks theoretical generalizations, one of those
scientists who do not hastily publicize fragmental ideas and
not fully matured concepts. Such men are not satisfied with
ready-made schemes, but through tedious and persistent work
form their own opinions and their own concepts in their
chosen field of knowledge. At the same time, Mykhaylo Horyn'
is by no means an office-type scientist; he (like all the others
convicted) did not closet himself within his profession, but
suffered the pains felt by the entire nationally conscious
Ukrainian intelligentsia. However, he perceived this discord
in Ukrainian social and cultural life not with acute emotion-
alism (as his brother Bohdan did in most instances), but with
the cool analysis and sober mind of a sociologist and researcher.
And he acted true to form in court, repudiating all charges
preferred against him by showing their tendentiousness and
baselessness. (This, of course, did not save him from being
sentenced to six years of imprisonment.)

*

Anyone following the development of young Ukrainian
prose would not fail to notice several short stories, published
in newspapers and magazines, which were written by a
linotype-setter from Zhytomyr, Anatoly Shevchuk. Even in
1962 critics had noticed in his writing "a culture of form,
psychological refinement, and purity of esthetic expression"
(see an article of E. Sverstyuk in the magazine *Zmina* [Change]
No. 12, 1962). Shevchuk's stories radiate the gentle kindness

---

1 In original, "to use forbidden hints" (transl. note).

of one in love with life and sunshine. His stories evoke in the human soul a desire to become better, softer, gentler. The manner of his writing is somewhat similar to that of E. Hutsalo. He has the ability to see and find artistic value in people and events which is not evident at first sight, and he can recreate the atmosphere of a provincial town and make an ordinary man the subject of poetry.

The process of Anatoly Shevchuk's creative growth is not yet completed. We believe that the young prose writer will successfully avoid the shortcomings that literary critics found in the works of E. Hutsalo, namely, excessive preoccupation with details and inability to develop large canvases which depict broader social problems. If Anatoly Shevchuk, being in feeble health, survives five years of "reforming", he too will have many new impressions for his works, which will excite the reader not by their formal perfection alone.

*

In the early sixties, Ukrainian periodicals began to publish excellent articles by Svyatoslav Karavans'ky. He entered Ukrainian literature as a translator and linguistics expert, as a self-taught scholar, and as the author of a fundamental work so extensive one would think only a collective effort could have accomplished it. However, no one knew how twisted and broken the life of the translator of Byron and Shakespeare was and in what circumstances the *Dictionary of Rhymes in the Ukrainian Language* was produced.

We shall not analyze the reasons that led the son of an engineer from Odessa to become a member of the OUN (although those reasons were predominantly of an objective nature). For this error of his youth Karavans'ky has paid more than an adequate price — almost seventeen years of imprisonment. It was amazing that when he was released he displayed such an unbelievable ability to work, as if he wanted to make up for all the time he lost during those two long decades in prison. He was involved in linguistic research and translation, wrote poems and humorous short stories, and practised journalism. In less than five years of freedom he tried almost everything.

A man with a nonconservative mentality, Karavans'ky managed to rapidly overcome the barrier of time and age, and immersed himself in the atmosphere of spiritual searching of the young Ukrainian intelligentsia in the early sixties. One of the proofs of this is the great popularity among young people of his articles dealing with errors in the language policy in Ukraine. These articles were consistent with Lenin's principles and testified (like his petitions submitted later from the camp) to Karavans'ky's journalistic mastery.

Having totally immersed himself in the public and cultural life, Karavans'ky forgot his past, but his past was not forgotten by those who were angered by his articles about the russification of Ukrainian education. Unable to find any formal reason to object to Karavans'ky's activities after his release from prison, they produced from judicial "Talmuds" a strange medieval decree, completely incompatible with the principles of socialist legality, which gave them the right, five years after his release under an amnesty, to send Karavans'ky back to serve more than eight years of his term for the offence committed in his youth.

Even if Karavans'ky physically survives the inhuman twenty-five-year term of imprisonment, his creative path, which proved to be so short, will be disrupted irrevocably. One more name will be added to the long list of ruined talents for which our nation may claim the world record.

*

Among such ruined talents (although of a smaller proportion) is Mykhaylo Masyutko. Stalin's "universities" in Kolyma,[1] the war, then an unjustified expulsion from the Institute, wanderings through Ukraine in search of work — all

---

[1] A notorious concentration camp (transl. note).

this did not contribute to the development of his creative potential.

When one examines those of Masyutko's works that were salvaged, one comes to the conclusion that in normal circumstances he would have been most productive in scholarly work. Masyutko demonstrated his ability for logical thinking in his brilliant defence during the court proceedings. In his satirical short stories and especially in his poems, one feels the trend toward a classical, folk-oriented manner of writing. His humorous short stories are characterized by acute perception of the present situation, by an ability to see unattractive backyards of "campaigns" and "achievements" behind the garishness of superficial fronts. His writing may appear to lack perfection of style and, above all, laconism, and it is difficult to say whether Masyutko would have been able to overcome this deficiency. Too little has been salvaged of his works. Those of the last few years (among them one novel) may be considered completely lost.

*

Before their arrest all those who were transported to Mordovia in 1966, to weave shopping bags or make night-tables, were leading active intellectual lives. They were published in the press, worked on dissertations and were considered to be experts in their fields.

Those who organized the deliberate campaign against Ukrainian intellectuals miscalculated their step. This time they were dealing with people of high education who were brought up in Soviet conditions and who were able to grasp the essence of Marxism-Leninism from original sources and not incidentally chosen quotations. They were dealing with people who had learned from the bitter experience of the thirties and forties. Notwithstanding the harsh conditions of camp existence, all the convicted continue to develop their intellectual potential and to worry about the same unsolved problems that had concerned them before their arrest. Therefore, their not very literate "educators" (some of whom still have dirty hands from the good times of Stalinism) can devise nothing better to counter their beliefs than putting them in prison camp and solitary confinement.

From the letters of prisoners cited below, as well as from other documents, it is evident that even those who, under the pressure of interrogators, partially admitted their guilt in court are now denying it, considering themselves to be unjustly and illegally punished.

Public interest (and not solely a contemplative one) should be aroused by the conditions of "re-education" of prisoners in the Mordovian camps, about which we learn from letters, from tales of those who completed their terms of imprisonment, and from Karavans'ky's petitions, as well as from his letter sent from camp No. 17-a. The facts quoted in those documents cannot fail to alarm everyone who has not lost an elementary understanding of humanity. Perhaps one could say that the prisoners deliberately use dark colours in their description of the "re-education" of prisoners, suggesting that in reality it is a refined system of cruel treatment of human beings? Then why doesn't the public verify these allegations? Why shouldn't the representatives of writers and artists visit Mordovia and investigate how the camp administration carries out the "re-education" of artist Zalyvakha, psychologist Mykhaylo Horyn', translator and linguist Karavans'ky, art expert Bohdan Horyn', literary critic and journalist Osadchy? After all, camp regulations do allow such visits by public representatives.

Over a year and a half has passed since the arrests were made. What changes have taken place since then? As before, Ukrainian intellectuals are grieved by the same unsolved problems. They express their anguish at every opportunity — from official rostrums (such as the Congress of Ukrainian Writers) and in private talks with friends, in letters to the press and to government institutions. There is no guarantee that signed or anonymous articles will not be circulated (or perhaps are already circulated) from hand to hand, containing materials about the russification of government services, schools, universities, and cultural institutions; about economic underdevelopment of most of Ukraine's regions, and about the forced emigration of Ukrainians to Siberia; about artificial changes in the ethnic composition of the Ukrainian ssr's population, etc., etc. Then what should be done? Should the KGB be left to solve these problems by sending a new group of "bourgeois nationalists" to weave shopping bags in camps?

Or perhaps it would be better to choose the alternative suggested by Mykhaylo Horyn' in his last word in court: "I am convinced that it will not be long before such problems will be solved not in the courtrooms but in discussion clubs. This will have a greater benefit for the cause."

Vyacheslav Chornovil,
City of L'viv,
Spokiyna St. 13.
April 20, 1967.

The circumstances force me to stress again the self-evident fact that ideas, thoughts, and evaluations of these or other phenomena which are contained in the collected materials do not necessarily coincide with my own ideas and evaluations. In selecting these materials, I tried to recreate a picture of the creative and ideological personality of each of the convicted.

I wish to thank most sincerely the relatives, friends, and acquaintances of the convicted — all those people without whose assistance I would not have been able to collect and prepare this manuscript. These materials should be considered a collective work of many people who are interested in the triumph of legality and justice.

Anonymous Letter from Camp No. 17,
Dubrava Administration of the Corrective-Labour Camps
(Mordovian ASSR)

The 17th Camp Branch of the Dubrava Camps Administration is located in the settlement of Ozerne, Zubova Polyana district, in Mordovia. It has two zones: the first, basic zone which houses about 700 women condemned for common crimes, and the second with 276 political prisoners, males. The head of the branch is Captain Novikov, the head of camp section 17-A (i.e., the men's zone) is Captain Annenkov, the chief medical officer is Sr. Lt. Zabaykin, the KGB plenipotentiary for the 17th Branch is Captain Ivan Romanovych Krut'.

The bulk of male prisoners are invalids. Second-class invalids — 208; third-class invalids — 51. The zone has only two cold, crowded, and poorly ventilated barracks. Food is transported from the female zone and, no matter how modest the prisoners' ration may be, they do not get their full ration. Bread is sour and poorly baked; it is not fit for consumption by healthy people, let alone by sick people, who form the majority of the camp's prisoners.

There is in fact a complete lack of medical help, which can be evidenced by the following incident. On January 7, 1967, the prisoner Mykhaylo Soroka, who spent 31 years in Polish and Soviet prisons (of them, 24 in Soviet ones) fell seriously ill with a myocardium infection. Cases of this kind require immediate and well-qualified medical help. But the doctor's assistant, a free woman, made her appearance four days later, on January 11. Only on the seventh day was he removed to the medical aid station (until then he was still in the barracks). All this time he (Soroka) was treated by the doctor's assistant, prisoner Mykola Yevdokimov, who was experienced but was unable to do anything under the circumstances due to lack of medicine and instruments.

The so-called hospital has only seven beds for 225 invalids, most of whom are quite ill and of advanced age. There are no medicines of any kind, and the prisoners are not allowed to receive them from relatives (not even vitamins, in spite of the miserable food rations). As for dentists, etc., no one has even heard of them. Theoretically, seriously ill inmates should be taken to the central clinic of the Dubrava Camp (Camp Section No. 3 in the settlement of Barashevo). But this is not always possible, as in the case of Soroka, when the sick are not fit to be transported (particularly on these dreadful roads).

Often it is useless to be sent to the central hospital. There were several cases when prisoners were sent from the camp to the central hospital because they were diagnosed as suffering from cancer, but doctors at the clinic, instead of releasing the prisoner because of his sickness (which they are authorized to do), would send him back to camp with a diagnosis of acute gastritis. Only death and the autopsy confirmed the validity of the initial diagnosis. People are released only when death is imminent within a few days after the release. How can anyone expect anything better from people who do not take a single step without orders from the KGB and the operational branch?

In the Third Camp (central hospital) the deciding voice belongs to the regimen director, Captain Kitsayev, who discharged Dr. Horbovy and sent him off to the camp, although his treatment was far from completion. Such cases are not rare. The head of the health department, Yeremeyeva, declared in Camp Eleven during Karavans'ky's hunger strike that she knew about the strike but would not undertake anything, as she had no instructions from the operational branch. Prisoner Ivan Maksym called on the surgeon many times in Camp Eleven for medical assistance, but the surgeon refused even to talk to him, accusing him of faking. This resulted in the prisoner's death. Medical personnel recruited from among the prisoners is no better, for only those who are in the service of the KGB and the operational branch are drafted. Medical education and knowledge do not play any role whatsoever. For example, such medically expert prisoners as Yaroslav Hevrych and Dmytro Verkholyak were dismissed from the health department and transferred to general work in the shop, although there is a shortage of medical personnel. But characters like Malykhin, who does not have and never has had anything in common with medicine but who is in the good graces of the KGB and of the operational branch, were and still are on the job. If Camp Section 17 has an experienced and conscientious doctor's assistant, it is only because the "medical practitioners" in the central hospital disliked him. Thus they sent him here to Camp 17.

In general, Camp 17 was set up to serve as a punitive camp. This fact is not denied by the administrative personnel, though officially the camp is not classified as such. In addition to invalids, they filled this camp with people who had no inclination to submit to the so-called educational work among prisoners and who could, by their activities or example, negatively influence the mass of convicts in this direction. For this reason, as far as the prisoners here are concerned, there is a strict policy of repression aimed at breaking the prisoners' health and crushing the slightest display of defiance or protest. With this aim, the organization of production (construction work and the manufacture of gloves) is based on a system of compulsion, high-handedness, and repression. Prisoners working on construction are not protected with warm work clothes (felt boots, quilted jackets), and the average temperature inside the shop is usually kept between 5° and 9°C (41° and 48°F). But down on the floor the temperature is usually below freezing. Normal work under these conditions and at this temperature, when one must use bare hands on the metallic parts of machinery, is completely out of the question. Nevertheless, prisoners are required to fulfill their quotas, although they are impossible even under normal conditions, let alone with defective equipment and in unheated premises, where prisoners are forced to remain for nine hours (the prisoner's work day being eight hours long).

One hour is allowed for the so-called lunch break and rest period. Not only is this not a rest period, it is an additional punishment, because it keeps people inside the cold building for one more hour. Lunch and dinner are served in unsanitary conditions, in generally dirty premises, without tables, so that prisoners are forced to eat at their working places, i.e., at the machines. There is no place to wash their hands, because the tiny wash-stand cannot hold enough water for all, and there is no water in the working area, and no towels, either. Smoking is prohibited in the shop or the corridor. And since there is no place for smoking, prisoners must smoke in the tiny entry hall leading to the street, where the door is constantly opened and there is always a draught (and this in temperatures of −30°C [24°F]).

The administration continually threatens those who do not

fulfill their quotas (at present, there is no one who *can* fulfill the quota) and will carry out punishments as soon as the term of job-training comes to an end (by the beginning of February, 1967). Since there are not enough people to do the work and second-class invalids enjoy the right not to work, the administration states openly that it will establish a local medical commission for the purpose of depriving cripples of their invalid prerogatives and of forcing them to work. This is stated quite frankly by the camp section head, Captain Annenkov. The fact of the matter is that until our arrival on December 29, 1966, this was a political camp for women, mainly women condemned for their religious convictions — a group least capable of offering resistance to the tyranny of the camp administration, or even of protesting against oppression. It must also be added that an overwhelming majority were women of advanced age. Thus, in the words of overseers, they were worn-out, ragged creatures who were forced to work in a place where the temperature seldom rose to 2 or 3 degrees above freezing and, more often, even remained below freezing. Inasmuch as the system of oppression became a tradition here, they intend to continue it in the future too. It is not surprising that the overseeers frankly say that the more we complain about them for violating our lawful rights, the more praise they receive from the authorities, and vice versa.

Did the prisoners try to complain about those numerous violations, oppressions, and injustices? They tried more than once, but there was no result. The camp's commandant, Captain Annenkov, would start shouting and would declare that things would remain unchanged. In reply to our complaint about eating in the cold and in unsanitary conditions, the chief engineer replied that it was not his concern and advised us to turn such problems over "to Van'ka Vetrov".[1] After many complaints, a medical inspector arrived from the health department of the Dubrava Camps Administration. In the first place, he refused to believe that the temperature in the shop was too low (he refused to measure it on the spot) and declared

---

[1] The equivalent in English would be, "Tell it to the marines." (transl. note)

that the quota was always fulfilled and overfulfilled here. After he was told that we recently dispatched a series of complaints signed by the shift foreman (a free man) in which mention was made of the shop temperature, he was only interested in finding out to whom these complaints were addressed and was displeased to learn that they went to the office of the Prosecutor General and not to the Administration.

In regard to the complaint of the writer Daniel about the shocking incident with Soroka's sickness, this medical inspector declared it all irrelevant (the sick man did not die while he was without medical attention) and tried to obtain Daniel's admission that everything in the camp was in order (he needed that for the report). But Daniel refused to make such an admission. It is not surprising that when prisoners demand what they are entitled to by law, the representatives of the Administration do nothing, and reply with impudence, "You can complain." They know that no one will pay the slightest attention to our complaints. Who can we complain to, when they, our educators of yesterday, sit everywhere in all the offices of authority. Their moral level can be evidenced by this fact: For about two or three years, Camp No. 7 employed as its medical officer a former operational branch plenipotentiary from Camp No. 19 who had been dismissed for an attempt to rape a nurse. At present he is employed as duty officer of the jail in the town of Ruzayevka in Mordovia. The present detachment commander in Camp No. 1, Senior Lieutenant Nekrasov, used to serve as a medical worker in the same camp. The supervision on the part of the prosecutor's office is no better than that of our medical doctors. (Our prosecutors often exchange chairs with camp commandants and administration officials, or the other way around; this was the case with the present deputy head of the Dubrava Camps' Administration, Nekachan.)

Correspondence and parcels were already mentioned. I wish to add that the delivery of packages containing literature, which we are legally entitled to receive, depends (as do the letters) on the whim of the KGB official (in this case, of Captain Krut'). This makes our rights illusory.

Among the camp's inmates are representatives of various nationalities of the Soviet Union. There are Latvians, Lithuanians, Estonians and Russians here; and (as can be expected) many Ukrainians.

But who are they?

[Here follows a roll of names of Ukrainian prisoners, whom the author (or authors) of the letter divides into the following groups: participants in the national liberation struggle of 1942-1954, as well as various illegal groups of similar nature; persons condemned for their religious convictions (Catholics, Baptists, Jehovah's Witnesses, etc.); those convicted for so-called anti-Soviet agitation, for attempted border crossing, and for similar offences; and those convicted for crimes committed in wartime. The roll contains: surname and first name of the prisoner, region, year of birth, date of arrest, term of sentence in years. The list contains a total of 114 surnames. Obviously, this is not a total number of Ukrainian prisoners held in Camp No. 17-A, because the lists of some of the groups end with "et al".]

Although all listed Ukrainians were tried in the courts of the Ukrainian Soviet Socialist Republic, they are held (and were always held) in the camps of Russia. This is one more proof of the refusal on the part of the Ukr. Soviet Republic to uphold its sovereignty — it does not enforce the sentences of its own courts.

The camp has only seventeen men in the category of prisoners capable of working.

The Head of the Dubrava Camps' Administration, Colonel Gromov, was known for his high-handedness in the forties and fifties in Kamyshlag (Kemerovo Region).

The Head of the KGB branch at the Dubrava Camps Administration is Lieutenant-Colonel Blinov.

Yaroslav Hevrych

Yaroslav Bohdanovych Hevrych was born on November 28, 1937, into a peasant family in the village Ostap'ye, Skalat District in the region of Ternopil'. After graduating from high school he studied for two years in a technical school, worked as a locksmith, and served in the army, where he received more than twenty citations for good service. After demobilization he began studies in the Stomatological Department of the Medical Institute of Kiev. He finished four years in this Institute before his arrest and was the union organizer of his class. Hevrych was one of the organizers and an active participant in the Bandurist[1] Ensemble of the Medical Institute in Kiev.

He was arrested at the end of August, 1965, while returning from a vacation spent with his parents in Kosiv, in the region of Ivano-Frankivs'ke. On March 11, 1966, at a closed session of the Kiev Regional Court, he was sentenced to five years in severe hard-labour camps (the Supreme Court of the Ukrainian SSR reduced this term to three years) on charges of anti-Soviet nationalist propaganda and agitation.

He is serving his sentence in the Mordovian camps for political prisoners (camp No. 11, village Yavas, presently — camp No. 17-a).

FROM HEVRYCH'S LETTERS TO FRIENDS

... The newspaper is very primitive. The speeches we are given are saturated with standard clichés to such an extent that we wonder if these people have become some kind of robots. However, I would like to ask you to send me all the issues of the university and institute weeklies. It's interesting to know how the students live ...

(September 9, 1966)

*

It was a great joy for all of us to receive your letter. It seems like a long time ago that we ate from a common pot and shared the same life and a common fate. It has been three months since we drank our farewell pot of coffee, presented you with the diploma of an experienced caveman, and saw you to the

---

[1] The bandura is a Ukrainian national instrument (transl. note).

gates. And you went to battle with a free existence while we all stayed behind to struggle with the life forced upon us.

The time has come to celebrate Dmytro's, Mykhaylo's, and Panas's birthdays. If it weren't for those celebrations, life would be completely dull. But on these occasions we can recall "freedom" and reminisce about the past.

There are no special changes in our life, although Opanas's [Zalyvakha's] occupation has been changed and he is a stoker now. In short, he's researching the esthetic affinity of a painter's brush with an oven-rake. It's a pity, but what can one do?

However Opanas will be Opanas, and he makes nothing of it all. He'll be working in three shifts now, because the boiler room operates twenty-four hours a day. Bod'yo [Bohdan Horyn'] works at the delivery of finished products; Ozerny is not here — he has been taken somewhere outside; Ivan [Hel'] is still working as a locksmith. Osadchy works at his old job. Polikarpovych [Ivashchenko] has trouble with his hands. He complains of pain in his joints but continues to work at his old job. Masyutko and Moroz spent quite a long time in a hospital because they ruined their stomachs . . .

(November 27, 1966)

*

. . . I am sincerely grateful to you for *The Centaur* by Updike and for the map, "The ethnic composition of the population of Ukraine", you sent me earlier. A strange thing happened to the map — it turns out that we aren't allowed to receive maps in any form.

Still, it's very rewarding to know that one is remembered not only by one's family. It helps one to maintain one's balance, gives him strength to endure all the difficulties of life. About ten days ago I received a letter from Tetyana Ivanivna, which brought great joy not only to myself but to all of us here. We shared it as we share everything, including our common fate.

Right now I'm completely separated from our boys because I have been transferred to 17 LO. For me it is undoubtedly a great punishment. You can see that I was destined to constant wandering. To tell the truth, it also has its positive features, but it is hard to bear. I often lie on my bench and think that possibly Slava [Menkush] or Euhenia [Kuznetsova] used to lie on the same spot, and I can imagine how hard it must have been for women to be here.

Right now I'm successfully mastering a new trade. I am a tailor. It sounds funny, but it's a fact. And, you know, I'm getting quite good at it. I'm sewing working gloves, and when I'm set free, I'll be able to promptly supply a pair of luxurious gloves to anyone who has changed from an intellectual occupation to a manual one (no matter for what reason!) . . .

(March 27, 1967)

Ivan Hel'

Ivan Andriyovych Hel' was born on July 18, 1937, into a peasant family in the village of Klits'ko, Horodok District in the Region of L'viv. [L'viv, a city in Western Ukraine, was under Polish occupation in 1937]. In 1954 he graduated from a secondary school for working youths in the city of Sambir and went to work as a locksmith in the truck factory in L'viv. From 1956 until 1959 he served in the army. After demobilization and until his arrest he worked as a locksmith in the electric vacuum factory in L'viv.

In 1960 he enrolled in evening courses in history at the University of L'viv but did not complete these courses because of his arrest. He is married and has a four-year-old daughter.

Hel' was arrested on August 24, 1965. On March 25, 1966, at a closed session of the L'viv Provincial Court, he was sentenced to three years in severe hard-labour camps on charges of anti-Soviet propaganda and agitation. He is serving his sentence in camp No. 11 (village Yavas) in the Mordovian camps for political prisoners, where he works as a locksmith.

*

To: *The Chairman of the Presidium of the Supreme Soviet of the Ukr.* SSR.

From: Political Prisoner, Ivan Andriyovych Hel', convicted under Article 62, Par I. of the Criminal Code of the Ukr. SSR, *to 3 years confinement in severe hard-labour camp.*

There have been many tragedies in the history of the Ukrainian people's struggle for their elementary rights, national dignity, and the right to existence. One of the greatest of these — in my opinion, second only to the infamous mass executions of the thirties and forties — were the numerous repressions of the Ukrainian intelligentsia in 1965 and 1966. Only nationwide protests prevented the persecution from becoming a mass phenomenon. I was among those groundlessly accused and convicted.

I shall not resort to a detailed analysis of the so-called anti-Soviet activities that formed the basis of my case and indictment, the methods of investigation, the juggling of facts, and the "handling" of the entire case by KGB agents. But I declare that the repressions of 1965-66 were flagrant violations of the law, a relapse to the days of the personality cult, and were attempts by the KGB to recover its previous status of an autocratic and irresponsible state within a state.

With their high-handed activities the KGB ignored not only a number of articles of the Constitution of the USSR and the Constitution of the Ukr. SSR, but also international law. Here are the most important violations:

Article 105 of the Constitution of Ukr. SSR and Article 125 of the Constitution of the USSR read: "In conformity with the interests of working people, and in order to strengthen the socialist system, the citizens of the USSR are guaranteed by law:

   a) freedom of speech;
   b) freedom of the press;
   c) freedom of assembly, including the holding of mass meetings;
   d) freedom of street processions and demonstrations."

Article 91 of the Constitution of the Ukr. SSR and Article 111 of the Constitution of the USSR: "In all courts of the Ukr. SSR cases are heard in public, unless otherwise provided for by law, and the defendant is guaranteed the right to defence."

In view of the fact that the trial, in violation of the Constitution, took place behind closed doors, the sentence should be annulled.

Article 19 of the Universal Declaration of Human Rights, signed by representatives of the governments of the USSR and Ukr. SSR, as members of the United Nations, states:

"Everyone has the right to freedom of opinion and expression; this right includes freedom to hold opinions without interference and to seek, receive, and impart information and ideas through any means and regardless of frontiers."

My political activities did not overstep the bounds of legality. I have been convicted absolutely without grounds. Therefore, regardless of my confession of guilt during the court trial, I do not consider myself nor admit to being guilty. I demand an immediate release and the indictment of the real violators of the law.

February 23, 1967
Ivan Hel'

Ihor Hereta

Ihor Petrovych Hereta was born on September 25, 1938, into a priest's family in the village of Skomorokhy near Ternopil'. In 1955 he graduated from secondary school and in 1957 enrolled in the Faculty of History at the University of Chernivtsi (in southwestern Ukraine). After graduating from university in 1962, he worked as a senior scholar at the Ternopil' Museum of Local Lore, and from the beginning of 1965, as the Museum's Assistant Director in charge of research.

He published several articles in the regional and national press about prominent cultural and scientific workers from the Ternopil' region. Before his arrest he was working on a guidebook for the region of Ternopil', which was commissioned by the publishing house, Kamenyar, in L'viv.

He was arrested in Odessa on August 27, 1965, while on an official trip. He received a suspended sentence of five years of imprisonment on February 26, 1966. After the trial he was unemployed for a while and later was reinstated in the museum as a senior scientist.

Bohdan Horyn'

Bohdan Mykolayovych Horyn' was born on February 10, 1936, into a peasant family in the village of Knisel', District Zhydachiv, Region of L'viv. From 1949 he lived with his family in the town of Khodoriv, and in 1959 he graduated from the University of L'viv in the Ukrainian Department of the Faculty of Philology. At the university he was a member of scientific groups and presented papers at the students' scientific conferences.

From 1959 he worked as a specialist in the methodology of cultural-educational work at the L'viv Provincial House of Folk Art, as a teacher of painting and drafting in the special school No. 7, and from June, 1962, until his arrest, as a research worker in the L'viv Museum of Ukrainian Art.

Beginning in 1960 he frequently published articles on the study of literature and art. He worked on the problem of the psychology of artistic creativeness and spoke on that subject at the inter-republican students' conference in Riga, twice at the conference of young writers in Odessa, as well as at the House of Writers of the Writers Union of Ukraine in Kiev. He often took part in discussions about art exhibitions.

Before his arrest he worked on a history of Western Ukrainian art, covering the second and the third decade of the twentieth century.

He was arrested on August 26, 1965, and was sentenced on April 13, 1966, at a closed session of the L'viv Regional Court to four years in severe hard-labour camps on charges of spreading anti-Soviet propaganda and agitation. He is serving his sentence in Mordovian camp No. 11 for political prisoners (village of Yavas), where he works as a cabinetmaker.

In camp he is preparing a monograph about the works of the painter, Panas Zalyvakha.

While in prison B. Horyn' contracted an eye disease which is growing worse in the camp and threatens him with blindness.

Mykhaylo Horyn'

Mykhaylo Mykolayovych Horyn' was born on June 20, 1930, into a peasant family in the village of Knisel', Zhydachiv District, Region of L'viv. After graduating from secondary school he entered the Faculty of Philology at the University of L'viv in 1949. From 1954 he worked as a teacher of Ukrainian language and literature, logic, and psychology and held the positions of Head of the District Methodology Office and of Inspector of Schools in the Strilkiv District of the former Drohobych Region. From 1957 until 1961 he was a principal in secondary schools in the Drohobych district and later in the Boryslav district. He was engaged in community work, gave lectures on methodology and history of Ukrainian literature at the re-training courses for teachers of the Drohobych region, and elaborated on individual themes, concerning the methods of teaching Ukrainian literature. He published two papers in this field in scholarly journals. He also spoke at the scientific UNDIP[1] conference dedicated to the hundredth anniversary of I. Y. Franko,[2] and at the republican pedagogical conferences. From March of 1961 until his arrest he worked as an industrial psychologist in the experimental scientific and practical laboratory of the psychology and physiology of work (first of its kind in the Soviet Union) at the truck factory in L'viv. He also conducted some scientific research on general psychology and the psychology of work.

Among the topics of theoretical and practical nature he prepared are the following: "Psychological requirements in the organization of the bench-worker's work area", "Questionnaire for the study of conditions and psychological atmosphere of work in a frame-press workshop", "Psychological characteristics of universal screw-cutting lathe operators", "Psychological-methodical instructions for the organization of the training process in workshops for apprentices", and others. He delivered a paper on "The peculiarity of control and its distinction from the concentration among workers of the machine-building industry" at the republican psychological conference in Kiev. In 1962 he was awarded a citation by the L'viv Regional Department of Popular Education for the paper delivered at the Eleventh Regional Pedagogical Seminar, under the title: "The development of pupils' imagination during literature lessons".

He often spoke about the culture of production and psychol-

1 Ukrainian Institute of Scientific Pedagogical Research (transl. note).
2 A famous Ukrainian writer (transl. note).

ogy of work at the truck factory and at enterprises of the L'viv *radnarhosp*[1] [economic region].

Before his arrest he worked on his research paper, "The role and interrelationship of control and concentration of the reflective activity of an individual (based on the materials of experimental studies in the machine-building industry)", which he intended to defend as his candidate's dissertation. He is married and has a daughter born in 1964.

He was arrested on August 26, 1965, and was sentenced on April 18, 1966, at a closed session of the L'viv Regional Court to six years in severe hard-labour camps on charges of anti-Soviet propaganda and agitation. He is serving his sentence in camps for political prisoners in the Mordovian ASSR (camps No. 1 and No. 11). In December of 1966 he was put in the camp prison for six months on unfounded charges of "preparing and spreading anti-Soviet manuscripts and essays in camp". In 1967 Mykhaylo Horyn' was denied a meeting (which is guaranteed by law) with his wife.

THE LAST WORD OF MYKHAYLO HORYN'
at the closed court session of the L'viv Regional Court on April 16, 1966 (Abridged)

Citizen Judges! Following the court's decision on my request to participate in the court trial without a defence counsel, I hoped to at least participate in the court discussion on an equal footing with my counsel, as was indicated in the statement of the presiding judge. As this did not happen, I shall dwell on some statements of the final indictment and of the indictment speech by the state prosecutor.

Is it possible to talk seriously about undermining the Soviet regime when the main documents were read by no more than two or three persons? During the period of almost one year, *The Deduction of Ukraine's Rights* was read by two people; *Scientific Papers of the Shevchenko Society* by two people;

---

1 In Russian, *sovnarkhoz.*

Ukraine — Its Present and Future by one person, my own brother; *Contemporary Literature in the Ukr.* ssr by two people, including my brother. If my object was to undermine the Soviet regime, couldn't fifty or a hundred of my close acquaintances have read the above-mentioned books, without having them photocopied, by simply passing them from one to another?

Besides, in order to come to such a conclusion, it is necessary to establish whether I shared the ideas of the above-mentioned documents. Did I promote those documents, or was I perhaps critical of them? On the basis of the witnesses' testimony, the court could be satisfied that I criticized many of those documents. I gave some of them to people with university educations, many of them scientists, who could evaluate them critically. The court must take into consideration the spirit of relationships between people of science, where the exchange of literature does not necessarily mean that they share the opinions expressed in those documents. I do not deny that I read those works with some interest because they raised questions which interested me, although I don't quite agree with their interpretation.

Concerning such articles as *Is It so Indisputable?* and *Thoughts and Reflections of a Perplexed Reader*, I must say that I agreed with them then and still do today. The articles, *The Trial of Pohruzhal'sky* and *Ukrainian Education in a Chauvinstic Stranglehold*, interested me because of their factual material, but I did not share their political generalizations. I think that the reason why *The Trial of Pohruzhal'sky* was circulated from hand to hand was that the Ukrainian press kept silent about the arson at the library. I consider that to be a mistake on the part of the government of the Ukr. ssr. After all, information is as much the national wealth as are the fields, forests, and factories. It belongs to the people and it should be managed only by the people.

In the final indictment I am accused of holding anti-Soviet nationalistic views. And the state prosecutor allowed himself to compare my activities with those of Ukrainian bourgeois nationalists. I have declared and I still declare that nationalistic views are alien to me. I was brought up as much on the works of Shevchenko and Franko as on the works of Dobrolyubov, Herzen, and Ogarev.[1] I consider them all to be my spiritual fathers. The first book that I bought for my library was the book of critical articles by Dobrolyubov. None of the witnesses at the trial confirmed that I preached nationalistic views or was enthusiastic about nationalistic literature. Even the witness Starak did not confirm the testimony he had given during the preliminary investigation.

All four questions which I asked each witness, as well as their answers to those questions, indicate that I did not propagandize anti-Soviet ideas, did not conduct any anti-Soviet discussions, and did not raise the subject of undermining the Soviet regime. As far as the facts of spreading literature are concerned, the act cannot be examined without taking into consideration their subjective motivation. I state once more that neither ideology, philosophy, legislation, nor the social and political system of the Soviet state are alien to me. When I criticized, I did not criticize the Soviet legislation, but the violation of that law in everyday life; I did not criticize the Soviet social system, but the separate aspects of the sociopolitical and economic life of our country.

Yes, I considered that the solution of the economic and legal problems of the *kolkhoz* [collective farm] peasantry is being delayed. The press made a lot of noise about the prosperity of *kolkhoz* members while they were receiving only grains and kopecks for a working day. That became the reason for mass pilfering in the villages. The situation was still further complicated by the fact that a *kolkhoz* member was not allowed to leave the *kolkhoz* without a certificate from the chairman of the village soviet and from the *kolkhoz* chairman. Having no passport, being dependent on the village administration, the peasant was morally depressed. All declarations about substantial changes in agriculture remained statements only.

I consider that the nationality policy towards the Ukrainian people is being distorted. The state prosecutor stated here that

---

1 Russian authors (transl. note).

the nationality problem is solved. I wish it were true, State Prosecutor! Can the nationality problem be considered solved, for instance, in the Russian Federation, where hundreds of thousands of Ukrainian children have no opportunity to attain at least grade eight education in their native language? Yet Russians do have such an opportunity in Ukraine! Does the law about the right of teaching children in their native language have any practical meaning for Ukrainians residing in Russia? Is there any practical meaning in the provision of the program of the Communist Party which literally states that every citizen enjoys full freedom to speak and to educate his children in any language he wishes? I think that for the residents of Vorkuta,[1] of the Far East, of the Kuban',[2] or of Central Russia — in other words, in places where thousands of Ukrainians live — this regulation has no practical meaning. There are no Ukrainian schools there.

The progress of the development of the national language in Ukraine is unsatisfactory. When a French scientist visited Kiev in the nineties, he remarked with amazement, "But I haven't heard Ukrainian spoken anywhere in Kiev!" Rusova[3] sadly wrote about this fact to Franko. I wonder what he [the French scientist] would have said about the linguistic relationship in the capital of Ukraine in 1966? And not only in Kiev!

In his time Lenin demanded that extraordinary care be taken in solving the problem of linguistic development. He stated that the chauvinism of a great power will exploit all possibilities in order to limit the interests of national minorities, who react painfully to the slightest hint that their national rights may be jeopardized and who distinctly remember the policy of tsarist Russia. Somehow these principles of Lenin are easily forgotten. They should not be!

But the attack of Russian tsarism on national languages was not accidental, for the tsarists understood quite well that the problem of language is a political one. We have not yet for-

---

[1] A coal basin and concentration camp area in northwestern Siberia (transl. note).

[2] An ethnically Ukrainian region of the Russian SFSR along the eastern shore of the Black Sea (transl. note).

[3] An outstanding Ukrainian scholar and social worker (transl. note).

gotten Valuev's circulars,[1] the Ems[2] decrees, etc. (that "the Ukrainian language never existed, does not exist, and cannot exist"). And the Ukrainian actors Kropyvnyts'ky, Sadovs'ky, and Saksahans'ky, before each performance of a Ukrainian play, had to stage a Russian play of the same length or a Russian vaudeville. In this way the tsarists imposed the Russian language and forcibly taught Ukrainians to forget their native one. And so today every patriotic citizen of Ukraine is especially grieved by the current violations of Leninist principles in linguistic development. Such facts already exist. In the magazine *Kommunist*, No. 48, 1965, there is an article by Yu. Desheriyev, M. Kommari, and M. Melik'yan, *The Development and Mutual Enrichment of the Languages of the Peoples of the* USSR, in which the authors cite statistics from the last census in 1959, according to which 10.2 million people of non-Russian nationality adopted the Russian language in their daily life. Are we to be proud of that fact? Should we not try to investigate the reasons which led to the emergence of a citizen, or rather of a person without kith or kin, who does not care what language he speaks? Today the Ukrainian language, tomorrow the Russian, and later he might as easily switch to English or German. A bastard of that kind is repulsive to me!

The State Prosecutor declared that he is also against such people and that we are fighting this type of person. As we can see, this fight is not too effective if in 1959 there were 10.2 million of them.

Speaking about love of the native language, the State Prosecutor declared that we should be loyal to the Russian language, using as justification Shaskevych's poem,[3] *The Native Tongue*. I would like to explain that by "Rus'ka"[4] Shashkevych meant "Ukrainian" language, because in those times the word "Ukrainian" was never or very seldom used.

---

1 Count Peter Valuev, the Minister of the Interior, whose edict of June 8, 1863, imposed major obstacles against the publication of books in the Ukrainian language (transl. note).

2 A secret Tsarist decree of June 18, 1876, forbidding the use of the Ukrainian language in print (with some minor exceptions) and banning the importation of Ukrainian publications from abroad (transl. note).

3 A nineteenth-century Ukrainian poet from Western Ukraine (transl. note).

4 Rendered in English as "Ruthenian" (transl. note).

I declare that I am not against the Russian language as a language of international communication, but I am against those theories of the academicians Bilodid,[1] Kommari, and Co., who preach bilingualism of national minorities. Someone by the name of Kravtsev went a step further, writing in the newspaper *Radyans'ka Ukraina* [Soviet Ukraine] that conversion to the Russian language in everyday use is progressive and inevitable. It it possible to ignore such pseudo-theories?

The State Prosecutor declared in his speech that he is also a patriot, that he loves Ukrainian song, and that in the twenties he used to listen to the Ukrainian bandura players who encouraged people to fight against Petlyura. But does the State Prosecutor know what happened to those bandura players and their banduras?

The privileged position of the Russian language in Ukraine produces statements of some chauvinistic elements, like the lecturer of the Kiev Medical Institute Tel'nova or the writer Aksenov. That is what we should fight against. Those are the items I criticized. Is this enough to accuse me of bourgeois nationalism? Does it give the right to the State Prosecutor to compare me to the Ukrainian bourgeois nationalists of the past and to those who live abroad at the present time?

The third problem that worried me was the losses to Ukrainian culture during Stalin's despotism. I was always revolted by the fact that citizens who had a sense of civic duty and Party members who had a sense of duty towards the Party witnessed crimes and did nothing about it. It was then that the philistine moral philosophy, "This does not concern me",[2] was born. Under the threat of reprisals, the broad masses of workers ceased to take part in the political life of the country. Politics were mainly concocted in the kitchen of Stalin who, according to Lenin, liked "spicy dishes". This moral philosophy was officially elevated to the level of state behaviour by Nikita Khrushchev, who announced at the congress that he knew about Stalin's crimes but was afraid to oppose him openly,

---

1 Prof. I. K. Bilodid, who served during the Khrushchev era as Minister of Education of the Ukr. SSR, advanced a theory of "two native tongues, claiming that Russian has become the "second native tongue" of Ukrainians (transl. note).

2 In original, *moya khata zkrayu* (Ukr. saying—transl. note).

fearing that he could have been exterminated and branded as a traitor to his fatherland. This from the leader of the Party and the head of the government! In that case, how could ordinary citizens act? Therefore I stated that remnants of Stalinism still exist in our public and political life, that this spirit ought to be rejected, and that the masses ought to be drawn into political life; that the only way we can safeguard ourselves from the repetition of events of the thirties is for every person to have a strong sense of civic duty.

The State Prosecutor said that the period of Stalin's reign cannot be completely condemned because, after all, with Stalin's participation the people achieved success in building socialism. But does Stalin deserve the credit?

It is a monument to the people who could work creatively in such difficult conditions. Do you know of an example in history, State Prosecutor, when one person's despotism could nullify the will to creative work of millions of people? Peter I could not achieve this, Stalin did not accomplish it, even Hitler could not do it. Do you need to be reminded of these well-known truths, State Prosecutor?

Therefore I say that this period was a very difficult one for Ukrainian people and Ukrainian culture, as well as for other nations within the Soviet Union. It is a great pity that the people responsible for those crimes, who allowed such injustices against humanity in hard-labour camps in the North, Far East, and Central Asia, are now receiving government pensions, occupy governmental positions, and did not have to answer for their crimes even by being publicly censured.

The State Prosecutor calls these "small shortcomings" and defends Stalin's high-handedness. What a thankless task! He is indignant that someone besides the government dared to criticize what "they themselves are criticizing". Since when is there a monopoly on the criticism of lawlessness, I would like to ask you, State Prosecutor! The State Prosecutor is indulgent towards the despotism of Josef Stalin. But does he know that in Ukraine in the thirties more than two hundred Ukrainian intellectuals perished or were silenced forever, while during the war only a few dozens perished? Which was worse for the Ukrainian culture — the years of war or the time of peace?

And so I declare that the fight against Stalin has only just begun. And the possibility of a revival of Stalin's despotism and lawlessness can be buried forever only when all the people begin to take part in the political life of the country, when a reliable apparatus is established to control the government, and when the elections are, first of all, transformed into an instrument of such a control. It will be possible when the instigation for policy changes in the realm of economics and culture comes not just from the "top", but also from the "bottom"; when the change in the material situation of *kolkhoz* members does not depend on the good mood of Kosygin alone, but is in the hands of the *kolkhoz* peasants themselves; when, finally, the feeling of civic duty in every citizen replaces the feeling of philistinism which is being so widely cultivated.

I presented my thoughts about the separate shortcomings of our society adequately. Having been brought up on the moral principles of Shevchenko, Franko, Dobrolyubov, and Herzen, I could not ignore those facts. I considered that I was responsible before future generations for everything that was taking place. Therefore I criticized them. The State Prosecutor tried to evoke an emotional atmosphere at the court session. However, I am convinced that in years to come such questions will be decided not in the courtrooms, but in the discussion clubs. This will have a greater benefit for the cause.

I declare once again that I was and still am a Soviet citizen. Anti-Soviet views are alien to me. I leave it to the court to consider this case soberly and impartially.

FROM M. HORYN'S LETTERS TO HIS WIFE

It is already our fourth day in Voronezh. Kholodna Hora[1] of Kharkiv is a large enterprise which swallows dozens of people every day and re-grinds as many human destinies and hopes. We lived in a special section, isolated from others by a corridor that could be locked the same way as our cell, which had double doors, double iron bars, semi-circular dungeon ceiling, no daylight, and no air.

---

1 "Cold Mountain", a prison in Kharkiv (transl. note).

In Voronezh we found ourself in a similar kind of cellar, only much damper. There is a letter "B" written on our doors instead of a number. Mentally ill prisoners used to live here all the time. One of them was still here when we were brought in. I say "we" because since Kharkiv there have been three of us living and travelling together: myself, Osadchy, and an old man . . .[1] years old, who comes from Berezhany — by the name of Ivan Vasyl'ovych Hirchanovs'ky. He was convicted for collaborating with the Germans and for being a member of the OUN. It appears that old cases, covered by twenty or twenty-five years of historical dust, are being revived again. Doesn't it look like a repetition of the last days of M. Khyl'ovy?[2]

Night. I cannot sleep because it is terribly cold. Sleeping on one mattress, without a blanket, in a cellar with a cement floor, is unbelievably cold even in summer. I didn't know about this, nor about many other things.

Morning. Everybody has influenza, especially Osadchy . . .

(Voronezh, June 14, 1966)

*

I'm thinking about the latest escapade of Iv.[3] There's no reason in it, no logic, not even the elementary propriety of form. Such language is used only by cobblers after the tenth glass of brandy. I am far from defending the people to whom this opus is addressed, but judging by the excerpts from it, Iv had one quart of beer too many before he started judging things he knows nothing about and doesn't even understand. In other words, it is all in bad taste and has nothing to do with artistic etiquette.

In my opinion an artist should create and not pay attention to the interpreters of his works. If the artist were to answer everybody who in his opinion tried to outguess him, he would be able to do nothing else but to brandish his argumentative sword, right and left. And when to create? A true artist is usu-

---

1 Illegible in the original.
2 A noted Ukrainian writer of the twenties and early thirties who committed suicide at the time of the purges, in 1933 (transl. note).
3 Meaning the article by Ivan Drach, *Oh, Be Damned Once Again!* in *Literaturna Ukraina*, attacking Ukrainian political emigrés.

ally a very bad sociologist or critic because of his mentality. He perceives things completely subjectively, he sees things in one dimension only, and his world-outlook, his world-expression, and his world-creation are of interest precisely because they are completely subjective.

A sociologist must base his evaluation of phenomena on objective criteria, elaborated by science. If a poetic soul enters this field, it brings unnecessary nervousness, emotional tension, and a whole lot of nonsense.

In other words, a shoemaker should know his trade and shouldn't try to be a tailor. Thus, old Osnovyanenko[1] came to my mind . . .

(Yavas, July 30, 1966)

*

. . . Breakfast — pea soup; dinner — borshch, macaroni; supper — millet soup and a small piece of herring.

Such is my diet. I receive sugar, 150 grams, once every ten days, bread every day. The portions here are the same as in cafeterias.

June 4th was the day I said goodbye to L'viv. During the night from 3rd to 4th I hardly slept at all. I kept thinking about everything I went through, judging and evaluating it critically. Somehow it happens to me that the moment I establish myself in one field, circumstances force me into an altogether different one. On the eve of my arrival in L'viv I was full of ideas in the field of pedagogical psychology. I worked out my own conceptions, not only to my own satisfaction, but also corroborating the articles and dissertations of many of my friends and acquaintances. You know about this. To achieve that I spent six years in pedagogical practice.

Then I came to L'viv. There were hardships of requalification, difficulties of getting acquainted with the new branch of science. It seemed that I wouldn't get anything started. And when many new ideas entered my head, when all there was to do was to write articles in the republican [Ukrainian] and

---

[1] A Ukrainian writer of the nineteenth century who coined the saying in the previous sentence (transl. note).

The Misfortune

Moscow magazines — another interruption and another re-qualification to the occupation of lathe-turner. It's as if fate itself tore me away from the place where everything was ready for the materialization of my ideas, as if it would not wait even a year for a final consolidation of my achievements. After all, if I hadn't been arrested until 1966, I would have been able to do so much more.

The Congress of Writers[1] surpassed all my expectations when it turned into a discussion of the language problem — a problem that the court told me is imaginary, false, and non-existent.

I have no doubt that this was also a special kind of diplomatic move, to disarm some passionate people, to declare that "we are also concerned about the fate of our native culture". It's a pity that none of our friends took a stand.

I read the materials from the Congress carefully. The problems of language and culture were much in evidence throughout the Congress. In that case, why have I been convicted? The Congress of Writers showed that these problems exist, that they are not far-fetched, and that they have to be solved.

Soon I am going to hand in my complaint about the papers that were confiscated during my arrest and about the missing letters. During three months of my stay in Sosnivka two letters were lost.[2] How can one explain it?

(Sosnivka, December 5, 1966)[3]

*

. . . After reading the materials on both the Congress of Writers and the Congress of Defenders of Antiquity,[4] I am convinced that both congresses were far more interesting and controversial than it appeared. The ideas of Honchar and Novychenko that appeared in the newspapers are most un-

[1] The Fifth Congress of the Union of Writers of Ukraine which took place in Kiev on November 16-19, 1966 (transl. note).

[2] The camp inmates are allowed to send only two letters a month.

[3] Three days after this date M. Horyn' was put into a camp prison, BUR, for six months.

[4] The founding congress of the Ukrainian Society for the Protection of the Monuments of History and Culture took place in Kiev, on December 20-21, 1966 (transl. note).

usual for such moderate men. So my imagination fills in the details left out. I doubt that *Literaturna Ukraina* will be able to retain the level of tension inspired by those two congresses, but even the material they have printed so far is worth praising. I read the article about Hrushevsky[1] in *Istorychny Zhurnal*[2] but I have no idea what public efforts were made in connection with his anniversary. Have there been any meetings, concerts, assemblies? Or was the whole celebration limited to some articles in *Literaturna* and another journal? In general, the press supplied us with a lot of materials to think about. So the time does not pass by in vain.

I recently finished working on Shopenhauer. Now, that is until December 9, I worked on Hegel, read Andriyashyk and H. Tyutyunnyk, and pondered about the psychology of teaching literature in schools. I have some rough drafts on the subject of "The development of memory during literature lectures" and "The development of thinking and of esthetic taste". If I were to add to these the material I've had published, it would produce a well-rounded theme. Something like "The psychology of teaching literature in schools"; I note in passing the problems of psychology in folk art. It's a pity that right now all these possibilities will have to wait . . .

(December 29, 1966)

Mykola Hryn'

Mykola Yevdokymovych Hryn' was born in 1928 in Western Ukraine [then under Polish occupation]. In 1948 he graduated from the L'viv Polytechnical Institute, Geophysical Department of the Geological Faculty. There, under the chairmanship of the geophysicist Subotin he completed his graduate studies, obtaining the degree of Candidate of Sciences. In 1963 he moved to Kiev, having won a competition for the position of senior research associate in the Geophysical Institute of the Academy of Sciences of the Ukr. SSR. He was considered an

---

1 The foremost Ukrainian historian, condemned in the USSR since the 1930s' (transl. note).
2 *The Historical Journal*, published by the Academy of Sciences in Kiev (transl. note).

able scientist with great potential. He was particularly known for his research of the problem of seismic modulations. He published many papers, and in 1965 the publishing house *Naukova Dumka* published his monograph.

He was arrested at the end of August, 1965, and was sentenced in March of 1966, in a closed session of the Kiev Regional Court, to three years in severe hard-labour camps on charges of anti-Soviet propaganda and agitation. Taking into consideration his total admission of guilt, together with the confession and condemnation of his associates, the Supreme Court of the Ukr. ssr changed this sentence to a suspended one. After his release from imprisonment he was reinstated at his work, but only as a junior research associate.

Panas Zalyvakha

Opanas Ivanovych Zalyvakha was born on November 26, 1925, in the village of Husyntsi, in the Kharkiv region. When he was still a child, his family (parents, two brothers, and a sister) moved to the Far East. Panas grew up, went to school and started working there. Little is known about that period of his life. In one of his letters from the camp, Zalyvakha wrote, "For me this is a continuation of the dormitories in which I spent almost twenty years." It has been said that he worked for a while as an ovenmaker and in other similar occupations. Later he studied at the Secondary Art School of the Leningrad Academy of Fine Art and in the Leningrad Repin State Institute of Painting, Sculpture and Architecture of the Academy of Fine Arts of the ussr, from which he graduated in the class of V. I. Oreshnikov in 1960.

In 1957 Zalyvakha arrived in Kosiv, in the region of Ivano-Frankivs'ke, to work. Here for the first time he became acquainted with Ukraine, its language, ethnography, and its spiritual life. All this made a radical impact on the artist's perception of the world. After returning to Leningrad he read Ukrainian books and learned the language. He came again to Ukraine in the summer of 1959. He spent some time on the shores of the Azov Sea and later stayed for almost a month in the region of Chernihiv (village of Burymka). He collected folk songs and took an interest in ethnography. After graduating from the Institute he was given a position as an artist in Tyumen' (Western Siberia) and served as a chairman of the local Art Council. He travelled to the far north (Khanty-Mansiysky National District) and to Tobol'sk, where he visited the grave of Hrabovsky[1]. His works were bought by the Tyumen' Picture Gallery and by the Khanty-Mansiysky Museum. In the summer of 1961 he came once more to Ukraine (L'viv, Ivano-Frankivs'ke, the Carpathians). In the fall of that year there was an exhibtion of his works in Tyumen', and he also took part in a regional exhibition in Novosibirsk.

In December of 1961 he came to Ukraine to stay and joined the Regional Association of Artists in Ivano-Frankivs'ke. In April of 1962, an exhibition of his works was arranged in Ivano-Frankivs'ke, but it was closed several days later by order of the Regional Party Committee (for the "decadent mood" of the paintings). In the autumn of 1962, he became closely acquainted with young Kievan artists, critics, and writers.

He did not exhibit very often (regional exhibitions and a zonal exhibition in L'viv). In most instances his works were rejected on non-artistic grounds. (For instance, his paintings and mosaics, *Fight and You Shall Conquer* and *The Prophet*, were rejected at republican exhibitions). Zalyvakha's works were reproduced in the national magazines *Mystetstvo* [Art], *Zmina* [Change], *Vitchyzna* [The Fatherland], etc. He was one of the creators of the Shevchenko stained-glass panel at the Kiev University (1964), which was destroyed on the order of Boychenko, secretary of the Kiev Regional Committee of the CPU (Communist Party of Ukraine).

He was arrested at the end of August of 1965, in Ivano-Frankivs'ke, and was sentenced in March of 1966, at a closed court session, to five years in severe hard-labour camps on charges of anti-Soviet propaganda and agitation. At the present time he is serving his sentence in camp No. 11 in Yavas, Mordovia, where he worked as a loader and later as a stoker. His paints were confiscated there and he was forbidden to paint in his spare time.

[1] A prominent Ukrainian writer (transl. note).

ZALYVAKHA'S LETTERS TO FRIENDS

TO V. KUSHNIR AND OTHER ARTISTS

Dear friends, greetings to you all!

Good day, Venyamin! Greetings to your studio and your work in it! Thank you for sending me the cover of the magazine *Mystetstvo*. Good! I received a package of books and paper from you and Halyna, and I'm using it. Unfortunately I can't use paints. It's forbidden now, although I was allowed to use them previously. I'm trying ink-drawing . . .

We are allowed to write two letters a month. Therefore I want to convey my greetings to all of you, my dear friends, and thank you for your warmth and for remembering us!

I received a book of Zerov's collected works from H. Kochur. Give him my sincere regards.

By the way, it's quite interesting to serve, or actually to work off, my term of imprisonment. For me it's a continuation of life in those dormitories where I spent about twenty years of my life. The masters wear uniforms instead of civilian clothes, and instead of entering reprimands in your personal file and placing them on the bulletin board, they send you to a camp prison. Actually, there is more candour this way. I've had a lot to think about, to examine, to perfect, and to convince myself of many things. Times passes very fast; while earlier, during the transport and in prison, I counted days, now I cross out months. There is very little spare time, and so it becomes more precious. I'm working on some sketches — perhaps I'll finish them when I'm freed.

Are there any new developments after that monumental propaganda about the immortalization of relics of the Zaporozhian Sich?[1] I read the resolutions in the newspaper.

If you happen to have any reproductions of the new monumental complexes I shall appreciate it if you send them to me, or any books or magazines with interesting articles about art.

Write to me about your life. Although I am here, in my thoughts I'm with you where culture and art are progressing. I'm alert in body and spirit. I don't despair! And I trust every-

---

[1] The main centre of Ukrainian Cossacks in the 16th to 18th centuries (transl. note).

thing will be all right! Otherwise it wouldn't be worth living. My hair is slowly turning gray but it doesn't worry me! Everything has its justification and its value. There are many sparrows and pigeons here. They take advantage of the abundance of barbed wire on which they like to rest. We feed those free birds and are proud of them because they are representatives of true freedom, without any institutions and without any codes...

I regret that I don't have Lesya's talent. There are so many interesting faces for caricatures here! ...

(Yavas, October, 1966)

*

TO I. SVITLYCHNY

Ivanko, my dear friend, my sincere greetings!

My cordial thanks for your concern and for your letters and parcels. I wrote an answer to your first letter, but perhaps you didn't receive it, so I'm letting you know again that I received the books by Rutkovych, Bubl'ov, Petrov-Vodkin, and others. It's hard to describe my joy! They are fine editions! ... Yesterday I began to read Zerov. Beautiful works! Convey my most sincere thanks to Kochur. I read Shamisso-Sverstyuk and found him brilliant! ...

I'm following the newspapers and periodicals, looking for Lina's[1] works in them. Somehow I couldn't find any. What's new in the field of film art? I was hoping to see an interesting production of the Odessa studio, *The Ships Are Sailing Westward*. But my hopes were futile. Are there any new films based on scripts by Drach and Lina? What's new in the world of theatre? Do write! I am very happy to receive your letters — they're a ray of light from the outside world. All the boys are well, and I conveyed your greetings to them all. Your friends and even those you don't know send their thanks to you. I look for your articles in magazines but so far, unfortunately, I haven't found any. I hope, however, that soon I'll see some! ...

(Yavas, October, 1966)

*

---

1 Lina Kostenko, Ukrainian poetess (transl. note).

Banduras are waking the past,
Trumpets are calling into the future . . .
L. Kostenko

Well, this is the way it is! You do deserve it, just watch that
you don't get dizzy! Let no harm come to you, dear monu-
mentalists — non-criminalists! I was very happy to receive your
letter, dear Alla, because it was the first I received from an
artistic soul. It cheered me, moved me, disturbed me and reminded me of . . . artistic searches. I beg you not to reject
comments on your work — at least accept it as an advance for
the future. It was well written. Why do you look for irony?
Have mercy!

I'd like to comment about your interpretation of colour:
"Colour is the essence, the soul, the history of people." Excuse
me, but this is absurd. Will the *colour* of pottery of the *Bronze
Age*, dishes, embroidery, etc. of the VII, X, XII, XIV, XVII,
XX centuries really tell you anything about the "soul and history of people?" It is a pity that Hryhory Ivanovych does not
have enough "dialectics". One has to be careful when using
this word. I'll simply give you an example. In Bukovyna [in
southwestern Ukraine] the rhythm of combinations of black,
red, and green, in the proportion of 1:1, is widespread; in
Volyn' [in northwestern Ukraine] entirely different combinations and different colours are used in different proportions.
One could give many such examples in order to convince you
that colour is not "the essence and the soul", etc. Our people
created beautiful examples of decorative-applied art. Later,
our ancestors adopted Christianity with its new artistic forms.
Thus, we got something like two parallel currents: on one
side, the inert art of the pre-Christian period — symbols, hiero-
glyphs, etc. (embroidery, ornamental art, carving, etc.) — and,
on the other, secular art — the art of cult and its varieties.
Boychuk [renowned Ukrainian artist] relied mostly on the latter. You, as I understand, rely on folk art, that is, on the art of
symbols. More accurately, you imitate it. Thus, Boychuk was
a greater dialectician. He was the true dialectician, or it is
better to say, he was simply consistent in his searches. The best

testimony to this may be found in the monumental Mexican works of recent years. (I have this book.) By the way, they studied in Europe. The best architects in the world, among them Niemeyer, as well as Japanese architects, also studied in Europe. It isn't imperative to study there. As you say, the main thing is to reveal a category of national thinking and its progress.

Apart from all this, there are in art, as in other fields of human activity, its own peculiar theories. Different artists of different nations are pushing forward and developing individual sectors as well as developing the general field of art . . . Apart from the fact that each branch of art has its own peculiar sphere of activity, they are also closely related to one another. Japan is an interesting example, with its understanding of Western philosophy and art, the emergence of new architectural forms, and in general, the penetration of foreign ideas into the Japanese ground. In my opinion, this feature was responsible for elevating the Japanese to the level of development they are enjoying now among the nations of the world. Look at Japan, at its diverse culture, its traditions and innovations, and compare it to what happened with China and its emperors, who created the Great Wall of China, the Curtain, etc. Don't think that I don't agree with you in principle. I told you that on one occasion. I simply think that so far there is no new movement in Ukraine, although with time there may be one, and you are working toward this aim. Because of this I have great faith in you. A pupil of *liknep*[1], Halyna Sevruk, perceived, probably subconsciously, the need to learn more and experiment further. (We all know from our own experience what folk art has given us.) *Liknep* is all right, though it doesn't answer all the questions; when it does so, then it will be bad. Striving to achieve the object that is shaped by the imagination — that is progress. After all, imagination is also in motion . . . It is good that Mexicans have studied their mythology[2] well. Unfortunately, we do not have one that is

---

[1] School for liquidation of illiteracy (transl. note).

[2] I liked the spelling of this word in Zerov's works. Not *mif* but *mit*, which is much easier to pronounce in Ukrainian than *mif*. — O. Zalyvakha. (transl. note: The word "myth" is currently rendered as *mif*. The noted Ukrainian author, Zerov, used the western Ukrainian *mit*.)

recorded and well arranged. We have only some knowledge from incidental sources. The same state of affairs exists in India. Take the school of dance, in which every movement of the body, even the movement of a finger has its meaning.

Greek art, following Egypt's, was based on national philosophy, on symbols, and on mythology. Do you and I understand the symbols used in our ornaments? In my opinion this is an important and complicated matter for further study and one that requires effort to be generally clarified . . .

I hope that no matter how our artists change, there is no possibility of returning to former confusion. Your works and your mosaics are reassurance. May God help you in your endeavour! I look upon your accomplishment as a great achievement of our monumental art. I am able to write now and to pursue an idea!

When you see our famous Slavko, give him my regards and thank him for being what he is. I received his letter as well as his parcel. His telegram arrived looking as though it had been typed on Ostap Bender's[1] typewriter, but with an English accent.[2] I am convinced about what he said, because only prominent people could afford such telegrams of greetings! . . .

I probably will not be able to thank everyone who sent me[3] his best wishes. It was a real celebration! We were very happy and proud! There were almost twenty telegrams! Please convey my most sincere thanks to H. Kochur. He understands, as we all do, the value of a kind word in certain circumstances. I was deeply moved by his concern. I received greetings from Ivan and a parcel of books. There was also a fine adventure novel by Smolych. I read it with great interest. I was pleasantly surprised that even writers make mistakes — there were twenty-five of them in that novel. And I used to blame myself for making an occasional error in my writing! It shows that to err is human! Now I have lots of books to read — if only I had

---

1 Hero of a humorous novel by Il'f and Petrov (transl. note).

2 According to telegraph rules, it is possible to send telegrams from Ukraine to other republics in the Ukrainian language, but in either Russian or Latin transliteration. Telegraph employees in Kiev at first refused to accept telegrams in Latin transliteration, but later accepted them, although distorting their contents (transl. note).

3 The reference is to O. Zalyvakha's birthday.

enough time! My cordial thanks to Ivan Dzyuba and my most sincere greetings! To Yevhen, who is a master of epistolary literature and who can compete with you in that genre, I also send my greetings and thanks for his birthday wishes. We read in the papers about the Congress of Ukrainian Writers, about the success of fine literature and the respect for writers and critics. Will there be a Congress of Artists soon?

I'm so tempted to work on murals. Have you completed your composition, *Mother*? It's going to be a magnificent work, Alla! Your letter brought me great joy because it was full of jokes, aphorisms, and wonderfully witty remarks! When I read it I felt as if I had drunk a bottle of champagne mixed with *samohon* (moonlight). I don't know how to describe such a drink in one word: would it be "moonpagne" or "chamlight"? It would be unusually potent and would hit you right between the eyes. I'm glad to hear that your group has gained a strong addition in the person of Viktor.

Is Venyamin becoming a monumentalist? I read in *Literaturna Ukraina* about new trends in paintings by a young graduate from the Kiev Institute. Is a new star really rising?

I'm in a hurry to close. It's time to go to work. Goodbye! Keep working for the glory of our art! My best wishes.

(November 30, 1966)

*

TO N. SVITLYCHNA

... I'm in a wonderful mood. Quoting Nekrasov, "Healthy, crisp air makes a tired man feel lively." I have warm felt-boots, hand-knitted socks and gloves, quilted pants, a warm jacket, and a winter hat. All this makes me look like one of Papanin's[1] heroes. The only thing missing is a moving ice-field ...

How is the Dnipro [Dnieper River]? It's probably frozen. Tell Halynka Sevruk not to send me any paints. They aren't needed. You keep painting, and I shall do so later ...

(Yavas, December 12, 1966)

*

---

[1] An explorer of the North (transl. note).

The Misfortune

Happy New Year to you!

Venyamin, my dear friend, and fellow painters, I send you my sincere greetings! I write this letter hoping that it will reach you, because not everyone received my New Year's greetings. But you may be sure that I was thinking of you all around twelve o'clock, turning my face towards the southwest. In my thoughts, or as I call them now, my imaginary films, I was with you, singing New Year's carols, walking along the snow-covered streets of Kiev and wishing people a happy New Year and Christmas!

Thank you very much for the newspapers, books, and for the kind words from you and Halynka. I wrote a letter to V. Chornovil but I'm not sure he received it. The letters from R. Korohods'ky, which were with the newspapers, were seized and we didn't receive them. I follow all the news on the pages of *Ranok* and the magazine *Mystetstvo*, and I hope that soon I'll see your works executed in the technique of monumental art! I read an article on Arkhipenko[1] by Korotych in *Vitchyzna*. It was a poor article except for some individual poetical assumptions. He wrote a great deal but failed to say much, referring to Shalyapin and Rakhmaninov! In my opinion, Arkhipenko has done more in sculpture than Cézanne in painting. Einstein failed to split the atom, yet he remained a great scientist.

Alochka promised to send me photographs of her works from Donets'k. I'm waiting for them. I believe it will be better in the future to send everything by registered mail. I try to sketch as much as circumstances permit. Thank you and Halynka Sevrukivna for the paper and the postcards . . .

Don't forget that when any of you are celebrating a birthday, all of us as a team join you in celebration because it isn't always possible to send greetings in time. So please convey our greetings to Lina on her birthday on March 19, and all our best wishes. We love her and are proud of her. Thank Halynka

---

1 Oleksander Arkhipenko (1887-1964), Paris educated, Americanized Ukrainian artist of world renown and extraordinary versatility, was the pioneer in problems of negative space in sculpture (transl. note).

Zubchenkivna for her letter and for Svaroh. My sincere greetings to you all!

There is a very interesting and meaningful article in the book *Moderne malarstvo* [Modern Painting] in the Czech language. It was written from the existentialist point of view, but this subject would be worth studying from another angle — the angle of traditions, national thinking, etc. Translate it and read it — it's worth the trouble. I wish all of you creative inspiration and success in your endeavours. Give my kisses to our creative women! I greet you with the coming of spring!

(March, 1967)

*

TO IVAN SVITLYCHNY

My dear friend! My sincere greetings to you, your glorious women and to all our friends! The epidemic of 'flu is over and I remained alive and well, God be praised. I continue, through manual work, "to atone for my sins". All my paintings were taken away from me and I was threatened with more severe punishment in the future. Painting is forbidden. In case you need some of my works, feel free to take them. Some of my paintings and sketches are in Ivano-Frankivs'ke. I fully depend on your judgment. I planned to do over many of my works, but there was no time.

I haven't had any letters since New Year's. Probably no one received mine either. They must have been delayed on the way — the frost is getting severe! We were visited by a "friend" from Frankivs'ke.[1] He expressed his love and concern, but somehow I couldn't recognize it because he had a very disgusting face.

Moroz, Karavans'ky, M. Horyn', and Masyutko were put in the camp jail for six months. They were found guilty of writing complaints to higher authorities. They are not reforming and they interfere with the re-education of others! Masyutko's

---

1 The author alludes to the arrival from Ukraine of a group of KGB officials who, by isolating prisoners for a period of time, demanded from each of them confessions and petitions for pardon.

health isn't too good, but all of them are keeping well and are optimistic. We all believe that love of our fatherland is not a crime but the sacred obligation of a citizen. This gives us strength and confidence that our belief is right, and makes us believe that sooner or later the real criminals will be exposed and justly punished. We believe and hope.

I have enough to read. I don't have time for "adventure" literature; I read about art and philosophy. I watch the sky and the stars. Looking at them, I follow the Milky Way to Ukraine, to the Dnipro. I'm glad that before too long a time I'll have the pleasure of seeing you all, my dear and unforgettable friends. Only a little over forty-two months are left, unless some miracle occurs. One wants to believe in miracles, especially in our times. Please give my regards to all who remember us and who believe in God!

Keep well and strong.

*

To: The Chairman of the Supreme Court of the Ukr. SSR
From: Zalyvakha, Opanas Iv., born 1925, convicted under Article 62, Part I of the Criminal Code of the Ukr. SSR, to 5 years of imprisonment in severe hard-labour camp.
Yavas, P.O. Box 385 — II.

DECLARATION

"Every man has the right to respect for his personality, to protection of his reputation, to freedom to seek the truth, to express and disseminate his ideas, to serve art, as far as this is compatible with moral law and the common good." (Pope John XIII. From the Encyclical of April 11, 1964.)

Every year progressive nations celebrate the anniversary of the adoption of the Universal Declaration of Human Rights. Members of the United Nations, among them Ukraine, signed this document to "reaffirm their faith in fundamental human rights, in the dignity and worth of the human personality and in the equal right of men and women, equal rights of the great and small nations."[1]

The signatures were affixed, but the contents of the Declaration were not put into universal practice.

For at the end of 1965, a wave of arrests of Ukrainian intellectuals rolled across our country, accompanied by accusations that had changed little since the times of Bohdan Khmel'nyts'ky: *mazepynstvo*,[2] separatism, German agents, nationalism, bourgeois nationalism, anti-Soviet agitation. I have been accused of "falling under the influence of hostile nationalistic propaganda", of having read literature not examined by Soviet censorship, and of having expressed my views.

Article 19 of the Declaration reads: "Everyone has the right to freedom of opinion and expression; this right includes the freedom to hold opinions without interference and to seek, receive and impart information and ideas through any media and regardless of frontiers."

The prosecution's materials contain no evidence of the crime mentioned in Article 62, Part I, because there is neither propaganda against the Soviet state or social system, nor any appeal to subvert the Soviet regime. On the contrary, there is only what is guaranteed by the Constitution of USSR, by the Soviet nationality policy, and by the Declaration on Human Rights. Here is an example taken from the letter, "To the writer Iryna Vil'de and her countrymen who do not fear the truth" by R. Rakhmanny: "We want to see factual proof of the improvement in Ukraine's situation . . . we want to see the Ukrainian people as masters of their house, not as an ethnographic mass." And here an excerpt from "The twelve questions for students of the social sciences": "6. All the nations here possess equal rights. 500,000 Russians settled in Ukraine during 250 pre-revolutionary years, and approximately 7 million came here during the years since. Why then do the

---

[1] The words "equal rights of the great and small nations" do *not* appear in the Preamble to the Universal Declaration of Human Rights, from which this quotation is taken (transl. note).

[2] *Mazepism*, derived from the name of the Ukrainian Hetman, Ivan Mazepa, who joined the Swedish King Charles XII during the Russian-Swedish war of 1707-1709 in the hope of ending Ukraine's increasing subordination to Russia (transl. note).

Russians consider themselves more as masters in Ukraine than the Ukrainians?"

The great words about equality and freedom must have a definite context. As the saying goes, "There are great words that are so empty that entire nations could be imprisoned in them." The Constitution of the USSR proclaims the equality of nations and independence of the sovereign republics of the USSR. I belonged to the 7.5 million Ukrainians living in the USSR outside the boundaries of Ukraine. In the Russian Federation alone, Ukrainians number over four million, yet there are no Ukrainian schools, no Ukrainian cultural and social life. Lomonosov called people who lost their language "living corpses". It is not surprising that as soon as I, the former "living corpse", came to consider myself as a Ukrainian and joined the cultural life in Ukraine, I immediately attracted the close attention of the KGB. It is dangerous to be conscious of one's own nationality. Indeed, nations have the right to ensure their own way of development without detriment to others, on the basis of equality and not guardianship.

The KGB fabricated an accusation and trampled on Soviet law and international commitments, so that they were quite naturally compelled to resort to secret court trials in order to prevent the truth of the flimsy evidence from reaching the public. I believe that these court trials are a continuation of the infamous pogroms against the Ukrainian nation that took place during the thirties, forties, and fifties. Why else would they need secret trials, fabricated investigations, etc. The KGB deliberately broke the laws governing the administration of justice and violated the Constitution of the USSR and the Declaration of Human Rights.

Art. 11 of the Universal Declaration of Human Rights reads: "Everyone charged with a penal offence has the right to be presumed innocent until proven guilty according to law in a public trial at which he has all the guarantees necessary for his defence."

I cannot and do not recognize the court verdict to be just if the legal proceedings were conducted illegally. The fabrication of the accusation is demonstrated by the conclusion of the "scientific" commission of experts in L'viv that T. H. Shevchenko's poem, *Dolya* (Destiny), found at my home, was the anti-Soviet nationalistic work of an unknown author. Isn't such trumped-up evidence a sufficiently clear expression of the long ears and ugly face of that great power, chauvinism? Over the centuries the oppressors tried in vain to destroy the Ukrainian culture and language; but the people withstood the onslaughts and they cannot be frightened now by any repressions, nor by the burning of libraries, nor by the destruction of the monuments of Ukrainian culture.

The KGB agents wrote in my indictment, ". . . a morally unstable person, having fallen under the influence . . .", etc., etc. But being a Ukrainian conscious of his national dignity is not a "harmful influence", but the duty of an honest man. To renounce one's own nationality is humiliating and immoral; the KGB agents who try to compel a man to renounce his identity are guilty of abusing their power, and deserve to be put in the dock.

I consider myself guilty neither before my conscience, nor before my people, nor before the law. I demand an immediate review of my case and my return from Mordovia to the "sovereign" Ukr. SSR, as well as the abolition of forced labor, in accordance with the Geneva agreement. I demand that criminal persecution be instituted against the real culprits — the chauvinists.

O. Zalyvakha,
Yavas,
April 5, 1967.

Myroslava Zvarychevs'ka

Myroslava Vasylivna Zvarychevs'ka was born into a peasant family on December 28, 1936, in the village of Trebukhivtsi in the Ternopil' region. In 1956 she graduated with honours from the Pedagogical School in Chortkiv, and in 1961 from the Ukrainian Department of the Philological Faculty of L'viv University. She was employed by the Scientific Library of L'viv University, worked as a proofreader for the newspapers *Vil'na Ukraina* [Free Ukraine] and *Lenins'ka Molod'* [Leninist

Youth], and as a literary editor in the Publication Department of the L'viv Regional Archive.

She was arrested on August 24, 1965. On April 18, 1966, she was sentenced, at a closed session of the L'viv Regional Court, to eight months of imprisonment on charges of anti-Soviet propaganda and agitation. After serving her term she was unemployed for a while. Now she teaches school in L'viv. In February of 1964, the newspaper *Lenins'ka Molod'* printed a review by Zvarychevs'ka of the novel by B. Antonenko-Davydovych, *Za shyrmoyu* (Behind the screen); the review was entitled, *A Ballad about a Son's Obligation.*

Dmytro Ivashchenko

Dmytro Polikarpovych Ivashchenko was born in 192?. He is a university graduate in philology. He took part in the Second World War, when he was wounded and decorated. Later he wrote articles dealing with problems of the Ukrainian language and literature. Before his arrest he worked at the Pedagogical Institute of Luts'k as a lecturer in Ukrainian literature. He is married and has children.

Ivashchenko was arrested at the end of August, 1965, and was sentenced in January of 1966, by the Volyn' Regional Court, to two years in severe hard-labour camps on charges of anti-Soviet propaganda and agitation. At present he serves his sentence in Camp No. 11 of the Mordovian camps for political prisoners (Yavas). He suffers from rheumatism. (It was impossible to obtain more detailed biographical data).

FROM IVASHCHENKO'S LETTER TO N. SVITLYCHNA

The book you sent me has always been my dream. I admire S-ko[1] not only as a brilliant poet but also as a fellow countryman — an honest, sincere man of whom I have the right to be proud.

I also value your present because it was a parcel of warm

---

1 Vasyl' Symonenko, a noted Ukrainian poet who died in 1963 (transl. note).

human kindness, a part of your great heart. And that is very important, because it gets very cold here. You cannot imagine how cold!

I wish I could tell you something sincere and very warm. But you must forgive me because during one September evening my soul was chilled by a gust of cold wind. Since that time my days are very grey, dull, and monotonous. I want to grab each of these days by the throat, choke it as hard as I can and throw it away so that not a trace of it is left.

On one occasion O-chy (Mykhaylo Osadchy), talking about himself and his moods, asked, "And how do you feel? After all, you survived the whole war; you marched from Odessa to the Volga and from the Volga to Berlin with an automatic rifle in your hand. You worked honestly during the post-war years. And here you are surrounded by former German policemen, collaborators with the Gestapo, former prison commanders, and the like."

What could I answer him? In our lives, unfortunately, paradoxes are a common phenomenon.

I live and I work. It's no novelty to me. Fate probably laid the path of my life with thorns even before I was born.

It will soon be a month since I began to suffer day and night from pains in my arms. (After all, I've been freezing in icy waters so often!) But it doesn't matter — I still manage to fulfill the required work quota. As they say, labour ennobles man.

Today is Sunday, the same as the last one and all the other Sundays in prison (there have already been fifty-four of them!), ragged, frustrated, dishonoured. I look at it, on its wounded, soiled breasts, blood-covered lips, and tattered Sunday skirt. And such sorrow seizes me.

Real autumn has already started here. The sky is heavy with clouds. Almost every day it rains. The rain is nasty and cold. The leaves on the birches do not become yellow, but wither and die prematurely.

Sadness fills the evening. As soon as dusk settles, gloom creeps out of the surrounding forests, marshes, and lakes and advances slowly, making little progress, yet still methodically, unceasingly. Like the fog, it covers everything and fills every creature.

I often become uneasy when I see how the young, gay birches suddenly drop their branches in a terrible grief and whimper in painful sorrow.

And this is just the beginning of autumn . . .

(Yavas, September 18, 1966)

Yevheniya Kuznetsova

Yevheniya Fedorivna Kuznetsova was born on October 28, 1913, in the town of Shostka in the Sumy region, in a worker's family. In 1935 she graduated from the chemical technical school in Shostka and was assigned to Tambov. From then on she worked outside the borders of Ukraine (Tambov, Leningrad). In 1937 she settled in Moscow, where she worked in one of the scientific research institutes of the defence industry and obtained two patents (for her numeral inventions on explosives). In 1962 she returned to her homeland. She lived in Kiev and worked for two years in the Institute of Communal Hygiene and for a year (prior to her arrest) as a laboratory worker in one of the Departments of the Chemical Faculty of the Kiev University.

She was arrested on August 25, 1965. On March 25, 1966, she was sentenced, in a closed session of the Kiev Regional Court, to four years in severe hard-labour camps on charges of anti-Soviet propaganda and agitation. At present she is detained in camps of the Mordovian ASSR (at first in camp No. 17, now in camp No. 6).

Yevheniya Kuznetsova's indictment and sentence mention that in 1964 she wrote three articles that touch upon social-political problems: *My Deliberations, Lessons of History,* and *Nationalists?*

FROM YEVHENIYA KUZNETSOVA'S LETTERS

I'm trying every possible way to bring my health back to the perfectly normal state it was before my imprisonment. There are no bounds to my indignation about the heartless attitude toward me on the part of the doctor of the isloation ward[1] (in Kiev), who did nothing to improve my health, not even so much as giving glucose injections, vitamins, and the like. I told her that I couldn't travel and asked that they treat me in Kiev. But they wouldn't listen to me!

In September of 1965 I was examined in the psychiatric ward. I returned to the isolation ward with the diagnosis — healthy. I suspect that the physicians and the investigating officer tried to find my sicknesses because it was necessary for them to know that I had been ill at one time. Of course, in the histories in polyclinics there are no indications that I was ever ill with anything, for I was healthy. Your father[2] staunchly maintained that I had never been ill.

Why should they even have been asked such a question — about my health?

Then in February of 1966 I was suddenly taken ill. I am still trying to learn from the physician the cause of my weakness. The pain was under the right shoulder-blade, as if someone had pierced it with a wire. The heart, the head — as if they were seized in a cluster of light rays that led to unconsciousness. The legs and hands trembled as if they were charged with a current. After two such attacks I lost my strength. The noise in my head was so fierce that I didn't know what to do. The confusion and pain were so severe that I have to tell someone about it all.

After sentence was passed I requested a gynecologist, for I felt pain in the lower abdomen. No disease was discovered. After February 26[3] I began to recover. The headache above the eyes stopped, the noise ceased. I became happy. I rested a great deal, for I was very weak. In camp I slowly began to recover. Right now I'm awaiting a transfer to the central hospital, where I wish to be examined after all the analyses made in Kiev so that I'll know definitely, that is officially, where I took ill, what my state of health is now, and whose fault it is.

About the food — it would be desirable to have more vita-

---

1 The prison of the KGB on Volodymyr Street, No. 33, in Kiev.
2 Kuznetsova's former husband.
3 The indictment in the case of Kuznetsova and others was compiled on February 21, 1966.

mins. We can spend up to five rubles in the canteen, if we have earned it. Last month I knitted nets and did not fulfill the quota, so this month I hadn't enough money to buy anything in the canteen. I buy mainly oil, without which I cannot get along, for I become weak. There is no sugar; it is issued every ten days, 150 grams (about ⅓ lb.), right in the canteen. It's enough to have sweet tea three or four times — thus one can live. I had very poor food when I was a child, especially in 1933, but I survived even that.

I concentrate my attention, my strength, and my free time on accumulating knowledge. Unfortunately there is just enough time to look through the newspapers and to read some articles in the journals. I have started a few notebooks . . .

(Pot'ma, October 22, 1966)

*

The other girls and I were very happy that we are not forgotten in our homeland. When your package came, we were like children: we were happy, we rushed at the books, we kissed them and cried for joy while reading the letter.

"O life! I am rocking on thy waves." I'm again in the east — in a camp. After twenty-seven years of living in Russia I pined so much for my native land. I often stood on the platform of the Kievan railway station[1] to feel the breath of Ukraine — the trains fill the Moscow air with the aroma of its berries, orchards, honey, and ripe wheat.

I can also endure this sorrow. Time passes quickly, for production work claims nine hours a day. We are awakened at 5:30 in the morning, and by 7:00 we must go to work. I pay no attention at all to the locks — it's easier that way. Instead I watch the surrounding forest of proud spruces.

In summer there were many flowers in our yard here. These Ukrainians are interesting people. They certainly love the soil. They cultivate it as if they were spreading butter on a slice of bread. They'll do everything in their power to make this plot of ground bear something. In the autumn there was even a "women's revolt" here, for it was rumoured that male brick-

---

[1] One of Moscow's railway stations (transl. note).

layers would do the whitewashing. When our women heard, their feminine pride was aroused: "We won't permit it. This is woman's work!" We whitewashed, painted, scrubbed so hard that some were even stricken with radiculitis.

We are fed three times a day in the mess hall. We receive 2,415 to 2,420 calories, but then there is a smaller ration, one of 1,328 calories, for those who are disobedient. We may buy five rubles' worth of food every month in the canteen (if we earn the money and if there is no violation of the rules). The regulations do not provide for fresh fruit.

We make the best of everything. We feel the lack of sugar deeply; when I receive the ration of 150 grams for a ten-day period, I make sweet tea and drink it on an empty stomach so that most of it will get into the blood. I arrived here in a very weakened condition. A general weakness after the investigations . . .

(Pot'ma, December 3, 1966)

*

Your New Year's wishes, carols, books, gifts make me happy even in the cell. I, too, profoundly believe in the final triumph of justice. We (the boys and I) are not guilty. They never had a reason to imprison us. I shall return home with a big sack of knowledge, compassion, reproaches, love, which I'll distribute according to the tradition: To God what is God's, to Caesar what is Caesar's. In advance I send best wishes to you and to all countrymen on the occasion of March 9, the birthday of Taras Hryhorovych [Shevchenko].

(Pot'ma, January 14, 1967)

*

There is still so much to be straightened out in life, and only science can prove and solve the contradictions. It is very hard to disclaim scientific evaluations. Thus in analyzing the situation in Ukraine prior to our imprisonment, we see that we are not guilty and so we could not have been imprisoned.

We all feel the adverse effect of an unfamiliar climate.

The Misfortune

As for Mykola Hryn', I think that everyone blames him too much. Of course, he did not conduct himself well at the trial, it was all due to his nerves. I noticed this when I saw him the last time in the hall of the court. He made it miserable for all — for himself and for his friends. If he has realized all this, then of course he'll never commit anything like it again and will regret acting the way he did.

(Pot'ma, January 14, 1967)

Oleksandr Martynenko

Oleksandr Ivanovych Martynenko was born on October 2, 1935, in the town of Nova Horlivka, Donets'k region, in a worker's family. In 1941 the family moved to the village of Hradyz'k in the Poltava region. His father was executed by the Germans in Dnipropetrovs'k in the winter of 1942 for supporting the partisans.

In the village of Hradyz'k, Oleksandr completed, with distinction, the seven-grade school and was admitted to the geological-prospecting technical school in Kiev. After graduating he worked only a few months before being called up for military service. Upon demobilization, he enrolled in the Faculty of Geology (Department of Geophysics) of the Polytechnical Institute in L'viv. From 1962 he worked as a senior engineer of the geological-prospecting research institute in Kiev. He worked on the problem of the programming of seismic oscillations and was preparing his candidate's dissertation.

He was arrested on August 28, 1965, and was sentenced on March 25, 1966, at a closed session of the Kiev Regional Court, to three years in severe hard-labour camps on the charge of anti-Soviet nationalistic propaganda and agitation. He is imprisoned in camp No. 11 (Yavas) of the Mordovian political camps.

FROM THE LETTERS OF O. MARTYNENKO

Perhaps you know, as no one else in Kiev, what life is like here. The main rule is—tomorrow will be the very same as yesterday.

I am very grateful to you for sending me the little collection of sonnets.[1] And not only I, for many of us are interested in things like this. Please convey sincere thanks to the translator for the valuable gift.

(September 29, 1966, Yavas)

*

At present it is dull here, a cold wintry murk. We go to work while it's murky and cold, as we return from work — it's the same. And so it looks like a long polar night in the camp.

Your letter revived memories of the life in Kiev that will never return. But it seems that the recollections become more or less blurred, and thank God. Very seldom are there letters, very seldom. That means that I actually had no friends. Oh yes, one scoundrel like Peredenko and the rest. I can't forgive myself for near-sightedness. It is not said in vain that when God wishes to punish someone, He at first takes away reason. A horrible crowd — I don't want to write any more about them.

As for my work there are no changes so far. In general much is without change.

What kind of letter is this? I read it through and my hands are dropping. Well I can't do anything, nothing can be done. May all this be damned!

(January, 1967, Yavas)

Mykhaylo Masyutko

Mykhaylo Savych Masyutko was born into a family of teachers on November 18, 1918, in the village of Chaplynka in the Kherson region. Mykhaylo went to school at an early age. After completing the seven-grade school, he graduated from the Workers' Faculty of the Pedagogical Institute in Kherson. From 1934 he studied at the Department of Language and Literature of the Pedagogical Institute of Zaporizhzhya, which he left after two years due to lack of funds. He took a position as a teacher of Ukrainian language and literature in the

---

[1] Apparently the sonnets of Shakespeare in the translations of D. Palamarchuk.

Volodar-Volyns'ky district of the Zhytomyr region. A year later, in 1937, he was arrested on the basis of a slanderous report and sentenced to five years on the charge of disseminating counter-revolutionary propaganda. He was not even nineteen years old at that time. He served his term at Kolyma. Several times he barely escaped death.

In 1940 his father died, and the mother obtained a review of his case, after which Masyutko was released and rehabilitated. He remained in the Khabarovs'k territory, where he taught German in one of the schools of the Serednekans'k district until 1942. From 1942 to 1945 he served in the army in the Patriotic War (W.W. II); the end of the war found him near Berlin. He was awarded a medal. After the war he returned to his family in Crimea (the village of Sarabuz), where he taught for a time. In 1946 he was appointed by the Minister of Education of the Ukr. ssr to the post of director of studies at the railway school in Drohobych. In 1948 he enrolled in the editorial-publishing department of the L'viv Polygraphic Institute (a little later he was a correspondence student of the L'viv Pedagogical Institute). He was an honours student and took an active part in the social-cultural life of the Institute.

In the latter part of 1952 he wrote a work for the scientific circle entitled, *Norms of the Communist Morality*, which was found to be "erroneous." During the state examinations Masyutko was dismissed from the Institute. In 1953 he graduated by a correspondence course from the Pedagogical Institute, taught in Volyn', worked for several months as a research worker in the Ivan Franko Museum in L'viv. In 1956 he obtained a diploma from the Polygraphic Institute in Moscow and went to teach in the village of Stayky in the Kiev region. A year later he joined his mother in Feodosiya and taught painting, drawing, and the Ukrainian language in a school and in a technical school. He retired subsequently and lived from a teacher's pension.

From then on he was intensely engaged in literary work, writing articles, short stories, novels. He also worked as a polygraphic artist, served as book art editor, mainly for the publishing house, Kamenyar, in L'viv. On rare occasions his writings were published in the republican press (*Literaturna*

Ukraina, Dnipro) and in the regional press of Crimea and L'viv. At the time of the Shevchenko jubilee in 1964, he gave radio lectures in Feodosiya on the creativity of Shevchenko and spoke on this topic on L'viv radio and television.

He is married and supports his 73-year-old mother.

He was arrested at Feodosiya on September 4, 1965. On March 23, 1966, he was sentenced in a closed session of the L'viv Regional Court to six years in severe hard-labour camps on the charge of anti-Soviet nationalistic propaganda and agitation. In prison, during the time of the investigation, he wrote an essay on the departure from Leninist norms in the Ukrainian nationality policy, which he forwarded to the presidium of the Twenty-third Congress of the CPSU.

Despite his poor health (a duodenal ulcer and a recent complex operation in the cardiac region), Masyutko was compelled to work in the Mordovian hard-labour camps as a loader on an emergency brigade. As a result, the post-operative stitches tore apart and his health grew much worse.

In December, 1966, Masyutko was placed for six months in the camp prison on the unfounded charge of "preparing and distributing anti-Soviet documents in the camp".

During the search at Masyutko's residence, the authorities seized his novels and short stories, which formed an entire volume of material for the preliminary investigation. Although they did not figure in the indictment, these works were confiscated. From the record of the investigation only the titles of a number of articles and literary works are known that were written by Masyutko, namely: the satirical stories (or humoresques), *The Revolutionary Grandfather*; *Blood Replies in Blood*; the novel, *Chimera*; the article, *Literature and Pseudoliterature in Ukraine*, and others.

All that are left are manuscripts of some verses, a few satirical tales, as well as some unpublished articles.

EXCERPT FROM THE DIARY OF 1951

. . . I have not yet kept a diary. But one should have one. Just now I have passed through the most disturbing time of my life. It will be interesting to look at these lines when I'm old, for each word conceals so much suffering and heartache, sorrow and worry, anger and love.

But will it be interesting? Will I really be old some day? Will I at some time be able to read this without a fervent anxiety in my heart? Maybe then, when I am many years old and my body is tired from all the adversities, my soul will also be tired. Do I know when I was old and when I was young?

Was I young then, when at the age of eighteen all the doors of hope were closed before me and I wrote:

Over this cold earth, I shall wander
and death will follow me with a bayonet,
and I shall often appear to you in your sleep,
on the snow with my head smashed.

And was I young at the age of twenty-five, when I was torn from the work that meant so much to me, that was so meaningful, and sent to a place of death? Which of us was the younger — that grey-haired grandfather who calmly led me to distant places where shells burst, or I, who counted my life by minutes?

Was I really young then, too, when I was preparing to live a quiet and peaceful life? To quietly count off day after day, to perform, painstakingly, all the obligations set by life and society, to expiate the "sin" of youth already thrice atoned, and to think of nothing else. Oh, this is the most difficult — to think about nothing! To be satisfied with that which is. Nothing excites the soul, the heart beats normally, serenely. And such an existence in this wide world was called life?

Was I really young then?

I didn't keep a diary and don't regret it. Why should I have kept one? So I could read in old age the old thoughts of youth?

When I look back, I see myself as I was very recently. I was never so young in the most blossoming years of youth. And now I am so old, older than I shall ever be in the most advanced years of old age.

What happened to me? I ask myself. Was this the youth which I overtook so late, or was it the love which I nourished within myself so long? . . .

Yes. That is where love began. From that moment when I

felt the close threads of morals and the restricted framework of behaviour that prevent people from being happy without a struggle.

Oh, how cruel these people are to themselves! Why have they voluntarily put their hearts into the fetters of morals?

But in looking back, I think: If happiness had come immediately, would I really have felt that happiness and that love? No, because their greatest value lies in the impassible paths to them, in the difficult and unquenchable aspirations.

And I thank mankind for ensnaring our passions in the nets of morals and thereby creating love. . . .

Easy, easy, my only friend who proudly call yourself "I". After all, nothing has happened to you. You have only looked back, you have only looked into your past! You see that it is made up of only the hardest blows of fate. If happiness had suddenly come to you — it would have disturbed the dialectic of your life. All that happened this time was that you received the next blow predestined for you.

You wanted to escape from the morass of life, but you forgot that there isn't a single bush to which you could have clung, and so you sank only deeper into that morass. You wanted, in the midst of the cruel adversities of winter, to warm the soul, and you only felt much colder.

Ha, ha, ha! You wanted to find your Halychanka,[1] having forgotten that long ago you lost the right to search for her.

(1951)

TO THE PROSECUTOR OF THE UKRAINIAN SOVIET
SOCIALIST REPUBLIC

Copy to: The Head of the KGB *administration[2] for the L'viv Region from citizen M. S. Masyutko, resident of the city of Feodosiya, 20 Stepova Street, at present held in custody in the city of L'viv, at 1 Myr Street, in the investigation isolator of the* KGB *Administration.*

---

1 Halychanka — a girl from Halychna or western Ukraine (transl. note).
2 In the original: *UKDB* (transl. note).

On September 4, 1965, on orders from the prosecutor's office in L'viv, a search was made in my apartment in the city of Feodosiya, where I reside permanently, by the officials of the Crimean administration of the KGB. Confiscated were a number of typewritten articles, which in the search report were referred to as "anti-Soviet nationalist materials", as well as my own works, both typewritten and in my own handwriting, such as literary criticism and art-study articles. Moreover, transcripts of little-known poetic works of various pre- and post-revolutionary authors and of some folk songs were confiscated. Pre-revolutionary books and a typewriter were also taken away from me.

Among the confiscated so-called "anti-Soviet nationalist materials" were the following articles: *The Night of Stalin's Death*; *The Trial of Pohruzhal'sky*; *Class and national struggle at the present stage of mankind's development*; The reply to[1] V. Symonenko's mother, H. R. Shcherban'; Speech at the evening meeting dedicated to V. Symonenko's thirtieth birthday by I. Dzyuba; *Literature and Pseudo-Literature in Ukraine* by M. Masyutko; To the authoress Iryna Vil'de and to her countrymen who do not fear the truth by R. Rakhmanny;[2] *Ukrainian Education in a Chauvinistic Stranglehold*; Dwight Eisenhower's speech at the unveiling of the Shevchenko monument in Washington; Reply to the cultural workers of the Ukr. SSR from the Ukrainian cultural workers of Canada and the U.S.A.; *Present-day Imperialism*; *The Last Work of Mykola Khvyl'ovy* by M. Hryshko; *From the Documents of the Latest History of Ukraine Burnt in Kiev* and *Oration at the Funeral of V. Sosyura* by A. Malyshko.

After the search I was taken into custody by the officials of the Crimean administration of the KGB and later, on orders of the prosecutor's office in L'viv, I was transferred there, where I have been held under arrest ever since September 7.

At the very first interrogation in Feodosiya, I explained to

---

1 The Ukrainian title of this article may be translated to read *either* "to" or "from" Symonenko's mother (transl. note).

2 A well-known Ukrainian journalist now residing in Canada (transl. note).

the investigators that the confiscation of my literature and my detention were groundless; none of the confiscated material can be called anti-Soviet literature, for which one can be arraigned in accordance with Article 62 of the Criminal Code of the Ukr. ssr. Article 62 clearly states that liable for legal prosecutions are persons engaged in various types of agitation aimed at the overthrow, the weakening, or the defamation of the Soviet rule, or who are keeping literature for this purpose. Meanwhile, in all the so-called "anti-Soviet literature" taken away from me, there is not even a mention of the words "Soviet rule" in a negative context. On the contrary, Rakhmanny's article, *To the authoress I. Vil'de*, deals with the struggle for the strengthening and consolidation of the authority of the existing Soviet government in Ukraine; my own article, *Literature and Pseudo-literature in Ukraine*, affirms that the establishment of the Soviet rule in Ukraine, before the lawlessness of Stalin's personality cult, led to the flowering of versatile and original talents in literature, fine arts, and cinematography.

I have explained to the investigators of both the Crimean and L'viv administrations of the kgb that Article 62 of the Criminal Code of the Ukr. ssr gives the right to prosecute for agitation aimed at a certain definite goal, but not for every idea that displeases some individual officials or individual institutions. I understand Article 62 and believe that it could not be understood in any other way; it does not envisage prosecution for ideological speeches or articles, even though they might have been evaluated, from the point of view of Marxism-Leninism, as ideologically intolerant, ideologically fallacious, or even ideologically hostile. That this interpretation is correct is evidenced by the facts in our post-personality-cult society. The criminal code does not provide for the prosecution of churchmen who promote an ideology completely opposite to the communist one. The criminal code never brought the anti-Party group of Molotov, Malenkov, and Kaganovich to trial, despite their open opposition to the official Party line. Nor does the criminal code prosecute the publishers of books of outright anti-communist content (for example, *Demons* by F. Dostoyevsky, or *Communist Partisan Activities* by Dickson and Hellbrunn).

I repeatedly explained to the authorities that one cannot identify articles or speeches that disagree with communist ideology with those that are anti-Soviet in nature; such persecution would be a revival of the lawlessness of Stalin's time, which was condemned from the lofty tribunes of the Twentieth and Twenty-second Congresses of the CPSU. Despite all that, the authorities refuse to understand it and continue to demand from me admission of "anti-Soviet activities".

I learned some time later that large groups of people were arrested in Kiev, L'viv, and other cities of Ukraine for possessing or circulating the same kind of materials as were taken away from me. It seems the authorities take the following approach: We will bring you to trial for illegal dissemination of literature even if it is not declared as anti-Soviet. The criminal code, however, does not envisage prosecution even for the dissemination of ideologically incompatible literature. It must be, in fact, anti-Soviet literature, literature slandering the Soviet rule, calling for revolt against the Soviet rule, calling for the sabotage of measures undertaken by Soviet authorities. None of these characteristics apply to the literature that forms the basis of the accusations against me and many others.

It is perfectly clear why the criminal code does not outlaw articles or speeches advocating ideas which are ideologically undesirable or inadmissible from the point of view of communist ideology. To combat them, the Communist Party is armed with organs other than the courts: the press, radio, television, cinema, universities of Marxism-Leninism, the Society for Dissemination of Political and Scientific Knowledge,[1] departments of Marxism-Leninism at higher institutions of learning, ideological education in secondary and technical schools, etc. An ideology must be fought with ideology, not with prison, for when prison becomes an arm of the ruling ideology, its services, as is evidenced throughout history, turn out to cause the worst damage. The experience of the times of Stalin's personality cult has shown that the use of suppression

---

1 Presently known as Society "Knowledge" (transl. note).

to cover up social deficiencies leads to antagonism between the government and the people, because behind every groundlessly condemned individual stand not only scores of his relatives and friends, but also the weight of opinion of the entire public. Prison cannot be used to combat ideological speeches and articles for yet another reason, namely, because such speeches frequently uncover social and political deficiencies which should be taken into consideration rather than covered up by acts of repression.

However, the question arises: Where is the borderline between ideologically incompatible and anti-Soviet speeches and articles? It should be clear to every jurist that if an article is directed against the state government, if it calls for a struggle against this government (in this case the Soviet government), it must be treated as anti-state (in this case, as anti-Soviet). But if it does not call forth aggressive action against the state but is critical in character; if it criticizes specific actions on the part of certain institutions, even those of the state; if it advocates an ideology which is contradictory to the existing one but does not incite any anti-state activities, then it cannot be called anti-state (or anti-Soviet).

Among the materials taken away from me are materials philosophical, sociological, literary, and socio-economic in character. Can the investigation authorities, or even the court, determine the extent to which these materials are related to Article 62 of the Criminal Code? Of course not. The investigator or the judge is only a jurist, but for this purpose a person must have, in addition to legal training, professional education in philology, philosophy, sociology, and political economy. Moreover, I have learned in the course of the investigation that the authorities of the L'viv KGB cannot be fully objective for another reason. They consider criticism of the GPU, NKVD, and MGB,[1] and the old practices as directed against themselves. Such criticism is supposed to have occurred in those of my own works confiscated during the search. That is why I suggest to the investigation authorities and, at the same

---

[1] The predecessors of the KGB: the State Political Administration (GPU), the People's Commissariat of Internal Affairs (NKVD), and the Ministry of State Security (MGB) (transl. note).

time, demand on the basis of my right under Article 197 of the Criminal Procedure Code of the Ukr. ssr, that a competent commission be formed of disinterested parties, to deliver a judgment on the relation of the confiscated materials to Article 62 of the Criminal Code of the Ukr. ssr.

The investigation authorities reject my suggestion. They claim that they have themselves determined the relation of these materials to Article 62.

I can understand that it is possible to accuse without going into the root of the matter, and even to condemn without making a fine analysis. But I consider it advisable to give a thought to what kind of influence this could have on public opinion. The unavoidable conclusion is that people are condemned for their words, for voicing their thoughts, as they used to be in the days of Yezhov or Beria, the times of terror and repression. And then the desire to defend the Soviet rule will turn into its antithesis. These will be an anti-Soviet agitation such as no enemy of Soviet rule could devise.

I have told all this to the authorities who are investigating my case and the cases of the L'viv group. I do not know whether they purposely misunderstand me, or are not able to understand. Insofar as the investigation authorities, it seems, are duty-bound to follow certain general instructions in connection with the investigation of similar groups in other cities, I am addressing this letter to you in your capacity of Prosecutor of our republic, in whose power it is to steer the investigation of all groups onto the correct course.

October, 1965

FROM MASYUTKO'S LETTERS TO HIS WIFE

A few days ago we were visited by a representative of the administration, and he allowed me an interview; that's probably why your letters arrived, because I told him that I wasn't receiving all your letters and that you weren't getting all of mine. He told me that the parcel with shirts and underwear may be issued to me, but our local executives have not done so.

I'm very sorry that you didn't receive my previous letters and that this brought you such sad and despairing thoughts. I wrote to you the day after you left. That letter was brimful of compassion for the tears you shed, for your suffering in the rain and the cold. On that day I stood in the rain for a long time, hoping to get a look at you, but as it turned out, I didn't get to see you at all. I can understand that having received no letters from me after all this time, you could have had the worst thoughts and feelings . . .

(October 19, 1966)

*

How sorry I felt for you on that cold, rainy day when you were crying at the gate, trying to visit me. How I pitied your tears! I wrote all about it in my letters. But when I realized that my letters didn't reach you, I started to write more restrained ones in the hope that they would find their way to you.

You ask me to be submissive. I'm not very rebellious out here, but when it is necessary to stand up for myself, I try to do just that.

Speaking of Sinyavs'ky, his wife arrived here, and when she found out that he worked at such hard labour, she wrote to the proper authorities and he was summoned and offered work of his own choosing. In my job I must pull loads weighing 90 kg and more. The strain tears apart the fresh scar where I had the operation, so that it is almost impossible for me to cough and to breathe deeply — I have such a sharp pain in my chest.

Out here it is not as you think it is; if one is submissive, he can perish. Although it doesn't help much to write what I am writing now, nevertheless, it's better than to be absolutely silent.

(October 26, 1966)

*

My dearest! When I was in the hospital I prepared two portraits, yours and mine. I painted them and had beautiful Hutsulian[1] frames made for them here. I was so happy that I'd be able to send them to you in time for your birthday, but unfortunately, the circumstances are such that I won't be in a position to send them to you that soon. I don't expect to be able to send them to you for about six months.[2] I was also planning to send you a congratulatory telegram, but now I won't be able to do that either.

As of December 9, 1966, I have a new job; I'm tying nets, that is those net-like shopping bags that people take to market. Before that I worked as a loader in an emergency brigade; I'm writing you about this so that you will know and not worry so much; during the next six months I will be able to write letters only once every two months.

On the whole, I don't lose heart; it's even easier for me here now, as on my old job I often had to work hard both day and night. I beg you to be steadfast and enduring. We will outlive it all.

(December 11, 1966)

FROM A LETTER TO HIS MOTHER

By now I'm sure you've been informed about the result of the examination of your complaint. I've been informed, too, and I have acquainted myself with its contents. Is it really worthwhile to write these complaints so pitifully?

(March 22, 1967, Yavas)

Yaroslava Menkush

Yaroslava Mykhaylivna Menkush was born into a peasant family on February 16, 1923, in the town of Pustomyty, L'viv Region. She was educated in L'viv, graduating from a specialized secondary school as a designer. Widowed since 1944, in the same year she gave birth to a daughter who is now finishing the conservatory in L'viv.

---

1 Hutsuls — Ukrainians living in the Carpathian Mountains in southwestern Ukraine, famous for their elaborate carving and embroidery (transl. note).
2 A hint at a six months' term in camp prison.

From her thirtieth year she resided permanently in L'viv, working as a teacher of sewing and design, and as a clothes designer. Her last place of work, from 1962 until her arrest, was at the L'viv Project-designing Institute of Light Industry, where she was a designer. On March 25, 1966, she was sentenced by a closed session of the L'viv Regional Court to two and a half years of severe hard-labour camp on the charge of anti-Soviet nationalist propaganda and agitation. (The Supreme Court of Ukr. ssr reduced her sentence to one year.) Upon her return from Mordovia (camp No. 17-a) she was not reinstated in her former job, but was refused a residence permit and expelled from L'viv. At present she is unemployed.

Valentyn Moroz

Valentyn Yakovych Moroz was born into a peasant family on April 15, 1936, in the village of Kholonovo, Horokhiv district, Volyn' region. After graduating from secondary school, he entered the Faculty of History at the L'viv University. As an active member of the historical science circle, he often delivered research papers. After graduating from university in 1958, he worked in his native Horokhiv district in the Volyn' region as director of studies in a secondary school and as a history and geography teacher in the school for working youth. He lectured at pedagogical conferences in Luts'k and delivered lectures on historical subjects in the villages of his district. From February, 1964, he taught modern history at the Lesya Ukrainka Pedagogical Institute in Luts'k and from September, 1964, recent history in the Pedagogical Institute at Ivano-Frankivs'ke.

While working in the villages, he prepared, without any assistance, his candidate's dissertation on the subject, "The Luts'k trial in 1934 as an example of revolutionary collaboration of the Polish and Ukrainian peoples in their joint struggle against the Fascist regime in bourgeois Poland". He did not defend this thesis due to his arrest.

He is married and has a five-year-old son.

Towards the end of August, 1965, he was arrested, and

in January, 1966, he was sentenced by the Regional Court of Volyn' to five years in severe hard-labour camps on the charge of anti-Soviet propaganda and agitation. He stayed in camp No. 1 of the Mordovian political prisoners' camps (village Sosnivka); at present is in camp No. 11 (village Yavas). In December, 1966, together with M. Horyn', M. Masyutko, and L. Lukyanenko, he was sentenced to six months in the camp's prison.

FROM LETTERS TO HIS WIFE

I feel much better here. You understand — after the cell, and mainly after being in the company of criminals; it was loathesome, not only to talk to some of them, but to stay in the same place with them.

They say here that Drach died[1] on July 15. A notice appeared in *Literaturna Ukraina* of July 22. I haven't seen the paper yet myself. That's how it goes. You think the man is alive, yet he is already dead! . . .

(July 29, 1966)

*

I'm now very interested in the problem of individuality. I see that it is one of great importance in the development of humanity in general. Inanimate nature represents unity, similarity, lack of individuality. With the appearance of a live being, there appears an individual, but only in the physical sense. For, in the spiritual sense, there is absolutely no difference between one monkey and another. Human beings had their beginning in the dissimulation of the spirit, in the appearance of a spiritual world of their own, original and unstandardized . . .

(October, 1966)

*

---

1 This proved to be a false rumour (transl. note).

Well, that's how I live. My work is as simple as mooing: lift up, put down. That's good — it leaves my mind free. I'm reading Cicero, Hobbes, Alberto Moravia.

(November, 1966)

*

I haven't yet received the Kant and Russell you wrote about. Recently I finished reading Hobbes . . .

(December, 1966)

*

However, the German language is now[1] the winner. I have more time for it now, although even before I used to devote some time to it every day (except Sundays). I intend to make my finishing dash in the course of these six months, and then come to a full stop. Even now I can always make out what I read in the paper. Next I'll start to learn English. The place here is full of teachers!

I've started reading Kant now . . .

(January, 1967)

Mykhaylo Ozerny

Mykhaylo Dmytrovych Ozerny was born into a peasant family in 1929 in the village of Verkhne Synevydne in the Skole district of the L'viv region. After obtaining a degree in pedagogy, he served in the army, worked for some time in the House of Pioneers in Ternopil', and later taught in various schools, including the Doruhivs'ka Secondary School in the Ternopil' region, until 1961. He tried unsuccessfully to obtain employment in the city of Ternopil', where his family resided. Two years before his arrest he managed to get work in the Ripnyans'ka secondary school, Rozhnyatyn district of the Ivano-Frankivs'ke region, where he taught German, as well as the Ukrainian language and literature.

---
[1] After commitment to the camp prison.

He is married and has two small children.

He was arrested towards the end of August, 1965, while returning from a vacation in the Carpathians. He was sentenced on February 7, 1966, by the Ivano-Frankivs'ke Regional Court, on the charge of anti-Soviet nationalist propaganda and agitation, to six years of severe hard-labour camp (the Supreme Court reduced the sentence to three years). He stayed in camp No. 11 (Yavas) in Mordovia; later he was transferred — present location unknown.

His articles dealing with language and literature were published in the press (for example, in the column *Around the World* of *Literaturna Ukraina* early in 1965).

From his Letter, Written in Prison
TO THE PROSECUTOR OF THE IVANO-FRANKIVS'KE REGION

It is hard to judge how much disgrace and heroism there is in my life. Let people pronounce judgment over us. I am far removed from Ukrainian bourgeois nationalism. I am equally far removed from pseudo-patriotism. My credo is that no one can succeed in building happiness on human sorrow . . .

*

NOTE DROPPED BY M. OZERNY
in the inner courtyard of the jail at Ivano-Frankivs'ke:

Oh, brother of mine! I know you are here; I heard your song. I confessed. Do not grieve. The devil is not as terrible as he is painted. I am proud of you. I have *Perturbations of the Heart* (a collection of I. Drach).

Mykhaylo Osadchy

Mykhaylo Hryhorovych Osadchy was born on March 22, 1936, in the village of Kurmany, Nedryhaylivs'k district, of the Sumy region, into the family of a *kolkhoz* peasant. After graduating from secondary school, he studied at the Faculty of Journalism of the L'viv University, from which he graduated in 1958. He worked as editor and senior editor at the television studio in L'viv, and from December, 1960, he worked as a lecturer at the L'viv University. In 1963-64 he served as instructor for the press of the L'viv Regional Party Committee. Prior to his arrest he was senior lecturer in the department of journalism at the L'viv State University and deputy secretary of the department's Party organization, in charge of ideological education. For one year he edited the university newspaper.

From 1962 and up to his arrest he was a member of the CPSU. He also was a member of the Union of Journalists of the USSR.

Completely on his own, without enrolling in a post-graduate program and without any faculty supervisor, he wrote a candidate's thesis on the subject, *Journalistic Activities of Ostap Vyshnya[1] (1919-1933)*, and defended it successfully on June 25, 1965. Because of his arrest, the Supreme Attestation Commission did not confirm his graduate degree.

As a journalist and specialist in literature, he contributed to the republican and regional press and periodically published poems and short stories. The Kamenyar Publishing House put out a collection of his poems, *Misyachne pole*, [Moonlit field], the entire edition of which was destroyed because of the author's arrest.

He is married. His son, Taras, was born on April 19, 1966 (the day after the pronouncement of the sentence).

He was arrested on August 28, 1965, and sentenced on April 18, 1966, by a closed session of the L'viv Regional Court to two years' imprisonment in severe hard-labour camps on the charge of anti-Soviet propaganda and agitation.

Confined to camp No. 11 (village Yavas) of the Mordovian political prisoners' camps, he works as a joiner. As a result of the prison and camp regimen, he contracted a stomach disease. During a search in the camp, in December, 1966, a notebook

---

[1] Pen name of the noted Ukrainian author and humourist, Pavlo M. Hubenko (1889-1956). He was banished to Siberia by the Soviet regime from 1934 to 1943 but was later rehabilitated (transl. note).

containing translations and paraphrased songs from Lorka and from the works of poets from Baltic republics, as well as original verses, was taken away from Osadchy.

Thirst cannot be endured for long. A man happily enjoys the coolness of a spring, finds a healing oasis in the desert, and the clever inhabitants of Madagascar drink fresh water from ravenal trees without causing themselves any harm.

Men quench their spiritual thirst at the well of life and work, in the inexhaustible depth of books, in love and song on the moonlit field of dreams.

The swift-winged splashing of the shallow Sula, the splendidly triumphal flow of the Dnipro, the golden flame of the sunflower, the silvery path of a rocket — all these are a source of inspiration and daring. Poetry is the wings which will interrupt their flight only when the earth becomes empty of air and life.

FROM M. OSADCHY'S LETTERS

Volodya, my big request is not to write anything and not to go to anyone with humble petitions, because the only result is your humiliation and my own; they do as much good as last year's snow could do for the development of jet technology. Volodya, I said at our rendezvous and I wrote that the court trial did not disclose any criminal intent in my action, as it is impossible, even by applying the most terrifying moral and psychological pressure, to disclose something that does not exist. I was completely baffled by my lawyer, who was three times as scared as I was and who was afraid to touch even slightly upon the gist of the case. The basic documents of Soviet legislation and juridical sources were simply denied to me, and I had never taken an interest in them before. So I found myself in a complicated situation, although my intuition kept telling me: Something is wrong, something here is not as it should be. I decided, therefore, no matter what might happen to me, to deny at the trial all that had been sucked out of fingers[1] during the investigation. My truth was so convincing that even the Supreme Court withdrew practically all the charges, leaving only two episodes, which were in no way proven either. In a future letter I will, possibly, try to write you the contents of my declaration to the Central Committee. Unfortunately it obviously hasn't been read by anyone, because the time that it took for the reply to get to me and the time that my declaration was en route to its destination were equal, ten days each way. Who exactly could have had the opportunity of learning what was in it, and when?

In view of this, Volodya, there is no "crime" in my actions, and I don't understand how it can be in any way "criminal" to read any kind of literature. To give an example, I quote the nineteenth chapter of the Declaration of Human Rights, which I read for the first time here in camp:

"Everyone has the right to freedom of opinion and expression; this right includes freedom to hold opinions without interference and to seek, receive and impart information and ideas through any media and regardless of frontiers."

The fact that my convictions didn't clash with the official ones was not even disputed by the investigation; nor was I accused of it. The fact that I did not collect and did not disseminate any information, except that on literature and works of art, was evidenced by the investigation, but nothing else. The fact is that my trial was a whim of the small toe on the left foot of the masters of this world of ours — but what have I to do with it?

Volodya, since you are free, perhaps you have learned what it is that I am supposed to confess? Something that I have not committed? Since you have already sent that kind of letter, without my consent, I think a way must be found to get it back.

Volodya, death, my death, may be tweny years or so nearer or farther away, but my life, even if I could be released this very minute, has been cut shorter — so what does it matter? Volodya, I want you to grasp this. In spite of all the blows and tribulations[1] of fate, I will be led by, my guiding star will be,

1 Invented, fabricated (transl. note).

my desire to be of service to my people. This was written once by Ivan Franko, and I will repeat it to my last days.

Yes, Volodya, my health has already been seriously undermined; I believe that in this respect even worse results must be expected. My prospects in life, which are already truncated, do not worry me much. Even if I leave nothing to the people in the way of lasting literature or literary criticism, still if my troubles should inspire at least some of those close to me to greater flights of fantasy and urge them on to more work — then I will know my life has not been wasted.

The roar, the howls, the grinding noises of machinery and timber are affecting the state of my nerves and cause complications in both the new diseases and the old ones that I brought here with me. But I stand firm and trust that somehow I'll survive to cure my frail body at some later date. By the way, the Declaration of Human Rights, quoted above, was promulgated by the General Assembly of the United Nations in 1948. Our government has ratified it. It goes without saying that, having read here the comments on the Criminal Code, and specifically on Article 62, I was even more astonished by the tragic and deliberate judicial error that sent me here. I don't mean the trial, because the honour of the uniform[1] compelled them to act as they did, but the arrest itself and the difficult investigation.

Everything passes, everything vanishes when there is an assured faith — I wrote that in one of my poems when I was nineteen or twenty. We've already had a few snowflurries; soon it will be winter, then spring and summer — that is my only consolation, that is the only truth, because it is difficult to reach another one.

(Yavas, October, 1966)

*

Lately I've read a lot of Goethe's poems about love. The old German fellow obviously knew how to fall in love and to live by the spirit and the body of woman.

I also read some very interesting articles in No. 10 of the

---

[1] Meaning considerations of institutional prestige (transl. note).

journal *Novy Mir* [The New World] and in No. 12 of the journal *Neva*. The article in the latter is entitled *America and the Americans* and deals with some interesting aspects of the problem of the city-village relations, spiritual trends, and the progress of the people, their habits and traditions. This was an essay, a new genre in our literature. Furthermore, I read the book by Chatuyev, *Zelimkhan*, about the tsar of Ingushetia and Chechnya, something similar in style to the book of Ivan Ol'brakht, *Mykola, Hay*. I felt a breeze of fresh mountain air, of the immeasurable height of the human spirit, and of a longing to hear the full swing of action. What sweet happiness — to feel in the arms, in the body and, above all, in the spirit — the spaciousness, that sweet and fresh feeling of spaciousness that we value so little in our mindless childhood and which we dissipate so uselessly.

Right now I want to learn as much as I possibly can about Eastern literature. I have before me a small volume of poems of Makhtum-Kuli translated from the Turkmen language. It's pleasant to feel the embrace of his wisdom, experience and quick-witted speech. This feeling of rapture exalts a man and turns him into a noble being . . .

(Yavas, February 14, 1967)

*

I told them here how little Taras used to catch reflections of the sunbeams on the floor. Funny — you know, no matter how I strain my memory, I can't picture in my mind's eye what he looks like and how he gets up on his feet. Write to me in detail about the things he does.

I have selected *Chornotrop* (collection of poems by V. Mysyk — V. Ch.) as one of the best books of Ukrainian poetry of the past year, and Pluzhnyk has given me a sea of delight . . .

(March 3, 1967)

*

Some of your letters, those of the tenth, the fifteenth, and the twentieth, are still wandering in the mails. Mountain passes are high.

Recently I finished reading Andriashyk's novel, *Lyudy zi strakhu* [People of Fear], and it left me dissatisfied. The author's efforts to show the historical background of Galician customs and the public and social life before and after 1917 are so feeble that they actually burst the seams of the author's own inadequate state of preparedness and his hazy understanding of the true situation toward the end of the 1910s and the beginning of the twenties. He himself has no clear knowledge of it, so what can be expected from the heroes he has unleashed into the world? It's true that here and there he tries to break through the restrictions of his knowledge of that period. Then some of the monologues and author's thoughts sound, though somewhat unnatural in the mouths of the heroes of 1919, fresh, timely, and stirring in this day and age. These droplets of fresh dew on the coarse, withered, furrowed surface of the novel arouse in the reader a few thoughts of his own to compensate him for the time wasted on reading.

The story, *Spraha* [Thirst] by Roman Ivanychuk in the first issue of *Dnipro* is likeable in places, and some episodes are dealt with skillfully and with a knowledge of the subject, with a compassion for social throes. But the composition is very loose and the ending is false, with the result that all the finer qualities of the story turn out to be just like the snowman who soon melts and vanishes.

The book by Korniy Chukovs'ky, *Miy Whitman* [My Whitman], is most interesting. Also very attractive is the article by one Shenkman in the journal, *Voprosy filosofiy* [Questions of philosophy], No. 12, 1966, about the freedom of spiritual production, including the artistic creativity of men of letters, not as a manifestation of a social-group assignment, but as an acquisition of a people's humanistic ideals, which connect their past, present, and future. The writer stands above the social demands of the day and often succumbs, therefore, to ostracism, or to something even worse. These are, approximately, the thoughts of that article.

As you see, I'm stuffing my beaten-up head and keep on dreaming of independent literary work in both translation and poetry and in literary criticism, but my wings are clipped. However, it doesn't matter. The last issue of *Literaturna Ukraina* contains Kozlanyuk's letters and in one of them — to a lovely girl — Kozlanyuk asks her to reassure his mother with these words: Convey to her that even Napoleon had to endure prison. With the same thought I console you, too, my beloved Oksana . . .

(March 18, 1967)

*

Right now Guillone Apollinere is clearing the metal shelf of my memory. As the day takes morning away from night, so he clarified for me many questions about the sources and inspirations of Mezhelajtis — the greatest contemporary poet of the Union. His creations are not merely reminiscences of Apollinere's experiences, moods, thoughts, and rhythmo-melodic verse structure; they are whole armfuls of images that Mezhelajtis snatched from Apollinere (as I, in childhood stole the sweet pears of old Stepanyda), hiding them inside his shirt front. For example, Mezhelajtis's collection, *Lyudyna* [Man], contains the poem *Ruky* [Hands] with this line: "My days die like people, it is very sad to bury them . . ." Apollinere writes: "I have found in myself the courage to look back. The corpses of days mark my road." I can't make any more comparisons because the book *Lyndyna* isn't available to me now, but I'm not reproaching Mezhelajtis. I'm only saying, how late poetic discoveries reach the consciousness and the imagination of unsophisticated poets. Some strange and comical dreams run through my mind: as if I were in a library, then in the isolator. This is probably because I, in an adult way, have developed an intense longing for a solid library — for the one about which the Romans said that in it the dead speak. In the distance I smell the paper pollen of libraries, their wisdom-filled tranquility, the sweet moments of discovery of spiritual truths.

My dear one, I'm completely blameless that my telegram

sent on March 30 was not forwarded until the third of April. O, gods, what are you doing to mortals ! . . .

(April, 1967)

Ivan Rusyn

Ivan Ivanovych Rusyn was born into a peasant family on November 8, 1937, at the farmstead Burtal' in the Horodok district of the L'viv region. In 1954 he enrolled at the L'viv Polytechnic Institute, from which he graduated in 1959 as a specialist in engineering geodesy. He was given employment in the design and planning institute, "Kiev regional projects", where he worked as a geodesic engineer until his arrest. He took post-graduate courses by correspondence at the construction engineering institute in Kiev.

He was a member of the amateur choir, Zhayvoronok [the lark], at the Academic Building of Scholars in Kiev.

He is married and has one daughter, born in 1965.

He was arrested on August 28, 1965, and sentenced on March 25, 1966, by a closed session of the Kiev Regional Court to one year of severe hard-labour camps on the charge of anti-Soviet agitation and propaganda. He served his sentence in camp No. 11 (Yavas) of the Mordovian political prisoners' camps. Since his return he has resumed his former employment.

Mefodiy Chubaty

Mefodiy Chubaty was born into a peasant family in 1938 in the village of Velyki Hayi in the Terebovlya district of the Ternopil' region. After completing school, he graduated from a secondary cultural education school, served in the army, studied in the orchestral department of the secondary school of music in Ternopil'. He graduated from the school of music in 1965, but his arrest prevented him from obtaining employment.

He was arrested towards the end of August, 1965. On February 25, 1966, the Ternopil's Regional Court imposed on him a suspended sentence of four years on the charge of anti-Soviet nationalistic propaganda and agitation. At present he is employed as a teacher in the school of music in the town of Zboriv, Ternopil' region.[1]

Anatoliy Shevchuk

Anatoliy Oleksandrovych Shevchuk was born on February 6, 1937, in Zhytomyr, into a workman's family. His father worked at a footwear factory and is now retired. In 1954, Anatoliy completed secondary school and enrolled in technical school No. 1 in Zhytomyr. In two years he received a construction master's certificate but could not work due to poor health. He found employment as a linotypist in the Zhytomyr regional printing office, where he worked until the day of his arrest. He became very skilful in his trade and was considered to be the best linotypist of the region. He was mentioned in the regional press as the outstanding tradesman. The last report about Shevchuk and his wife, both linotypists, appeared in the newspaper, *Radyans'ka Zhytomyrshchyna* [The Soviet Zhytomyr Region], in May, 1966, a few days before the arrest.

He is married and has a six-year-old daughter.

He suffers from a progressive heart disease and acute rheumatism. He has endured two rheumatic attacks. Since the beginning of 1960, Shevchuk's short stories appeared in the republican and regional press. Some ten of his stories were published. His works received favourable comments in the journal, *Zmina* [Change], and in the newspaper, *Literaturna Ukraina*. In 1962, his works were discussed by the commission for assistance to young authors of the SPU [Writers' Union of Ukraine]. He prepared a collection of short stories for publication with the publishing house, Radyans'ky pys'mennyk, that received laudatory reviews (one of them — by the writer I. Senchenko—was confiscated during the search by the Zhytomyr KGB).

He was arrested on May 23, 1966, and on September 7 of the same year he was sentenced at a closed session of the Zhytomyr Regional Court to five years of severe hard-labour camps on

---

1 We have no further details about Chubaty.

The Misfortune

the charge of anti-Soviet propaganda and agitation. At present he is in camp No. 11 (Yavas) of the Mordovian political prisoners' camps.

FROM COMMENTS ON THE WORKS OF SHEVCHUK

It is particularly pleasant to point out that the writings of writers with secondary school education — as in *Ira, Stop Reading!* by Anatoliy Shevchuk — are distinguished from the works of many professional writers by the culture of their form, psychological refinement, and esthetic purity. Those who love to appeal to the "mass reader" should ponder this: there is less and less room for literary artisans.

(Ye. Sverstyuk, *Problems of the young prose, Zmina,* No. 12, 1962.)

FROM A. SHEVCHUK'S LETTERS TO HIS BROTHER

I finished reading your story in *Dnpiro.* I like it. Remarks: the first part is slightly disconnected from the second. That is, the figure of the teacher, with his fairly long judgments about humanity and its evolution, disappears in the second half and is no longer mentioned. The gun (in this case — the teacher) didn't fire, but only clicked in preparation to shoot. All the same, I read it with interest and, when I compared it with the work of other short-story writers, the comparison was in your favour. I read and recognized the prototypes. Your teacher is probably a hybrid of Yefrem Solomonovych and Stepan Stanislavovych.

Please send me Updike and, if very interesting, Sartre. Also send me that book, *About Books and Book-Lovers*; I long to read something of that sort. I'm reading Joyce in *Vsesvit* [The Universe]. Haven't finished it yet. I have the impression of a certain intention in his style . . .

(January, 1967, Yavas)

*

I don't know whether *Literaturna Ukraina* will find me here. Try to correct the address. Write what you hear about the congress.[1]

Just now my neighbour brought me the latest issue of *Vsesvit*. We have Ukrainian books here, too. If you have something of interest, please send it by parcel post. You know my tastes. I had no time, after all, to look at Shcherbak's book. If it's interesting and still available, please send it. Have the selected works of Symonenko appeared in print? ...

(January, 1967, Yavas)

*

The boys are now reading *In the Middle of the Week*, so I'll look at it carefully at a later date and write about my general impression. Right now I'm reading articles from issues of the journal *Byloye* [Bygone] for 1906, stitched together into one book. They're mostly about the Decembrists and members of the Narodnaya Volya [People's Freedom]. There is also an autobiography of Drahomaniv. The news that you've purchased a dictionary for me has, of course, melted my heart with joy. My sincere thanks.

Some time early in March I'll send some of my works. I'm too lazy to copy them. Time seems to float past my present life, and the constancy of feelings give it quietude and indifference to outward irritants. It's like some outer-space existence, between the sky and the earth, where everything around you is dominatd by uncertainty and petrified expectations. But it would seem that everything should be just the opposite. I don't try to determine what is better and what is worse. It's a sort of semi-Bohemian life coloured with the implacable force of one's surroundings. This force never loses sight of you; it's as if you don't notice it, you simply float with the current and give movement to other currents hidden inside you. And that force somewhere in the distance lashes a grey, fidgety, and slippery thing, a *something* which could be called despair. That force just keeps on lashing and lashing it, urging it to

---

1 Of Ukrainian writers.

slink up to our Bohemian milieu and to creep into it, to poison our souls. And it wriggles and yelps, but does not advance, because there's no road for it here. And so, day in, day out, this crawler yelps in the distance but cannot retreat. At times I think it's necessary in the end to tear apart the curtain of that strange tranquility and primitive well-being.

I read somewhere that a Franco-Roumanian film called *The Nameless Star*, based on a play by M. Sebastianu, is now in the making. I remember we heard that play on the radio and were fascinated by it. And now this film will certainly appear on the screens, but we won't see it here; the only more or less decent film shown here was *Ivan's Childhood*. As a rule, they feed us all kinds of film strips à la *Youth of Maxim*. By the way, have any works of Sebastianu been published as a separate book in our country? I seem to remember reading another of his plays in *Rumynskoe obozreniye* [The Roumanian Review]. Generally speaking, it would be very pleasant to read something new by Sebastianu. We have here the journal *Vitchyzna* [Fatherland] which contains A. Maurois' *Prometheus, or the Life of Balzac*. I read about S. Zweig's book on Balzac, but this work is interesting and original. In the summer of last year, in Zhytomyr, I read *Chagrin* by Balzac and was most pleased with it. I'm trying not to waste any time on poor books; there are so many good ones that I can't possibly read them all in my lifetime. I read Dzyuba's interview in the newspaper, *Nove Zhyttya* [New Life]. Among the better books of prose by young authors, he mentions the works of Yu. Shcherbak, Andriyashyk, and of Hryhor Tyutyunnyk. Have you had a chance to get acquainted with this material? It should be interesting.

So far no letters have come from Zhytomyr but, obviously, they will write about Mother's illness. My child wrote me a letter once, in which she said that she was well and was helping her mother to bake pastries; mother shaped them and daughter dipped them in egg white.

Kazbek tobacco smokes well in the pipe. I smoke a pipe sometimes, and sometimes roll-your-owns of shag tobacco. I bought ten packages of Prima — I'm really living!

*

A few days here were almost spring-like; the snow thawed gradually, and the air was filled with something exciting and heart-aching. But today it's a bit colder, cloudy, and there are light snowflurries. I'm writing this letter at work. We have a small nook here in a corner of the shop where one can sit in peace and quiet. Soon we'll go home (!) As usual people will line both sides of the road, waiting for us to pass by, and we'll glance (there is a better Russian word, *glazeya* [gaping]) at that grey throng that exudes ignorance and incomprehension. The ones who await a visit also glance around, hoping to catch sight of a relative. We pass there every day, and on both sides people who call themselves *free* are stamping their feet in the cold. What is this? Is anyone really free? We're all dependent on something, and sometimes through our own will we find ourselves in an even greater dependence, but all this together is incomprehensible, as life itself is incomprehensible.

Anatoliy
(February 24, 1967)

Svyatoslav Karavans'ky

Svyatoslav Yosypovych Karavans'ky was born on December 24, 1920, in Odessa, into the family of an engineer. In 1938 he graduated from Odessa secondary school No. 119 and enrolled in the Industrial Institute (and at the beginning of 1939, he also enrolled in the correspondence course of the Institute of Foreign Languages). Even during his school days he wrote poetry and short stories, some of which were published in youth magazines. He also tried his hand at translating while in the institute. Dissatisfied with his chosen profession, he voluntarily left the Institute in 1940 and joined the army, intending after completing his service to enroll in the faculty of literature at the university. In July of 1941, the detachment in which Karavans'ky served was surrounded by the Germans in Western Byelorussia. Avoiding capture, Karavans'ky managed to get to Odessa at the beginning of 1942. There he enrolled in the faculty of literature at the university, where he joined an illegal group of Ukrainian youth connected with the

OUN. He organized a bookshop and transferred the profit from the sales of books to student groups and to the Ukrainian theatre. Karavans'ky was persecuted by the Rumanian political police.[1]

He left for Rumania in 1944, and later in the same year he returned illegally to the liberated Odessa. However, on the third day of his return, while attempting to establish contact with his former associates, he was arrested. He did not commit any actions (neither armed nor through propaganda) directed against the Soviet government during his stay on the liberated territory. During interrogations, Karavans'ky was promised freedom if he agreed to inform the police about attitudes among the students. He rejected this offer. On February 7, 1945, the Military Tribunal of the Odessa Region sentenced Karavans'ky to twenty-five years of imprisonment. He served his sentence in many hard-labour camps of the North and the East. He worked on the construction of a railway in Pechora, felled trees in Magadan, mined gold in Kolyma, worked on the construction of the highway between Taishet and Lena, and sewed overalls in Mordovia.

When the conditions in hard-labour camps improved slightly after Stalin's death, he resumed his literary work. He wrote poems, tales in verse, plays, and made translations. Some of his works, sent from the camps, were even published in republican publications (for instance, in *Literaturna Hazeta* [Literary Gazette]). In 1954 he began a major project — the preparation of a dictionary of rhymes in the Ukrainian language.

After sixteen years and five months of imprisonment, he was released on December 19, 1960, on the basis of the decision of the Dubravny ITL (Corrective Labour Camp) which was based on the Decree of September 17, 1955, Art. 2, dealing with amnesty. His sentence was reduced by half — to twelve years and five months.

After returning to Odessa, Karavans'ky completed a course for mechanics, specializing in the repair of calculating machines. He worked as a mechanic in the provincial auto-

---

1 Odessa, as well as other southwestern regions of Ukraine, was occupied for a time by Rumania during World War II (transl. note).

mobile workshop; as a senior mechanic at a factory which manufactured adding machines; as a mechanic in the servicing section for calculating machines; as a book-hawker; as a translator in the editorial office of the regional newspaper, *Chornomors'ka Komuna*; as a part-time correspondent of the magazine *Ukraina*; as a subscription salesman for Soyuzdruk (publishing house); and then left for several months for Intu (Komi ASSR) to increase his earnings. The frequent changes of work were caused by the fact that at times he was able to find only temporary work or because he was dismissed from work after his past in the camps became known.

The intensity of Karavans'ky's literary work after his release from imprisonment was amazing. He completed the work started in the camp on the dictionary of rhymes in the Ukrainian language (1,000 printed pages). He translated many English poets, prepared a book, *The Biographies of Words*, frequently wrote articles to newspapers and magazines on linguistic problems, had a column in the magazines *Ukraina* and *Znannya ta pratsya* [Knowledge and Work], and newspapers *Sil's'ki Visti* [Village News] and *Ukrains'ke Zhyttya* [Ukrainian Life] and others, prepared a collection of humorous short stories and feuilletons for the publishing house Mayak, and published short interludes. In agreement with the publishing house Dnipro, he was translating Charlotte Bronte's novel, *Jane Eyre*.

S. I. Karavans'ky actively participated in Ukrainian community life. He organized subscriptions for Ukrainian publications in workingmen's hostels in Odessa, collected Ukrainian books for libraries in Kuban', addressed extensive proposals to public and government organizations concerning such matters as the nationwide observance of the jubilee of M. Lysenko,[1] the introduction of the dubbing of all films in the Ukrainian language, the creation of special councils of spectators at film studios, the improvement of sales of Ukrainian books, etc. In 1965, disturbed by the growing russification of Ukrainian schools and universities, he wrote two articles (an accusation of the Minister Dadenkov and *About One Political Error*), which he sent to official institutions.

[1] The outstanding Ukrainian composer (transl. note).

Karavans'ky was married in 1961. In 1962 he enrolled in the correspondence department of the Philological Faculty of the Odessa University where he made good progress in his studies.

On September 4, 1965, when arrests were made in Ukraine, Karavans'ky's home was searched but nothing illegal was found. The next day Karavans'ky sent a categorical protest against the unjustified search to official organizations and to the press. Somewhat later he handed letters to the Consuls of Poland and Czechoslovakia in Kiev, explaining the violations of Lenin's principles of nationality policy in Ukraine and describing the arrests of Ukrainian intellectuals in August-September of 1965.

For all this Karavans'ky was arrested on a street in Odessa on November 13, 1965. Since there was no formal cause for a trial, on the recommendation of the KGB, the General Prosecutor of the USSR, Rudenko, revoked Karavan'ky's 1960 release. Upon his decision Karavans'ky was sentenced, without an investigation or a trial, to eight years and seven months in severe hard-labour camps (the term which remained from the original sentence of twenty-five years). As a protest Karavans'ky went on a hunger strike. At the end of November of 1965, he was deported to the Mordovian camps (camp No. 11, Yavas).

In the camp Karavans'ky wrote a number of petitions to official organizations and to representatives of the public, for which he was twice sentenced to punitive isolation for ten days. On October 8, 1966, he was sent to a camp jail, BUR, for a term of six months. He was formally charged with failing to fulfill the required work quotas (which the majority of prisoners fail to accomplish). In the solitary confinement cell and three times in the prison jail, Karavans'ky went on hunger strikes, demanding a meeting with the public prosecutor. In all, since his arrest, Karavans'ky went on five hunger strikes, which were usually broken on the ninth or tenth day by forced feeding.

During those brief periods when he was not sitting in the prison jail or in solitary confinement, Karavans'ky managed to finish the translation of Bronte's novel, *Jane Eyre*, and also wrote several chapters of his book, *The Biographies of Words*.

On January 3, 1967, a search was made in the house of Karavans'ky's wife in Odessa. Among the confiscated documents there were drafts of statements written by Karavans'ky's wife concerning the illegal arrest of her husband, as well as the manuscript of Karavans'ky's poem written in camp under the title, *To the Heirs of Beria*. In 1967 the camp administration deprived S. Karavans'ky of the right (guaranteed by law) to have a meeting with his wife.

To the Prosecutor of the Ukr. ssr

PETITION

by citizen Svyatoslav Yosipovych Karavans'ky, residing in the city of Odessa, Chornomors'ky shlyakh, 56, Apt. 47.

I beg you to indict the minister of higher and secondary education of the Ukr. ssr, Yury Mykolayovych Dadenkov, according to the articles of the cc Ukr. ssr [Criminal Code of the Ukrainian Soviet Socialist Republic] which provide penalties for:

1. Violation of national and racial equality (Art. 66, c.c. Ukr. ssr).

2. Opposition to the restoration of Leninist principles of opportunity for higher education in the Ukr. ssr (Articles 66, 167, c.c. Ukr. ssr).

3. Failure to implement the resolutions of the Twentieth Congress of the cpsu concerning the liquidation of all traces of the personality cult, and obstructing the restoration of normal conditions for the development of the Ukrainian socialist nation (Article 66, c.c. Ukr. ssr).

4. The training of unqualified teaching cadres and the disorganization of the educational process in the system of secondary and incomplete secondary education (Article 167, c.c. Ukr. ssr).

I base my petition on the following facts:

1. During his tenure as minister of higher and secondary education in the Ukr. ssr, Yu. M. Dadenkov committed serious mistakes; as a result people of Ukrainian nationality, whose native tongue is Ukrainian, do not enjoy the same rights in entering the *Vuzy* [higher institutions of learning] as do those whose native tongue is Russian. Russian language and literature are a compulsory part of the *Vuzy* entrance examinations,

and so the graduates from Russian schools are more successful in passing this examination with higher marks than the graduates from Ukrainian schools. Furthermore, entrance examinations for special disciplines are also conducted in Russian, and this, too, makes it difficult for graduates from Ukrainian schools to pass special subjects. And so Ukrainian speaking applicants get lower marks in competitive examinations. Because those with higher marks in the competitive examinations are accepted by the institutions, the majority of students entering the *Vuzy* in Ukraine are graduates from Russian secondary and incomplete secondary schools. Most of the institutes on the territory of the Ukr. ssr demand from their entrants an examination in the Russian language and literature. To this petition are added two clippings with the announcement of admissions to the Dokuchayev agricultural institute in Kharkiv and the credit-economic institute in Odessa.

As a result of such a faulty anti-Leninist approach to applicants to the *Vuzy*, Ukrainians comprise a considerably lower percentage in comparison with the percentage of Ukrainians in the production of material amenities on the territory of the Ukr. ssr. Among those who entered the Odessa Polytechnical Institute in the 1964-65 school year, Ukrainians amounted to 43%. Of 1,126 Ukrainians who applied for admission, 453 were accepted, i.e., 40%. But of 1,042 Russians who forwarded documents to the institute, 477 were accepted, i.e., 46%. This is the result of the system of admission, which makes it difficult for Ukrainians to enter institutions of learning. This established practice of admission to the republic's higher and secondary institutions of learning is anti-Leninist and constitutes an indirect restriction of the rights of citizens because of their nationality. Actions of this kind must be punished according to Article 66 of the c.c. Ukr. ssr.
"Article 66.
Violation of national and racial equality.
Propaganda or agitation for the purpose of arousing racial or national hostility, or dissension, or the direct or indirect restriction of rights, or the establishment of direct or indirect privileges for citizens depending on the race or nationality to which they belong, shall be punished by the deprivation of

freedom for a term of six months to three years or by exile for a term of two to five years."

2. In the resolution of the cc RCP (b) [Central Committee of the Russian Communist Party (bolsheviks)] of November 29, 1919, concerning the Soviet regime in Ukraine, Lenin himself wrote the following:

"In view of the fact that Ukrainian culture (language, school, etc.) has been suppressed for centuries by tsarism and the exploiting classes of Russia, the cc of the RCP enjoins all members of the Party by all means to remove all hindrances to a free development of the Ukrainian language and culture. In view of the centuries-long oppression, one can observe nationalist tendencies within the backward part of the Ukrainian masses; in treating these tendencies members of the RCP must show greatest patience and caution and counter them by explaining in a friendly way that the interests of the toiling masses of Ukraine and Russia are identical. The members of the RCP on the territory of Ukraine must implement the right of the toiling masses to learn and to use their native tongue in all Soviet institutions, and always counteract attempts to relegate the Ukrainian language to an inferior position. On the contrary, they should aspire to transform the Ukrainian language into an instrument of the communist education of the toiling masses. Measures should be taken at once so that all Ukrainian institutions will have a sufficient number of employees with a command of the Ukrainian language and that in future all the employees will be able to speak the Ukrainian language." (Lenin, *Works*, Vol. 39, pp. 334-337.)

As a result of Lenin's instructions, higher and secondary specialized education in Ukraine was ukrainized during the twenties and thirties. Teaching in the higher institutions of learning was conducted in Ukrainian. This paved the way to an education for the majority of the Ukrainian working masses and created conditions for a normal development of the Ukrainian socialist nation.

During the period of the Stalin personality cult, this Leninist principle of higher education in Ukraine was forgotten. Later the Party passed resolutions to enable the ministry of higher and secondary specialized education in the Ukr. SSR, headed by Yu. M. Dadenkov, to liquidate the remains of the personality cult. But in most higher and secondary specialized institutions of learning in Kiev, Kharkiv, Odessa, Dnipropetrivs'k, and other cities, the instruction is still not in the Ukrainian tongue. The ministry allowed the Ukrainian language to be "relegated to an inferior position", against which Lenin had forewarned. And it continues to tolerate the elimination of Leninist norms in the organization of higher education in the Ukr. SSR.

3. A normal prerequisite for the development of any socialist nation is the training of cadres of the national intelligentsia. During the time that Dadenkov has held his post, the training of such cadres has not been restored in the Ukr. SSR. The Ukrainian intelligentsia is being trained in isolation from its people, its culture, its language. The cadres of lecturers at the *Vuzy* of the Ukr. SSR "do not understand" the Ukrainian language. In the Ushyns'ky Pedagogical Institute in Odessa, which trains cadres for the secondary schools, instruction is not offered in Ukrainian because the lecturers "do not know" the language. At the Mechnikov State University in Odessa, in the Ukrainian section of the Department of Philology, which trains Ukrainian philologists, most of the disciplines (the history of the CPSU, foreign languages, logic, psychology, foreign literature, Marxist philosophy) are not taught in Ukrainian. This is a direct result of the minister's negligent attitude towards his duties: (a) The textbooks required in the Ukrainian language for the *Vuzy* are not being published — manuals for foreign languages, textbooks on logic, on foreign literature, anthologies of foreign literature, etc. (b) There are no cadres of national teaching intelligentsia being trained. There is no doubt that such a state of higher education in Ukraine ruins the normal conditions for the development of the Ukrainian socialist nation.

4. As a result of the "relegation" of the Ukrainian language to a secondary position in the system of higher education, graduates of universities and pedagogical institutes have no command of the Ukrainian tongue. Such instructors working in Ukrainian schools do not teach their subjects in Ukrainian. Fifty per cent of the graduates from the Odessa University and

the Odessa Pedagogical Institute decline to teach in Ukrainian schools because they do not know the Ukrainian language. Such a situation interfers with the normal pedagogical process in Ukraine.

Thus Minister Dadenkov's negligent attitude toward his duties affects the training of cadres and interferes with the normal work of the institutions of popular education.

All the facts I have presented attest to the abnormal work of the ministry of higher and secondary specialized education of the Ukr. ssr, headed by Yu. M. Dadenkov.

I beg you to take these facts into account in ascertaining the degree of guilt of Yury Mykolayevych Dadenkov.

February 24, 1965
(S. Y. Karavans'ky)

Appended to the petition are two newspaper clippings:
1. A clipping from the newspaper *Kolhospne selo* [Collective-farm village], July 4, 1964, on the admission of students to the Dokuchayev Agricultural Institute in Odessa, and 2. A clipping from the newspaper *Znamya kommunizma* [Banner of Communism] (Odessa), June 5, 1965,[1] on the admission to the Odessa credit-economic institute.

ABOUT ONE POLITICAL ERROR

According to Article 9 of the "Law on the ties between school and life" adopted in 1959, in the Russian-language secondary schools of the union republics, study of the national language is not obligatory and is carried out only at the request of the parents.

Lenin expected to bring the Ukrainian language into all aspects of the republic's social and political life. In that case there is no doubt that a knowledge of the Ukrainian language should be obligatory for those who acquire education in the territory of the Ukr. ssr.

From a juridical point of view, Article 9 of the "Law on the ties between school life" is anti-constitutional, for it contradicts both the Constitution of the ussr and the constitutions of

---

1 Inaccurate dates in the original.

the union republics. The Constitution of the Ukr. ssr states: "The equality of rights of the citizens of the Ukr. ssr, regardless of their nationality and race, in all fields of economic, governmental, cultural, and social-political life, is an inviolable law. Either direct or indirect limitations of rights or the establishment of direct or indirect privileges for citizens depending on their race and nationality and also any propaganda of racial or national exclusiveness or of hatred and contempt are punishable by law" (Article 103).

The language of a nationality is a clear expression of its national image. But where are equal rights if one language must be taught in school, but another (in this case the language of the basic part of the population of the republic!) is taught only at the request of the parents?

This article of the law is discriminatory, for it places the language of the republic in an inferior position and degrades the dignity of the citizens of the republic who use the native tongue. It is also wrong from the viewpoint of the international communist upbringing of the children. When parents are reluctant to teach their children the language of the republic whose bread they eat, the child is imbued from its infancy with chauvinistic views, unworthy of Soviet people, of the exclusiveness of its own nationality — a direct departure from the standards of international communist education.

Article 9 of the law is absolutely wrong from the pedagogical point of view. In the practice of Soviet education, there was never a precedent when the teaching of subjects was left to the discretion of the parents. Leaving the question of whether the children should study this or that subject to the parents is a profoundly unpedagogical measure. The parents often do not understand what advantage or harm they cause a child by the decision they make. It can be said that one of the very responsible aspects of international upbringing is being transferred to the discretion of the parents. Such "democratic solution" of this very question could be justified if the question of the language of instruction in the *Vuzy* were solved in our country in a similar democratic way. But it is in this sphere of popular education that, for decades (during the personality cult of Stalin and Khrushchev), the instruction has been given in Russian and a knowledge of the Russian language has been required at the entrance examination. After decades of discriminatory measures against the Ukrainian language, to place the question of teaching it at the discretion of the parents is, to a great extent, strange and unpolitic. This action could be justified if the question of wages for the various categories of workers and employees were submitted to the judgment of the citizens. For the public is not any less interested in the just distribution of material amenities in the country, all the more so since this distribution is one of the basic principles of communism.

As a result of the adoption of Article 9, the number of Ukrainian schools on Ukrainian territory has decreased. In Odessa and the Odessa region in the 1962-63 school year, there were 821 Ukrainian schools; in 1963-64 the number was reduced to 693, and in 1964-65 to 603. Of that number in Odessa, respectively, there were 10, 8, and 6 schools instructing in the Ukrainian language. (The total number of schools in Odessa is 104). The few Ukrainian schools that survived are under the threat of being closed. All this is the result of the anti-Leninist, discriminatory Article 9.

How are the Ukrainian schools being closed? Even before the Ukrainian language was removed from the *Vuzy* in Odessa, the parents only reluctantly sent the children to Ukrainian schools because of the impossibility of continuing their education after graduating from a Ukrainian school . . . Indeed, the graduates from Ukrainian schools are only a small percentage of the total number of graduates from the Odessa *Vuzy*. The system of admission that existed till recently, and still exists in some places, gave preference to graduates from Russian schools. So the parents, who earlier reluctantly sent the children to Ukrainian schools, now (after the appearance of the discriminatory article) began to demand that Ukrainian schools adopt the Russian language of instruction. At first a few Russian classes appear in a Ukrainian school, then their number gradually increases, until finally the school becomes entirely Russian. Ukrainian parents, who speak Ukrainian, come to the schools and beg that their children be transferred to "Russian" classes. Such a request is dictated not by an indifference towards the native tongue, but by those discriminatory obstacles which for decades have barred the road of graduates from Ukrainian schools to the attainment of education, and which still exist in some places.

Characteristic of the parents' attitude is the request of citizeness Balok, a resident of the village of Kryva Balka, to transfer her child to a Russian school. Citizeness Balok, in a conversation with me, stated that she wishes to have her child attend a Russian school, because she herself at one time had completed seven grades in a Ukrainian school and had gone to Odessa to continue her schooling. And here, because she spoke Ukrainian, her classmates laughed at her. Citizeness Balok had to terminate her education, and she wishes to have her daughter taught in such a way that no one will jeer at her.

One cannot listen calmly to such confessions. How could such discriminatory acts penetrate into the environment of the Soviet people — who are militant internationalists — discriminatory acts that compelled the child of honest workers to quit school and to ask that her child be enrolled in a Russian school, so that in future the child would not become a victim of national discrimination? This same thought prompted many other Ukrainian parents to insist that their children be taught in Russian schools. After all, it is no secret that in Odessa (and in other places in Ukraine, including Kiev) among a certain chauvinistically inclined part of the populace, derision of the Ukrainian tongue and of the Ukrainian nationality became a very popular pastime. Such acts were observed in autobuses, in offices, libraries, institutions of learning. Madame Mel'nyk, a lecturer in history at the Party school in Odessa, declared in the presence of students that she did not like the Ukrainian language and did not wish to make use of it. Such a declaration from a pedagogue, an educator of the Ukrainian masses, is in this case more than characteristic.

All this shows that, during the time of the Stalin personality cult, discriminatory tendencies towards the Ukrainian language and the Ukrainian nationality developed in Ukraine. These tendencies were bolstered in recent times by the so-called "Law on the ties between school and life", as a result of which the number of the Ukrainian schools in Odessa, in the

Odessa region, and indeed all over Ukraine decreased catastrophically. The number of Moldavian schools in the Odessa region has also become smaller. Furthermore, in the Russian schools the vast majority of pupils refuse to learn the Ukrainian tongue. It is not taught at all in the schools of the Volgrad district of the Odessa region, in the town of Izmail, and in the Izmail district.

Thus Article 9 of the "Law on the ties between school and life" is directed against teaching the national tongue in the schools. What true internationalist could be worried by the fact that a child learns the language of a brother-nation? Only chauvinists can lock their children in narrow national frameworks, hiding behind theories of the exclusiveness of their nationality. Article 9 of the law placed the cards in the hands of these chauvinistic elements, kindled and fanned chauvinistic sentiments among parents and pedagogues. The director of the Odessa Ukrainian School No. 125, O. I. Kryuchkov, for example, incites the teachers and parents to introduce the Russian language in the school as the medium of instruction. Not having received permission from anyone to do this, he twice arranged meetings of the parents, who voted to adopt the Russian language of instruction in the school. Rather than trying to improve teaching techniques, to master the Ukrainian language himself, which incidentally he cannot speak, and to acquire, at least by a correspondence course, the pedagogical training which he also lacks, this "educator" does everything to install the Russian language as the means of instruction in the school.

This law also develops undesirable tendencies among the pupils. Pupils being instructed in the Russian language are divided into two categories: those who study the Ukrainian language and those who do not. Thus, instead of levelling the national differences among the pupils, the school fosters and emphasizes them. The division of the children into two categories also engenders discrimination. The appearance of improper nicknames, such as *khokhol*,[1] *katsap*,[2] etc., has been observed amongst Soviet children in Odessa schools.

[1] Derogatory term for Ukrainians (transl. note).
[2] Derogatory term for Russians (transl. note).

The children whose parents refused to teach them the Ukrainian language develop a contemptuous attitude toward the Ukrainian language and nationality. Among the children who do study it there arises a feeling that their nationality is inferior; the study of their national language is not obligatory, is of secondary importance, and can be derided openly by chauvinistically inclined elements.

No less painful is the effect of this law upon the pedagogical process and upon the teachers who offer the Ukrainian language. For the instructor is constantly aware that the pupil may refuse to learn the Ukrainian language; therefore, God forbid, one must not give him a low mark. After all, the study is not obligatory. If the pupil is given a low mark, he simply asks his parents that he be completely relieved of the study of the language. Such cases are very common. Thus the law places an entire category of Soviet teachers in an impossible situation; the normal process of teaching this subject is violated.

All these facts show that the adoption of one discriminatory law during the time of the Khrushchev personality cult created impossible conditions for the normal functioning of the Ukrainian school system. This law belittles the national dignity of citizens of Ukrainian nationality, strikes a blow at international communist education, and prepares the ground for the kindling of national animosity. It contradicts the last will of Lenin and, being basically discriminatory, encroaches upon the friendship of peoples of the USSR.

It is essential that the general public speak out against this situation. It is dreadful to commit a political error, but it is much more dreadful to be afraid to rectify it. The desire to rectify the error compelled me to write this article.

On my part I suggest the following measures;

1. To revise at once Article 9 of the "Law on the ties between school and life".

2. To transfer the teaching in the higher and secondary specialized institutions of learning in the Ukr. SSR to the Ukrainian language in order to facilitate the education of the broad masses of the Ukrainian people.

3. To set up a co-ordination committee between the Ministry of Education of the Ukr. SSR and the Ministry of Higher

and Secondary Specialized Education of the Ukr. ssr to establish normal conditions for the training of graduates from Ukrainian secondary schools in the institutions of higher learning and the technical schools of the republic.

4. To remove chauvinistically inclined instructors from among cadres of popular education.

5. To apply decisive measures to stop discriminatory acts against the Ukrainian language and Ukrainian nationality.

6. To select for the teaching staffs of Ukrainian schools people who can instill love for the native tongue and culture.

7. To stop the pedagogically erroneous practice of setting up Russian classes in national schools, which leads to the russification of national schools.

8. For a truly international training of national minorities, the system of poular education should include schools offering Yiddish, Armenian, and other languages of instruction.

9. In the institutions of higher learning which train teachers, special attention must be given to the training of national teaching cadres, to establish groups and courses which would graduate qualified cadres for national schools.

10. To inform the general public of all the measures taken. Only the implementation of these points will make it possible to remove in practice, in the Leninist manner, all the hindrances to a normal development of Ukrainian education.

S. Karavans'ky

To the First Secretary of the Central Committee of PORP,[1] *Comrade W. Gomulka, from Svyatoslav Yospovych Karavans'ky, a citizen of the* USSR, *residing in the city of Odessa, Chornomors'ky Shlyakh Street, 56, apt. 47.*

PETITION

The Twentieth Congress of the Communist Party of the Soviet Union became a turning point in the history of the communist movement. It condemned the policy of unjustified, unwarranted repressions, which took place in the USSR during the

---

1 Polish United Workers' Party.

time of the Stalin personality cult, against a large number of Party and non-Party citizens, including representatives of the Ukrainian intelligentsia. Unfounded accusations charging the Ukrainian intelligensia with "nationalism", with "betrayal of the fatherland", etc., were a tool in the hands of unscrupulous opportunists, which made it possible for them to revise the Leninist nationality policy.

These lawless purges removed from the ranks of the Party such prominent Leninists as S. V. Kosior, V. Ya. Chubar, M. Skrypnyk, D. Zatons'ky, P. P. Postyshev, and thousands of other Party activists, who joined the Party prior to October and during the revolution, when V. I. Lenin directed the Party. This crime against the Party was attended by a crime against the Ukrainian intelligentsia. Thousands of writers, artists, teachers, scientists were accused of "nationalism" and were liquidated. It suffices to mention the names of those who were executed by firing squads and who are now [posthumously] rehabilitated — stage-director L. Kurbas; the writers I. Mykytenko, M. Zerov, D. Zahul, M. Irchan, O. Vlyz'ko, D. Fal'kivsky, M. Kulish, I. Dniprovs'ky, O. Sokolovs'ky — and those persecuted without cause — Ostap Vyshnya, B. Antonenko-Davydovych, V. Gzhyts'ky, Z. Tulub. This far from complete list of outstanding names shows what a blow was dealt the Ukrainian culture and the Ukrainian intelligentsia during the period of the Stalin personality cult, just on the eve of the Great Patriotic War [World War II]. Literally tens of thousands of the rank-and-file of Ukrainian intellectuals were destroyed. These unwarranted pogroms no doubt contributed to a degree of activization of nationalistic organizations on the territory of the Ukr. ssr during the Great Patriotic War.

After 1945 several attempts were made to renew the unfounded repressions against the Ukrainian intelligentsia; repressions also took place against Jewish intellectuals.

The Twentieth Congress condemned these actions against the representatives of various nationalities. Unfortunately, during the last month incidents in Ukraine speak of attempts to renew the unwarranted persecution of the Ukrainian intelligentsia.

In February of this year I approached the Prosecutor of the

Ukr. ssr with a petition, asking for the indictment of the Minister of Higher and Secondary Specialized Education in the Ukr. ssr, Yu. M. Dadenkov. The Prosecutor did not reply, and only in a private conversation with him did I learn that my petition had been forwarded to the Ministry of Higher and Secondary Specialized Education. After a study of this petition, Minister Dadenkov implemented a whole series of measures to remove the discriminatory rules of admission to schools of higher learning and to secondary special training institutions of the republic. My petition was thus substantiated, and since it helped to disclose shortcomings, it should be regarded as beneficial to the cause of communism. But unfortunately, for reasons unknown I was subjected to persecution.

On September 4 of this year, five representatives of the Odessa regional division of the KGB arrived at my home and conducted a search. They did not turn up any incriminating material. Later I learned from the questions I was asked at the hearing that a copy of my petition to the Prosecutor had been found in the possession of a Canadian citizen, Ivan Vasylyovych Kolyaska.[1] This was the reason for conducting the search in my apartment.

I succeeded in establishing that Ivan Vasylyovych Kolyaska is a Canadian communist who has been a Party member for thirty years. In 1964-65 he studied in the Higher Party School of the CC UCP in Kiev and, presumably, returned to Canada in 1965. Since this is so, I wonder why the fact that my petition was found in his possession caused so much worry to the custodians of state security? It seems to me that it is much more important for the security of the Soviet state to remove from our life as soon as possible the obvious distortions of the Leninist nationality policy — such as anti-Semitism, Ukrainiphobia, national discrimination, and other manifestations of bourgeois ideology — and to bring to justice those guilty of violating the Soviet Constitution. Why is it that a Canadian communist who is fighting world imperialism shoulder to shoulder with us

---

1 Should be Kolasky. Upon returning to Canada, Kolasky compiled *Education in Soviet Ukraine*, an indictment of Soviet policy, published by Peter Martin Associates, Toronto, 1968.

　　　　　　　　　　　　　　The Misfortune

should not know about the violation of Leninist policy that took place and still occurs in Ukraine and in other Soviet republics? These unpleasant truths are the result of the absolutely erroneous nationality policy that developed in the USSR with the personality cult of Stalin and Khrushchev. The article, *About One Political Error*, which I have enclosed with this petition, outlines the mistakes in nationality policy in the realm of education.

Comrade Kolyaska was a communist for thirty years. If after a stay of one year in Kiev, under the effect of reality he began to doubt the justice of the russification of Ukrainian life, of discrimination against the Ukrainian language and culture, of removing the Ukrainian people from Ukraine and placing a non-Ukrainian populace, primarily Russian, in the towns of Ukraine — then this fact should have compelled the leadership of the CPSU to ponder whether it is carrying out the right nationality policy in Ukraine, whether this is the Leninist policy, and whether it serves to strengthen the international communist movement.

Unfortunately, the facts show that an altogether different viewpoint predominates in the CPSU leadership. At the time when my apartment was searched, twenty-eight representatives of the Ukrainian intelligentsia were arrested in Ukraine, among them the journalist, I. Svitlychny. Critic I. Dzyuba was dismissed from work at a publishing house, charged with "Ukrainian bourgeois nationalism", and denied the right to engage in ideological work.

It has been almost a month now, but the press has not yet announced the causes of these arrests. In Kiev, unknown sources circulate rumours that these people allegedly wished the separation of the Ukr. SSR from the USSR. No doubt these are unfounded accusations, for neither by their activities nor by their views have these people ever voiced such desires (the publications of I. Svitlychny do not even contain an allusion to such views). But even if this were so, why accusations of "Ukrainian nationalism"? In the world socialist system the states of the socialist camp—Czechoslovakia, Rumania, Poland, Yugoslavia, Hungary, Bulgaria, the German Democratic Republic — co-operate in a fraternal manner. Perhaps under the present conditions of the development of the communist movement it would be expedient if the Ukrainian socialist nation should be a separate unit in the general socialist camp? At any rate the Constitution of the USSR guarantees the union republics the right to leave the USSR. And if this is so, then the accusation of those who want to take advantage of this right of "bourgeois nationalism" is entirely unfounded and cannot possibly serve as a cause for arrest. From this point of view, the communists of Poland, Rumania, Czechoslovakia, Hungary, and the German Democratic Republic could also be accused of bourgeois nationalism; for they found it necessary to develop their socialist economy within the framework of independent socialist states. Such unfounded accusation of the Ukrainian intellectuals of bourgeois nationalism would simply be strange and would testify to the fact that in this case we are dealing with a lack of understanding of the spirit of the Leninist nationality policy.

Representatives of the Ukrainian intelligentsia are accused of bourgeois nationalism systematically every five to ten years. The regularity of these accusations make the matter strange and incomprehensible. Is the Ukrainian intelligentsia so thoroughly bourgeois (fifty years after the October revolution!) and hostile to the socialist order? Is there not another cause in Soviet reality which brings about the recurrences of nationalism? In general, what is nationalism? Is it nationalism to desire the development of the national culture, of the native language? Is it even the desire for a separate development as a state, is it the legitimate right of every nation, the result of its economical, cultural, and social development? All these questions require profound communist rethinking and explanation, for they play a primary role in the world communist movement.

Marxist dialectics teach us that all phenomena have causes, and in order to liquidate negative social phenomena, one must liquidate their causes. The inclination towards so-called "nationalism", no doubt, has its objective causes, deriving from the anti-Leninist nationality policy carried out in Ukraine for the past thirty years. It consists of the russification of the population and of the mass-transfer of Ukrainians from Ukraine to Siberia, Kazakhstan, and other remote areas, as well as of the settlement of a non-Ukrainian, mainly Russian, population in Ukrainian towns. Of course, such a policy is anti-Leninist and has nothing in common with Marxism. It is a policy which harms the international communist movement.

The unfounded repressions against representatives of the Ukrainian intelligentsia, which began this month, the series of distortions of the nationality policy in the Soviet republics of the USSR, compel me to turn to you, as a prominent leader of the communist movement, with this petition. I believe that both the proletarian solidarity and the communist conscience, as well the perpetual concern for the fate of the world communist movement, a concern for the purity of communist ideas, the principles of Marxism-Leninism, will compel you to examine my petition with Party-like conscientiousness. The gist of my petition can be reduced to the following:

1. Since the nationality policy in the socialist countries is very important to the development of the international communist movement, the communist parties of the world should exchange ideas on the nationality question.

2. In order to carry out such an exchange of ideas, I recommend that an international conference of the communist parties of the world be called.

3. To work out at the round table of the communist parties of the world the principles of the Marxist-Leninist nationality policy, the principles which the communist parties of the world must follow in their practical work of building communism.

4. To condemn at the round table of the communist parties the attitudes of anti-Semitism, Ukrainophobia, national discrimination, and other manifestations of a bourgeois ideology which occur in the practice of separate communist parties. In particular, to investigate the inadmissible practice of discrimination against the Ukrainian population of the Kuban' region, who have been deprived since 1937 of all cultural and educational institutions in the native tongue.

5. To study separately the expediency of changing the

ethnic composition of a population — the expediency of the mass-transfer of representatives of a given nationality from the territory of their national republic.

6. To study at the round table of the communists of the world the permissibility of unfounded repressions and to condemn such repressions with all the strength born of principles.

With profound respect and ardent greetings,
September 27, 1965

(S. Y. Karavans'ky)

*

The consul of the People's Republic of Poland in Kiev, who was handed the above petition, promised to bring it to the attention of his government. The consul of Czechoslovakia, after having familiarized himself with the essence of it, refused to accept a similar petition addressed to A. Novotny. Both refused to forward the petition to other socialist countries, which have no representatives in the Ukr. SSR.

PETITIONS[1]
ADDRESSED BY S. Y. KARAVANS'KY FROM THE CAMP

*To the College of Advocates (Bar) of the Odessa region
from journalist S. Y. Karavans'ky
sentenced to eight years and seven months for the complaints
lodged against the Minister of Higher and Secondary
Specialized Education in the Ukr. SSR, Yu. M. Dadenkov*

PETITION

I request you to appoint an attorney to defend my rights before a Soviet court and to prosecute I. Petrenko, the author of the article, *Trylyky* [Triple-faced], which appeared in the Odessa newspaper, *Chornomors'ka komuna* [Black Sea Commune] on November 21, 1965.

In this article an attempt was made to slander me and to characterize my complaint against Minister Dadenkov and my article, *About One Political Error*, as "Bandera literature".

At the same time this article attacks "the writing of letters",

---

1 Abridged because in many petitions facts and thoughts are repeated.

i.e., of complaints to the higher authorities. Thus the author clearly speaks out in favour of suppressing criticism.

The occurrence of slander in the article *Trylyky* can be traced in the following main points:

1. In the article *Trylyky* it is said that with my articles I am trying to "hammer my Bandera ideas into the heads of honest people", that I am "cooking porridge [stirring up trouble] in OUN water".[1] This phrase alone compels me to ask competent authorities to examine the contents of my articles and to ascertain whether there is even one "Bandera idea" in them. My articles are based on the works of Lenin and the Soviet laws. Thus I. Petrenko assumes that the "Bandera ideas" can be based upon the works of Lenin. This is an aspersion on Lenin and on the contents of my articles.

2. It is said in the article that I "had taken upon myself the mission of supplying information of my own production for the benefit of unscrupulous foreigners eager for the rotten lure".

This assertion, too, is a slander. I know no "foreigners eager for the rotten lure" and have not supplied them with anything. My article and complaint spontaneously acquired wide circulation because they were based upon actual facts. No wonder, therefore, that some copies of the complaint fell into the hands of foreigners. I learned from the material of the interrogation that the text of my complaint concerning the Minister of Higher Education came into the possession of a Canadian communist with a thirty-year standing, I. V. Kolyaska, a student at the VPSH [Higher Party School] in Kiev. Although I do not know him and did not hand him the complaint, I am amazed that a Canadian communist with a standing of many years was placed in the category of "foreigners eager for the rotten lure".

3. In the article *Trylyky* it is said that I juggle figures fetched from thin air. But the author does not mention a single one and does not indicate where I have manipulated figures. Having been a correspondent of the journal *Ukraina*, I was able to gather data about the schools and institutions of

---

[1] The reference is to Karavans'ky's past association with the OUN (transl. note).

higher learning of the republic in the official institutions and departments of popular education, and made use of material from Soviet newspapers.

4. In the article *Trylyky* it is also asserted that, while I was imprisoned, "for a long time, tirelessly and assiduously, I wrote and distributed anti-Soviet leaflets". My file actually contains a document, written in pencil in 1953, directed against the high-handedness of Beria. This is true. But to identify the Soviet regime with the tyranny of Beria, as Petrenko does, having called the anti-Beria pamphlet an anti-Soviet document, is more than strange, and casts an aspersion upon the Soviet system and also upon me.

5. The article which was supposed to have convinced everybody that my articles are really anti-Soviet is not at all convincing. For not a single quotation from my article is adduced and refuted. On the other hand, Petrenko does not spare such expressions as "black and despicable soul", "miserable prophet", "wretched renegade", "rogue". In addition to indicating the low level of culture and the primitive spiritual world of the author, such a style brings to mind the sad times when criticism was not tolerated. Lacking arguments against my argumentation, Petrenko resorts to profanity — rude, slanderous, and boorish.

6. Petrenko's article also discloses the fact that the mistakes, about which I wrote, were made; and in 1965 the Ministry of Higher and Secondary Specialized Education applied a series of measures to rectify them. Thus the graduates from Ukrainian schools were given the opportunity, when applying to the institutions of higher learning and to technical schools in Ukraine, to write the examinations in Ukrainian (instead of Russian), and at the conference of rectors (August 16, 1965), they considered the question of transferring most institutions of higher learning in Ukraine to the Ukrainian language for instruction.

7. Accusing me of manipulating figures, Petrenko himself juggles the facts, trying with generalizations to deny irrefutable facts. Thus he writes, "In most schools and institutions of higher learning of the republic, the instruction is in Ukrainian". It is possible that the total number of the schools where

the Ukrainian language is used is actually greater, but during the last five years this number has considerably decreased due to the increase of Russian schools. As for the institutions of higher learning, Petrenko would like to see the wish as the reality. . . .

My address: Mordovian ASSR, Stn. Pot'ma, p/v Yavas, Box 385/11.

January 9, 1966.

TO THE PEOPLE'S COURT OF THE OCTOBER DISTRICT OF THE CITY OF ODESSA

. . . In the article I. Petrenko had to resort to "disclosure" of my past to shut my mouth in the present. Why was it necessary to mention my past? I was released from prison in 1960, and for five years neither the militia, nor the prosecutor's office, nor the KGB reminded me of my past. On the contrary, the officers of the KGB advised me to keep it quiet. Mention of my past became necessary only after the appearance of my complaint. What else can this be called if not a suppression of criticism? As long as I did not write complaints I was not "three-faced", nor a "renegade", nor a "rogue'. On the contrary, my works were published in republican newspapers and journals. The reference to my past is a method which serves one purpose — suppression of criticism and persecution.

Since the past has been mentioned, it would be relevant to recall that people's acts or deeds are the results of certain circumstances. It was a whole series of circumstances that gave rise to the activity of underground anti-Soviet organizations during the occupation of Ukraine. The main cause was the demoralizing influence of the personality cult upon the hearts and souls of those Soviet citizens who experienced its repressive actions and could not reconcile themselves with it. . . .

It was this situation that led to the re-activation of underground organizations during the occupation. Therefore, Petrenko plays the buffoon in vain, calling me a "victim of the cult", for I truly was and am a "victim of the cult", as our entire much-suffering Ukrainian people were a "victim of the cult" — they experienced under Stalin the harshest, most unjust persecutions and repressions. And only opportunists, who do not "remember their kin", can forget this and pour slops on those who, driven to despair by the Stalin terror, turned from the right road and lost their way.

It seems to me that now, after the Party has disclosed and condemned the deviations of the period of the personality cult, they could also grant amnesty to those who in their younger years, under the effect of Stalin's injustices, found themselves in the enemy camp. It seems to me that Ukrainian culture and Ukrainian intelligentsia in the past have suffered so many unfounded persecutions and so many innocent victims (Les' Kurbas, Mykytenko, Zerov, Kulish, Irchan, Gzhyts'ky, Dniprovs'ky, Sokolovs'ky, Chubar, Skrypnyk, Kosior, and countless others), that it is possible now, if only as a compensation for the former groundless mass-extermination of the Ukrainian intelligentsia, to free not only one guilty Ukrainian journalist, but all Ukrainians who are incarcerated for political motives. . . .

Accordingly, if one examines my activity during the occupation period in relation to the entire complex of historical events, he will see in all its monstrosity the true cause of my mistakes in life — the repungnant personality cult of Stalin.

Petrenko resorts to mentioning my past, distorting the content of my articles, and coarse abuse for one purpose — to frighten, to arouse fear in those who cannot reconcile themselves to violation of the public interests. He wants to restore the times of lawlessness, when for just criticism people were executed by firing squads. This credo of that heir of Beria is disclosed in the closing lines of the article: "So that other such victims would never forget that we will not permit dirty hands to touch matters of great purity, of especial value."

If only the "matters of especial value", the achievements of the Great October, had not been touched by the "clean" hands of the Beria manhunters, who exterminated millions of the best people of the Soviet nations, exterminated the entire Leninist guard, and took upon themselves the mission of presenting their own philistine ideology of dependence as a model of pure revolutionism.

January 16, 1966.

TO THE VICE-CHAIRMAN OF THE COUNCIL OF THE UNION OF THE
SUPREME SOVIET OF THE USSR

Deputy M. Stel'makh

The effort to strengthen socialist legality requires constant steadfastness and must encompass all areas of our life and all the branches of Soviet law.

However, side by side with actions which strengthen legality, there also occurs a strange indifference to socialist legality in our juridical practice, an indifference that paves the way for high-handedness and lawlessness.

Is this paradoxical? Nevertheless, it is a fact.

What else, if not a paradox, can one call the twenty-five-year prison term we still have in the USSR? Is this not a shameful contradiction of the humane principles of Soviet law? For the new code has set a maximum term of fifteen years for all categories of criminals. The twenty-five-year term is left over from the extermination policy of the adventurers Yagoda, Yezhov, and Beria.

What actually is the twenty-five-year term?

Let us begin with history. The term of twenty-five years was established in the USSR for the first time in 1939, during the Stalin cult, for the purpose of exterminating innocent Soviet people in the camps. From 1917 to 1939 the maximum term in the Soviet Union was ten years. The country survived the revolution, civil war, industrialization, and collectivization without the inhuman twenty-five-year term, and no harm was done. But now after socialism has finally prevailed in the USSR, we have retained the twenty-five-year prison term as an inheritance from the times of terror. Is this not a paradox?

And what is the twenty-five-year term like in practice? What does it mean to remove a person from society for twenty-five years (not months, but years!), to deprive him of freedom? What purpose does such a term serve? A person can be re-educated in ten, in fifteen years. But what in twenty-five years? What kind of re-education is that? And if one recalls the present "strict" conditions of imprisonment, then one can only conclude that twenty-five years of "strict" conditions can only destroy a person, physically and morally. . . .

Most of the prisoners sentenced to a term of twenty-five years are moved thousands of kilometres from their families, for they are deported from their republics (from Ukraine, Belorussia, Lithuania, Latvia, Estonia, Moldavia) to the Mordovian ASSR. It is clear that a term of twenty-five years under such conditions can be justified only under a policy of genocide. There are no other arguments for it.

What awaits a person upon release after serving a twenty-five-year term?

I was arrested at the age of twenty-four. After I have served the term I shall be fifty-four years old (I was free for five years "by mistake"). I had no employment seniority at the age of twenty-four (the war, occupation). But in order to earn a pension one must work another twenty years, i.e., until the age of seventy-four, or until death. All this would require that my health be indestructible. But how many prisoners, while serving out this savage medieval term, were felled by paralysis; how many died of tuberculosis, how many had to be placed in mental hospitals, how many committed suicide?

In a word, in my opinion, it is more humane to burn someone in an execution chamber than to kill him methodically over twenty-five years, without let-up, day after day. Anyone who defends such a term is inhuman. But our society is supposedly the most humane of all the progressive social formations! And if that is the case, how can one deprive the unmarried, the single prisoners, of love and married life for twenty-five years? Yet among the prisoners, buried alive for twenty-five years, are many bachelors who were imprisoned at the age of nineteen, twenty, twenty-five. It cannot be possible to justify sentencing them for twenty-five years to a monastic life and depriving them of marriage.

But perhaps Soviet law defends the practice of meting out life-sentences? Not at all. On the contrary, twenty-five-year sentences contradict the basic principle of Soviet law, which states that the punishment must be commensurate with the crime . . . Let us assume that two individuals, X and Y, committed the same crime in 1955. For this crime X was sentenced in 1955 to twenty-five years, but Y hid from the authorities till 1960. In 1960 Y is sentenced to only fifteen years for the same crime for which X was given twenty-five. For the same crime X and Y received a different punishment (the difference is ten years). And Y will be released five years earlier than X, although he was imprisoned five years later. Is this not a paradox? Is this not a terrible violation of the principles of Soviet law? Yet such cases occur in our judicial practice.

The existence of the twenty-five-year prison term brought about the so-called law of April 19, 1960. This law provides that if the prisoner serving a twenty-five-year sentence has been re-educated, the visiting assizes of the military tribunal can commute his term to fifteen years.

But how can it be ascertained whether a person has been re-educated or not? Officially, to all appearances, this is decided by the camp administration; actually the sanction comes from the KBG if the one sentenced to twenty-five years condemns his past in writing or agrees to co-operate. Thus this law places the people sentenced to twenty-five years in an extraordinary situation, if their release from the camp depends not upon the definite end of the term, not upon the firm letter of the law, but upon the whim of the KGB. What is this if not a vestige of lawlessness? Are the people sentenced to five, ten, fifteen years released by a court? Not at all. But the prisoner sentenced to twenty-five years, after having served fifteen, is tried again: Has he been re-educated or not? Is it worthwhile to release him or not? What justification is there for such cruelty to a human being?

First of all, who gave the right to try the accused for one and the same crime twice, three times, and more. (For the court refuses to release the "accused" and puts their "case" off till next year for at least three and more times. Certain prisoners, Batistikov and others, were tried three times by the military tribunal and three times the court refused them. Some prisoners lived through five and six refusals.)

This is humane, is it not? The prisoner has been kept alive for fifteen years by the hope of freedom and yearns for it with all his being, but they show it to him, buoy him up with hope, and then withhold it. . . .

Can this be called the re-education of prisoners? I do not know from what archives of the Inquisition this method was unearthed, but it has nothing in common with re-education.

Yet the KGB use the "re-education" of political prisoners as a basis for determining whether they should be released. "If you become re-educated" — if you condemn your past and all the rest — you will be released; if "you are not re-educated", you stay put. The desire to be free can compel a human being to agree to anything. But is this re-education? In the system of such "re-education", freedom figures as a fata morgana, as a temptation, as a fetish which compels the prisoners "to become re-educated". It seems to me that to conduct business operations in which the means of payment is human freedom is as inhuman, immoral, and evil as pouring out precious water before a man who is perishing of thirst.

One must add to all this that the release by a tribunal is illusory, for the one released, to the end of his life, lives under the threat that he may be apprehended to finish the term. For the Prosecutor of the USSR can reject the request of the KGB to release a prisoner and can return a person to the camp to finish the twenty-five-year prison term. Such cases abound. I personally, having served sixteen years and five months of the twenty-five years, was released from the camp on December 19, 1960. For five years I was free, having in no way violated Soviet laws. I worked as a mechanic, translator, as a correspondent of the journal *Ukraina*; I published my translations of the verses of English poets in the republican press. And yet, on November 13, 1965, because I wrote a complaint concerning the Minister of Higher and Secondary Specialized Education in the Ukr. SSR, Dadenkov, I was arrested by the order of the Prosecutor of the USSR (without sentence, without trial, without a hearing) to serve eight years and seven months to complete the twenty-five-year sentence.

How can one evaluate such actions of the Prosecutor of the USSR?

What can one call this juridical practice, when a person is released and then is put in prison again for the same offence? Is it possible that in the twentieth century, at the dawn of the cosmic era, a person does not merit elementary human treatment, but is treated like some inanimate object, like a dumb beast that can be driven from one shed to another? Only a complete lack of self-respect, a complete lack of human dignity can compel a human being to treat a fellow man so cruelly. It seems to me that the Prosecutor who signed the order for my arrest, and who on the evening before still listened to the radio and watched television with his wife and children, forgot when he came to work that he lives in the twentieth century and imagined himself a contemporary of the great inquisitor, Torquemada, or of the Mongolian conqueror, Genghis Khan. My arrest cannot be comprehended by the logical categories of the twentieth century, for it is an act of indisputable lawlessness. If the KGB were not satisfied with my conduct and if I in some way had violated the Soviet laws, I should have been tried. But no, I was *not* tried. I was arrested to finish the old term. Evidently there were no reasons for a trial. Why then was I arrested? Can one call such a practice legal, when one reason is given for a person's arrest, but juridically altogether different causes are advanced — in this case, the old matter? This is nothing less than illegality, veiled by juridical subterfuges. Does this not recall the times when Stalin, in exterminating the opponents of the cult, charged them with unfounded contradictory accusations?

Thus a twenty-five-year prison term arms the KGB with the weapons of arbitrariness and lawlessness, if a person can be subjected to repressions without trial and hearing for some trifle or simply because of suspicion.

It follows from the above that the twenty-five-year prison term is an absolutely paradoxical phenomenon and that it is inadmissible in our society for the following reasons:

1. Historically the twenty-five-year prison term originated in the USSR as a tool of high-handedness and lawlessness;

2. In practice, the twenty-five-year prison term is a method of physical and moral extermination of men;

3. The prison term is doubly severe in view of the contemporary "hard" conditions of detention of prisoners in camps;

4. This term is anti-social, for it produces old men without pensions and sexually depraved unmarried bachelors (homosexuals, onanists, etc.);

5. The twenty-five-year prison term contradicts the principles of communist humanity;

6. The term contradicts the principles of Soviet law;

7. The twenty-five-year prison term engendered the unjust decree of April 19, 1960 and created the unheard-of practice of re-sentencing those already sentenced, which opens the way to lawlessness and cruelty to human beings deprived of freedom. The principle, "I can pardon whom I wish to pardon and I can punish whom I wish to punish", is a high-handed and lawless one;

8. The twenty-five-year prison term empowers the KGB, without trial and hearing, to arrest former prisoners and deprives them of protection by the law;

9. The twenty-five-year prison term is without precedent in the juridical practice of socialist countries.

All these considerations compel me to turn to you with the request that you place before the Supreme Soviet the question of liquidating this outrageous vestige of the personality cult — the twenty-five-year prison term — and to introduce in the USSR a single maximal term in conformity with the new Soviet legislation. (February 14, 1966)

TO THE CHAIRMAN OF THE ADMINISTRATION OF THE UNION OF SOVIET WRITERS

. . . In February of this year I directed to the Union of Writers a petition requesting it to raise before the Supreme Soviet of the USSR the question of removing the twenty-five-year prison term.

In March I received from the Union of Soviet Writers the following reply, signed by the Secretary of the Union: "Your petition addressed to the Union of Writers was forwarded to the Prosecutor of the USSR. The questions you raised in your petition are beyond the competence of the Union of Writers". . . .

I do not know whether the constitution of the writers' organization determines the sphere of competence of the Union of Writers. But when I recall that the SSP [Union of

Soviet Writers] unites people with a highly developed sense of civic consciousness who are supposed to stand guard over the public interest of the public, this reply seems to me first bureaucratic, then heartless, callous, and, finally, blasphemous. . . .

Can a writer, all the more the Union of Writers, withdraw from social problems and retire into the narrow framework of questions of fees only? Can a writer stand aside from any fact of our reality, from any social-political phenomenon? Can a writer remain indifferent to crimes committed before his eyes?

May I ask citizen Oryev whether it is within the competence of a Soviet writer to defend a woman who was raped in the office of a Minister then executed by a firing squad as an "enemy of the people"? Apparently citizen Oryev is of the opinion that such problems do not enter into the sphere of competence of writers? But what is within this sphere? Writing a slanderous pamphlet concerning an unjustly condemned, violated woman?

Can a writer — a man with a great soul, a man of thought, forever searching, struggling, a passionate protagonist of justice — disperse his capabilities, the passion and ardour of his soul, within the framework of incoming and outgoing numbers, to divide everything that is happening around him into things within and without his sphere? Who of the writers, or simply of the people with a high sense of civic duty, when faced with injustice will refuse to say with Radishchev, "My soul was wounded by the sufferings of mankind?" Would Radishchev and Shevchenko, Tolstoy and Chekhov, Gorky and Mayakovsky have divided sufferings into those within and those outside their sphere? . . . A writer cannot be indifferent to injustice, to the violation of public interests, to stagnancy, savagery, and barbarity.

How can one not recall the words that I. Franko spoke prior to his death to the young generation of writers: "Do not remain silent in the face of barefaced lying, of the grief of others, in the face of slander and injustice. Speak up!"[1] . . .

Citizen Oryev forwarded my official letter to the writers to the office of the Prosecutor of the USSR; he, apparently, is of the

[1] This is a free summary of Franko's poem cited in the original petition (transl. note).

opinion that the Union of Writers is an appendage of that office. It seems to me that for the progress of society, for its harmony, it would be much more practical, more humane, more just, and more natural that the office of the Prosecutor should listen to the voice of those who think creatively and critically — the writers — whose hearts and souls ache for their people and its future. The office of the Prosecutor is bold enough to maintain its absolute infallibility in all juridical questions, although it is known that during the fifty years of the Soviet regime, it was precisely these offices that were responsible for the greatest number of cases of misuse of power, highhandedness, and outright crimes. And if the office of the Prosecutor legalizes high-handedness and, in this case, advocates the retention of the cannibalistic twenty-five-year term, then there is even more reason for the writers' society to intervene in the affairs of that office.

The blood of the writers M. Kol'tsov, B. Yasinsky, V. Polishchuk, O. Vlyz'ko, M. Zerov, I Babel, L. Kvitka, P. Markish, A. Vesely, N. Loskutov, O. Mandelshtamm M. Kulish, M. Levidov, and dozens of others lies upon the conscience of the organs of justice. Upon the conscience of the same authorities lies the shame of the scandalous trials of writers, the decades of banishment of Ostap Vyshnya, Halyna Serebryaka, Zinaida, Tulub, Volodymyr Gzhyts'ky, and hundreds of other writers. The Prosecutor of the USSR is not an innocent lamb, but a lamb who admits gross errors and commits crimes against humanity.

It sounds paradoxical, does it not? A Prosecutor's office legalizing crimes!

Nevertheless, it is a fact. Therefore the activities of the Prosecutor must always be under the constant surveillance of people endowed with a high public consciousness.

To the Chairman of the Council of Nationalities of the Supreme Council of the USSR

PETITION

... The questions of interrelationship between nationalities should be of prime importance to the Council of Nationalities of the Supreme Soviet of the USSR.

But during the last thirty years the Council of Nationalities has investigated very few actual national problems. The work of the Council until 1953, while all the Soviet state organs were personally represented by Stalin, as Secretary General, certainly cannot be criticized nor condemned. This was a period when the Council existed only formally and did not carry out any government work. Unfortunately this inertia of inactivity still weighs upon the Council, which should be busy in removing a whole series of vestiges of the Stalin personality cult that still hinder and undermine the friendship of peoples of the USSR.

This friendship can develop successfully and grow stronger only if all the nations and peoples of the Soviet Union have equal rights in all branches of public and political life. This is an axiom which needs no proof. It is precisely this that compels me to apply to the Council of Nationalities with the request to take steps to remove the outrageous vestiges of national discrimination which still occur in our life.

First of all I wish to draw your attention to discrimination against the Jewish population, for the attitude toward the Jews is the litmus paper that shows the degree of international consciousness of a given society. The closing of Jewish cultural institutions, of newspapers, schools, theatres, publishing houses; the execution of Jewish cultural workers; the discriminatory practice in the admission of Jews to the higher and secondary institutions of learning — all these are phenomena which blossomed forth luxuriantly during the time of the Stalin personality cult. It would seem that the condemnation of the cult should also have put an end to these discriminatory phenomena. Unfortunately this has not happened. To quiet public opinion in foreign countries (he paid no heed to the public in this country), N. S. Krushchev was compelled to rehabilitate the unjustly executed and unjustly condemned Jewish cultural workers. And here he stopped. And where are the Jewish theatres, newspapers, publishing houses, schools? In Odessa, where there is a Jewish population of 150,000, there is not a single Jewish school. And the policies of admission to schools of higher learning? Again, in Odessa where the Jewish population amounts to twenty-five per cent, only three to five per cent of the Jews study in institutions of higher learning. This is the norm which secretly exists in the admission to institutions of higher learning. The Jewish youth of Odessa who forwarded documents to institutions of higher learning in other cities of the Union received the following reply: "But Odessa has a fine institution of higher learning, go to your own institution." Yet at the same time young people from the Urals, from Siberia, Moscow, Tula, and Saratov study at the institutions of higher learning in Odessa — they are provided with dormitories especially built for this purpose — but the local Jewish youth (as well as Ukrainians and Moldavians) have very restricted rights in respect to education.

Can such facts advance the friendship of peoples?

On the contrary, they help to develop in the Jews a feeling that they are an inferior nationality without equal rights, and drive them onto the road towards Zionism. And it must be admitted that never were the ideas of Zionism so popular among the Jewish population as now. This is the consequence of discrimination against the Jewish minority.

No less outrageous is the wholesale deportation of Crimean Tatars and of Volga Germans beyond the borders of their republics, and the liquidation of their statehood.

The deportation of the Tatars from Crimea is an act of crying injustice, and no arguments can justify it. How is it that in the twentieth century the society which aspires to construct the most just order on earth deports 900,000 people from the lands of their heritage for "treason to the fatherland" committed by its individual representatives? Who has been given the right, in the twentieth century, to extract from the archives of imperialism the arguments that, allegedly "historically", these lands are not Tatar, but Russian lands. If one were to be consistent in such considerations, then the Khabarovsk and the Primorsky territories and the Amur region should at once be handed over to the Chinese People's Republic, for these lands were wrested by force from the Chinese people by the Russian tsars.

Really, will the abolition of the statehood of the Crimean Tatars, their dispersion over the vast spaces of Kazakhstan and Siberia, the liquidation of their schools, newspapers, theatres,

200   *The Misfortune*

and native tongue be conducive to bringing the peoples closer together?

And the Volga Germans? In what way are they responsible to society for the crimes of Hitler? Is this really the Marxist approach to the solving of complex problems, to judge people not by social but by national criteria? Does not the slogan, "Proletarians of all countries, unite!" really apply to the Jews, the Crimean Tatars, and the Volga Germans? In the Soviet Union there are no Jewish bourgeois, Tatar capitalists, and German landlords. There are only workers.

How can young people be brought up in the spirit of internationalism when before their eyes entire nationalities are deprived of their rights to governmental autonomy and to education in the native and foreign tongues? How can there be a discussion of "togetherness" between the person who has been exiled from his own home and his native country and a person who has occupied this home and this country?

Of the same magnitude are the mistakes which were committed in the restoration of the national statehood of the Chechens, Ingushes, Kalmyks, Karachay, and other peoples. This act of justice concerning the small nationalities was not without blunders which emphasize to the small nations that they do not have fully equal rights. In accordance with the established order, immovable property, such as houses, buildings, cottages, is not restored to the families of the unjustly deported nationalities; after having returned to the land of their fathers, they must buy their houses from the local government or build new ones. Why is this? The people were deported unjustly! Thus, in having given permission to return, the decree of the Supreme Soviet failed to provide means to its implementation. As a result many Chechens, Ingushes, and representatives of other nationalities do not return to the land of their fathers. Does such a practice promote the friendship of peoples? It is the same as giving an expensive cake to someone after having eaten all the chocolate off it. Could such a gift be accepted as a gift?

During the period of the cult a number of outrageous injustices were also inflicted upon the peoples of the Baltic region, among them, the deportation to Siberia of the Estonian population from the border districts of Estonia. Their only guilt was that they lived near the border. This population could have been transferred to another district in the Estonian Republic. But no, the populace of the town of Silamyae was deported to Siberia.

In 1940, as is known, the Latvian Republic voluntarily joined the Soviet Union; therefore, no repressive measures should have been applied to the soldiers of the Latvian Army.[1] However, strange as it may seem, officers of the Latvian Army were requested in 1941 to attend tactical training from which they never returned. They were interned and their further fate is unknown. The fact remains that of these officers not a single living soul returned home, as is the case with those thousands of Latvians who were unfoundedly repressed and deported in 1940-41. One is led to think that, during the time of Beria's high-handedness, these Soviet citizens may have been exterminated in the camps in various ways. This fact, which in itself is a crime against humanity, cannot serve to strengthen the friendship of peoples. And in order not to allow similar cases in the future, the time has now come to start an investigation, and, if necessary, to exhume corpses, and to bring those who are guilty of the death of thousands of Soviet citizens of Latvian origin to answer for these crimes.

Great harm has been caused to the friendship among peoples by the perversions of the national policy in one of the largest republics of the USSR — Ukraine. The russification of Ukrainian institutions of higher learning, carried out after 1937, was condemned and partly revised in Western Ukraine, but in Eastern Ukraine, the school of higher learning is fully russified even today. This policy is built upon the argument that there allegedly exists a difference between Eastern and Western Ukraine. Why then have the Ukrainian people united into one Ukrainian Soviet State? To ensure that the entire Ukrainian people, once deprived of statehood, would be educated and would develop a single national organism. Nevertheless, in the

---

[1] Reference is to the army officers of the Latvian Republic, which was an independent, non-communist state from 1918 to 1939 (transl. note).

field of education a single republic is divided into two parts. Such a practice not only does not promote the friendship of peoples; on the contrary, it splits a single people into two, in the same way as a single nationality — the Ossetians — were split into two republics, Southern and Northern Ossetian ASSR; similarly the Buryat-Mongols were divided into the Buryat-Mongol ASSR and the Ust'-Ordyn and Agine national districts. Such arbitrary division does not promote friendliness among peoples but, on the contrary, divides them.

Another hindrance to the friendship of peoples is the absence of an amnesty for participants in the national uprisings of 1943-1949 in Ukraine, Latvia, Lithuania, and Estonia, which were directed against the Stalin personality cult and the Beria terror. Even now large numbers of Ukrainians, Lithuanians, Latvians, and Estonians live in the Komi ASSR (Vorkuta, Inta, Pechora), in Siberia (the Irkutsk and Kemerovo regions, the Krasnoyarsk territory), in Kazakhstan, and on the Kolyma. They were exiled on suspicion of having acted against the personality cult in 1943-1949.

It is no secret to anyone that there have been injustices against the Ukrainian people: the executions of Ukrainian public figures such as Chubar, Kosior, Zatonsky, Lyubchenko; the executions of the writers Mykytenko, Vlyz'ko, Fal'kivs'ky, and scores of others; the unfounded expulsion of the KPZU[1] from the Comintern; the extermination and the deportation, during 1939-1953, of the Ukrainian intelligentsia from the city of L'viv; the forcible en masse deportation of Ukrainians to Siberia; the forcible russification of the Ukrainian population of the Kuban', Bilhorod, and Starodub regions. All of these facts could not but arouse the indignation of the people, which resulted in the national uprising of 1943-1949. Most of the participants and even those who were eyewitnesses (of which there are more) still live outside their republic. In order to ensure the true friendship of peoples of the USSR, we must forget old controversies and return these victims of the Stalin personality cult to the territory of their republics.

---

[1] The Communist Party of Western Ukraine (transl. note).

The true friendship of peoples also requires a broad amnesty for the prisoners who are still (after fifteen, eighteen, twenty years!) rotting in prisons and camps for participating in actions against Stalin and Beria. If the friendship of peoples of the USSR is a true one, then it must be based upon human, friendly relations and not upon national hatred and fratricide. But now, decades after the events of 1943-1949, the camps and prisons of the USSR are still packed with prisoners — the participants in the uprising. Precisely in order to prevent the release of these people, the USSR has retained the barbarous twenty-five-year prison term. This term is being served mainly by Ukrainians, Lithuanians, Latvians, Estonians, Byelorussians, and Moldavians. Why is there no pardon for them? After all, we now magnaminously pardon those who put their hands to the mass extermination of Soviet citizens in 1937-1939, saying that there was such a time, that the people who carried out orders from above are not guilty. Why is there no such pardon for the Ukrainian women, Kateryna Zaryts'ka, Halyna Didyk, and Odarka Husyak, who were sentenced to twenty-five-year prison terms? Is it admissible to keep Kateryna Zaryts'ka in Vladimir Prison since 1947, Halyna Didyk and Odarka Husyak since 1950? At one time N. S. Khrushchev condemned the inhuman execution of a pregnant female revolutionary in Albania; in view of this, is it possible to approve the detention of women for eighteen years or more in a stone grave?

The genuine friendship between peoples is thwarted by the practice of settling Russian populations in the towns of other national republics. Thus in the Ukrainian SSR, the Russian populace systematically increases from year to year and the Ukrainian one decreases. Similar national migrations occur in Lithuania, Latvia, Estonia, Byelorussia, Moldavia, Kazakhstan, Kirghizia, and other national republics. Such colonization is contrary to the friendship between peoples. For instance, the appearance in Ukraine of large numbers of Russians (retired officers, retired KGB officials, and other privileged categories of citizens), who settle in towns and take over all the better positions, jobs, and professions, forces the native Ukrainian populace into low-paying work as unskilled labourers, sanitary workers, janitors, stevedores, construction workers, and agricultural labourers. Such unceremonious colonization of the ancient Ukrainian lands promises only animosity. Let us recall the butchery between peoples in 1917-1920 in the Caucasus and Central Asia. And in 1958, when the Chechens and Ingushes returned to their homeland, they were met in the city of Grozny by the Russians populace with the slogans, "Keep Chechens and Ingushes out of the Caucasus!", "Long live the Stalinist nationality policy!" Is this not undeniable proof that the colonization of the national republics does not lead to friendship but to enmity between nations? . . .

No less disturbing is the system of passport registration that exists in the Soviet Union. In keeping with this system a person must live where the military officials permit him to. He has no right to move freely about the country; or, to be more precise, he has the right to move to Siberia, to the Urals, and to Kazakhstan, but not to reside in the so-called "regime" towns. An inhabitant of Ukraine, for example, has no right to move to and live in Kiev, Odessa, or L'viv. A Lithuanian may not move to Vilnius and Kaunas, and a Latvian may not live in Riga. Why? What threat is there to the security of a communist society if Ukrainians live in Kiev? In 1948, the Soviet Union signed the Universal Declaration of Human Rights, which contains a provision for freedom of movement inside the country. Actually, this freedom does not exist. The present discriminatory residence-permit system opens the way to colonizing the towns of national republics with outsiders, primarily with Russians. Such a practice arouses antagonism, evident in all the national republics, between the local populace and the russified inhabitants of the towns.

To the facts of national discrimination one must also add the "errors" in the determination of boundaries of the national republics. The territory of the Byelorussian SSR does not include large areas inhabited by Byelorussians in the Smolensk and Bryansk regions. The Ukrainian SSR does not include the Krasnodar territory, parts of the Voronezh and Bilhorod regions, and the Tahanrih district of the Rostov region. Excluded from the Moldavian SSR are the lands inhabited by

Moldavians in the Odessa region, and from the territory of the Armenian SSR, the Upper Badakhshan Autonomous Region is excluded....

The development and the strengthening of the friendship among peoples of the USSR demand that these problems be investigated as soon as possible and solved in the most equitable manner.

On my part I recommend the following measures:

1. To stop every kind of national discrimination against Jews.
2. To re-establish the statehood of the Crimean Tatars and of the Volga Germans.
3. To return their immovable property to the repatriated families of people unjustly deported.
4. To repatriate the people of the Baltic region, Western Ukraine, Byelorussia, and Moldavia who were unjustly deported to Siberia.
5. To investigate the disappearance of the Latvian army personnel.
6. To proclaim a broad amnesty for all victims of the Stalin personality cult.
7. To release the women martyrs — Kateryna Zaryts'ka, Halyna Didyk, and Odarka Husyak.
8. To examine the discriminatory attitude towards the Ukrainian population of the Kuban', Bilhorod, and Starodub areas and to apply measures to eliminate this attitude.
9. To end all forms of educational discrimination against nationalities in Ukraine, Byelorussia, Moldavia, and other republics.
10. To condemn the practice of deporting the inhabitants of the national republics to Siberia and of populating their lands with Russians.
11. To re-examine the system of passport restrictions and to condemn the passport discrimination which contradicts the Universal Declaration and undermines the friendship of peoples.
12. To revise the boundaries of the national republics for the purpose of establishing exact ethnographic boundaries.

The Misfortune

13. To organize a broad discussion in the press of all the problems raised here.

"The socialist legality, the legality of the most perfect society in the world, must be based upon the most humane principles, for the communist society is the most humane and the most progressive one in the world."

This is an axiom which does not require proof. And this is why the high-handedness and lawlessness which occur in our juridical practice to this day arouse anxiety. The worst outrage is the USSR's retention of the twenty-five-year prison term, which is simply a method of genocide.

But there are many more negative elements that must arouse concern.

Andreyev, a witness of the International Commission which investigated the matter of the Katyn Forest in 1942, is serving his twenty-second year in Vladimir Prison. His testimony was embodied in the conclusion of the International Commission in 1942, which accused the NKVD of the mass execution of Polish officers.[1] This case was later examined again and the new examination rejected the preceding conclusion. But why was Andreyev punished so severely for giving false testimony? Twenty-five years of solitary confinement in prison! Is a false testimony under duress really such a terrible "war" crime to justify twenty-five years in a stone grave?

Volodymyr Horbovy,[2] a citizen of Czechoslovakia, is now serving his nineteenth year as a prisoner in the Dubravlag system; he was sentenced in 1947 by oso (special conference). All the persons sentenced by oso were rehabilitated long ago, and oso itself was liquidated, and its activity condemned. Yet

---

1 Officers of the Polish Republic who were taken prisoner when the USSR invaded (then) eastern Poland a few days after Nazi Germany in 1939 (transl. note).

2 Horbovy was arrested in Prague in August, 1947, at the request of the Polish government, and was convicted of war crimes. Subsequently a Polish court in Warsaw found him not guilty of any crimes, whereupon the Polish secret police, rather than allow his release, deported him to the Soviet Union.

Horbovy, who until his imprisonment had never resided in the Soviet Union, is kept under guard, for whose sins no one knows. The sentence by oso is altogether unfounded. Why then has a man been rotting nineteen years in prison? In 1935, while residing in the Polish Republic, Horbovy defended Bandera at the Pieracki trial.[1] Is this a crime? Horbovy is serving a term for "betraying the homeland". Which homeland has he betrayed? Has he committed treason? Should a citizen of the Republic of Czechoslovakia, residing in Poland, consider himself a citizen of the USSR?

A son of General Shukhevych,[2] Yuri Shukhevych, is also imprisoned in Dubravlag. Arrested in 1948 (at the age of fifteen) he was sentenced without cause by the same oso to ten years' imprisonment for a fictitious "connection with the underground". In the spring of 1956 he was released as a minor who had served one-third of the term. In the fall of the same year Prosecutor-General Rudenko repealed the release, arguing that Shukhevych "is the son of a nationalist leader". The prosecution of parents because of the children, and of children because of the parents, is the most repulsive vestige of the cult of Secretary-General Stalin, but nevertheless this was the manner in which the repeal was formulated. Placed in jail, Shukhevych served another two years, and on the day of liberation he was shown a warrant for his arrest and subjected to an investigation for anti-Soviet agitation, which he had allegedly carried out in his cell. Two cell "witnesses" were found and the case was given proper juridical form. It was thought that, in the face of a new term, the prisoner would be "re-educated" and would agree to everything asked of him. But Shukhevych did not agree to this. And he was sentenced, for the "cell" affair, to ten more years in a camp. Do we not see in the actions of Rudenko and the KGB the deliberate hounding of an innocent man? Was the practice of "cell" cases not

---

[1] On trial were several leading members of the Organization of Ukrainian Nationalists accused of organizing the assassination of the Polish Minister of the Interior, Pieracki (transl. note).

[2] General Roman Shukhevych (*1907), known as Taras Chuprynka, was the Commander-in-Chief of the Ukrainian Insurgent Army (UPA) until he was killed in a battle near L'viv in March, 1950 (transl. note).

condemned? How many more of such "cell cases" will Shukhevych have to suffer in the future? Is he doomed to spend the rest of his life in prisons and camps?

M. Soroka, a victim of the Stalin lawlessness, is still languishing in Dubravlag. Arrested in 1940, he was sentenced for no cause to eight years by the Beria gang. In 1949 after returning to L'viv, he was again arrested and deported to the Krasnoyarsk territory for the same thing as in 1940 — he was punished twice for one "crime". But there was no "crime". In 1957 the Carpathian military tribunal recognized his rehabilitation in respect to the case of 1940. Yet in 1952 M. Soroka was arrested for the third time, was accused of being involved in fictitious camp "organizations". For this "sin" he was given twenty-five years. Supposing Soroka actually had participated in these organizations — even then he would not merit such an inhuman term, for his "crime" has three mitigating circumstances:

1. From 1940 to 1948 M. Soroka served his prison term without being guilty, and having lost faith in the justice of the juridical authorities he looked for justice in something else.

2. The time when M. Soroka was serving his prison term was a period of lawlessness, and of the shameless extermination of prisoners; underground organizations in the camps were a kind of self-defence.

3. Neither the court nor the investigation established any concrete actions of these hastily produced "organizations".

Today, on his first conviction, Soroka is serving his twenty-sixth year in prison. And this is at the time when our legislation provides for fifteen years as the maximum term. Having served the full term, M. Soroka will have spent thirty-eight years in prison!

Communist humanity and socialist legality demand a reexamination of Soroka's case to ascertain by means of an open trial whether he merits such inhuman punishment, a punishment which can be justified only by a policy of genocide directed against the Ukrainian intelligentsia.

V. Duzhyns'ky, a talented artist, is also kept in Dubravlag. His guilt consists of the fact that in 1957 he displayed in the opera theater in L'viv the flag of the Ukrainian Zaporzhian host, the flag of our valiant forebears, the defenders of Ukraine and of the entire Rus' against the Turks and the Tatars. For hoisting the flag he was sentenced to a ten-year term in prison. Is this humane? Is it legal?

A group of intellectuals of the city of L'viv is also imprisoned in Dubravlag — S. Virun, M. Lukyanenko, I. Kandyba, and other organizers of the Ukrainian Workers-Peasants' Union. The program of this Union provided for the full retention of the socialist achievements in Ukraine and the granting to the Ukr. ssr of a greater political and economic independence within the system of the socialist commonwealth of nations. For this sin they were sentenced in 1961, M. Lukyanenko and I. Kandyba to fifteen years, S. Virun to eleven years. The constitution of the ussr guarantees the union republics the right of secession from the ussr. How then can people be sentenced for actions which do not at all contradict the constitution of the ussr?

A group of Ukrainian intellectuals of the city of Karaganda, Yu. Dolishny and others, are also serving a term in the Dubravlag system; they were sentenced for their attempt to open a Ukrainian school for their children, which is a right guaranteed by the constitution of the ussr.

The system of so-called "erroneous" releases is also a manifestation of suppression. A person is released prior to completing his term. He lives as a free man, and suddenly the kgb appears. Get ready for prison — you were released by mistake. This method provides the kgb with an opportunity to imprison a man without trial and hearing. Journalist Karavans'ky, who was sentenced to twenty-five years, was released in 1960 after serving sixteen years. He lived as a free man for five years, married, enrolled at a university, and suddenly on November 13, 1965 (five years later), he was arrested to serve another nine years, for the Prosecutor protested his release after a corresponding request had been received from the kgb. In a similar manner S. Soroka, V. Levkovych, and others were re-arrested and placed in Dubravlag.

No less shameful is the system of detention in camps:

1. The prisoners work for eight hours in shops harmful to

their health and are not allowed rest either on Saturdays or days prior to holidays.

2. The guaranteed norm of nutrition barely reaches 2,000 calories. (Theoretically, on paper, the norm provides for 2,400 calories, but because of the very low quality of the products and due to the low quality of baked bread [60% overplus[1]] the calories of the guaranteed ration barely reach 2,000.)

3. Of the money earned by the prisoners, fifty per cent is retained for the benefit of the state, and of the remaining, only five rubles per month can be used to buy goods from the canteen (under the special regime — only two rubles).

4. The canteen does not sell bread, nor butter, nor sugar, but only low-quality candies, fats, and canned vegetables.

5. A prisoner must first serve half of the term before he is entitled to receive food parcels from home.

6. After having served half the term he may receive three parcels (weighing five kilograms!) a year, providing the administration gives permission. But there is a host of pretexts for refusing to issue a parcel to the prisoner: failing to fulfill the prescribed quota, not participating in the camp police, not participating in cultural activities, failing to attend political information meetings, and hundreds of other reasons.

7. A prisoner may write only two letters a month.

8. A political prisoner, who is usually an intellectual — a student, a teacher, an engineer—must do hard physical labour. This is a means of moral suppression and of psychological mockery of a human being.

9. Prisoners may meet visitors during "the time when they are not working", i.e., on visiting days a prisoner must go to work and may have visits only in the evening and the night, when one should sleep and rest. Thus of three days of visiting, a prisoner spends only thirty-six hours with his wife or with other relatives (twelve hours are spent on going to and returning from work and at the work itself; at six o'clock in the evening he is admitted to the building for visits). Thus the system of detention strikes not only at the prisoners, but also at their relatives. . . .

---

1 Excess in weight of loaf over the weight of flour used. The excess is due (presumably) to non-flour additives (transl. note).

The interdiction of parcels, the starvation ration, the restricted use of money earned, is this really not extermination by starvation?

It is interesting that the entire "re-educating" work in the camps is based upon such starvation. Prisoner A. Hubych received a parcel. It was not released to him, and the man in charge of the detachment told him straight to his face: Join the camp police and you'll get the parcel. A. Novozhyts'ky, another prisoner, also received a parcel, but it was returned to his home on the grounds that Novozhyts'ky did not attend school. Has the system of "re-education" of the prisoners no other arguments in defence of education than the method of coercion by hunger?

What a progressive method of re-education! Exactly as animals are trained in a zoo: If you do this and that then you will eat; if you don't, then you can die of starvation. It seems to me that this method bears no resemblance to re-education and, for the communist society, it is simply shameful.

A characteristic detail: The weight of a parcel must not exceed five kg, and if it weighs five kg and one hundred grams, it is returned. If only all the rules and laws were observed as scrupulously. But they are not. Even this very firm rule is not always observed so carefully, for all the parcels arriving from abroad are released without any restrictions. Why? Does the rule provide for foreign parcels? Not at all. It is simply that the "trainers" of human beings are ashamed to admit to the rest of the world that they so savagely and contemptuously mock the human dignity of the prisoners.

The living conditions of the prisoners, too, are terrible. There are double bunks in the barracks and 1.3 square metres [approximately four square feet] of barrack space per prisoner. Such standards are unsanitary and depressing.

And the special regime? It is synonymous with death, with cremation camp. People are locked up for decades in concrete cells, without windows, always by the light of a little lamp. The food ration is minimal. The canteen sells only cigarettes, matches, toothpaste, soap, envelopes. One can make only two rubles' worth of purchases a month. The clothing is that of Buchenwald — black and white. Deprived of air and light, emaciated with the starvation ration, and stuffed seven to ten men to a cell, the people little by little lose their resemblance to human beings. There are frequent cases of suicide (for instance, the prisoner Susey), mutilation, and insanity. The prisoners open their veins and write in blood on the walls of the cell, "Death to Svyatkin." (Svyatkin is the KGB plenipotentiary for camp detachment No. 10.) One prisoner cut off his ears, placed them in a parcel, and addressed it to the Twenty-Second Party Congress. Driven to despair they tattoo on their foreheads the words, "Slave of the CPSU". This act is very severely punished, in the same way as sabotage and subversion, by execution by a firing squad (as with the prisoner Malay). All these terrors serve as tools of "re-education". The death cells of the special regime are regularly visited by members of the KGB, who recommend to the inmates that they condemn their past or recant their views so that they can be transferred from the "special" to the "strict" regime.

Detention in the "special regime" means the absolute physical and moral transformation from human being to animal. It is the ruin of a man. These camps of the "special" regime are a shameful reminder of the extermination carried out in the camps by Beria, Yezhov, and Yagoda.

And what is the attitude of the administration, especially of the KGB officials? Lt. Harashchenko, KGB plenipotentiary in the eleventh camp detachment of Dubravlag, takes the liberty of appearing in the room for visitors; when wives come to visit their husbands, he states in the presence of the husbands, "Why do you come to see him? Reject him!" Such "kind" conduct was not known even in the times of Beria. . . .

I am appealing to you and through you to the public with the request to turn your attention to these last outrageous traces of the Stalinist terror and to implement all possible measures to remove them. . . .

I am forwarding this petition to the Union of Journalists, for it unites people who by their very profession are called upon to defend the interest of society. I assume that the Union of Journalists will support my proposals, for they are obliged to do so by the "moral code of the builders of communism".

(May 10, 1966)

TO THE COLLEGIUM OF THE SUPREME COURT OF THE USSR
From journalist S. Y. Karavans'ky

PETITION

I request that you re-examine the question of whether citizen Rudenko[1] who systematically violates Soviet legislation, should continue to serve as the Prosecutor General of the USSR. He is not suitable for this important position and should be punished for his deeds, in keeping with Soviet law.

While he was Prosecutor of the Stalino (Donets'k) region (1938-1940), and later in the post of Prosecutor of the Ukr. SSR (1944-1953), and since 1953, in his capacity as the Prosecutor General of the USSR, Rudenko often flagrantly violated Soviet legislation. He sanctioned the murder of completely innocent Soviet people; knowingly held innocent people criminally responsible; introduced a system of complete juridical irresponsibility into the courts and the prosecutor's office, sanctioned the violation of Soviet procedural law; and transformed the judicial body of the USSR into tools of high-handedness and lawlessness. Thus while holding high government positions, he committed crimes punishable under Soviet laws. This can be substantiated by the following facts:

1. While he was Prosecutor of the Stalino (Donets'k) region, citizen Rudenko sanctioned the execution by firing squad of absolutely innocent Soviet people who are now rehabilitated; this crime is punishable under Art. 102, par. "E", and Art. 102, par. "Z" of the Criminal Code of the RSFSR[2] (a premeditated murder of two or more persons).

2. Citizen Rudenko, as Prosecutor of the Ukr. SSR, sanctioned in 1947 the arrest of the fifteen-year-old son of General Shukhevych,[3] Yu. Shukhevych, on the trumped-up charge of "connections with the underground". In 1947 he sanctioned the banishment of engineer Soroka for crimes he had not committed, basing his sanction on Soroka's 1940 conviction,

---

1 Rudenko was chief prosecutor for the USSR at the Nuremburg trials of German war criminals.
2 Russian Soviet Federal Socialist Republic, the largest of the "independent" republics of the USSR (transl. note).
3 Commanding general of the nationalistic Ukrainian Insurgent Army (U.P.A.), killed by Soviet forces in Western Ukraine (transl. note).

for which he was rehabilitated in 1957 by the decision of the Carpathian military tribunal. In 1956, in his capacity as the Prosecutor of the USSR, Rudenko protested Yu. Shukhevych's release on the grounds that, "He is the son of a nationalist leader." This remark testifies to the fact that the Prosecutor was well aware of young Shukhevych's innocence. Thus he is guilty of yet another crime, according to Art. 176 of the Criminal Code of the RSFSR, which reads as follows:

"The institution of criminal proceedings against a person known to be innocent by a person conducting an inquiry, by an investigator, or by a prosecutor shall be punished by deprivation of freedom for a term not exceeding three years."

"The same acts combined with an accusation of an especially dangerous crime against the state or any other grave crime, or with artificially created proof of the accusation, shall be punished by deprivation of freedom for a term of three to ten years."

3. Citizen Rudenko, as Prosecutor of the Ukr. SSR, introduced into the courts and the prosecutor's office an atmosphere of complete irresponsibility before the law, evidenced by their refusal to reply to the complaints and demands of citizens, which they should do in keeping with the law. Art. 109 of the CPC of the RSFSR (the corresponding article of the CPC of the union republics) states the following:

"A prosecutor, investigator, organ of inquiry, and judge shall be obliged to accept declarations and communications concerning any crime that has been committed or is in preparation and to make decisions concerning them within the period of not more than three days from the day of receiving the declaration or communication, or in exceptional instances within a period of not more than ten days . . . The person who has made the declaration shall be informed of the decision taken."

However, neither the prosecutor's office nor the court adheres to this article. In February, 1965, journalist Karavans'ky forwarded to the Prosecutor a request to arraign Yu. M. Dadenkov, the Minister of Higher Education in the Ukr. SSR. But he has not received any reply to this request. In 1966, he petitioned to the people's court in the Zhovten' district of the city of Odessa, asking for the arraignment of I. Petrenko on charges of libel. But he received no reply. Thus the court and the prosecutor have violated Article 109 of the CPC of the RSFSR and the corresponding articles of the CPC of the union republics. This negligence is the direct responsibility of the Prosecutor General. He does not observe the articles of the constitution which obligate him to ensure strict observance of the laws by all the ministers, institutions, and individual citizens on the territory of the USSR. Negligence in carrying out official duties is punishable under Articles 172 and 170 of the CC of the RSFSR.

4. During the time that citizen Rudenko held the post of Prosecutor General of the USSR, the courts repeatedly violated the Constitution of the USSR and those of the union republics. Article 115 of the Constitution of the RSFSR states: "In all courts of the RSFSR cases are heard in public unless otherwise provided by law, and the accused is guaranteed the right to defence."

However, this principle continues to be flouted by most, if not all, courts in the USSR. For example, on April 12, 1961, the collegium on criminal cases of the L'viv Regional Court heard, in a *closed* court session, the case of M. P. Lytsyk and O. V. Vodynyuk. Yet the text of the verdict states that the case was heard in "an open court session". Such a shameless violation of the constitution is characteristic of most (if not all) courts since citizen Rudenko became Prosecutor General. On September 10, 11, and 12, 1963, the Volyn' Regional Court heard in a closed court session the case of Yu. Sachuk, even though the accused had twice appealed to the court for an open trial. Even now he does not know why the court and the prosecutor deemed it necessary to try him in a closed court (perhaps an order from the KGB?). On March 21 to 25, 1966, also in a closed court session, the Regional Court of Kiev heard the cases of E. Kuznetsova, O. Martynenko, and I. Rusyn.

Another symptom of the current disdain for Soviet law is the reduction of the role of the legal profession to that of assistants to the judge and prosecutor. When the defendant Sachuk, on September 10, 1963, discovered that the Volyn' Regional Court Session would be closed, he refused to answer the judge. The trial proceedings stopped. Three times the court withdrew for deliberation and three times Sachuk refused to answer; when the court began to question the witnesses, Sachuk sang the "Internationale" and stopped them once more. The court again withdrew for deliberation and called in the lawyer, Ploskonos. The lawyer, instead of supporting Sachuk's legal request for an open court session, took the side of the judge and the prosecutor, and intimidated Sachuk in a private conversation to agree to a closed court session. This lawyer's conduct is typical of the actions of the entire legal profession since Rudenko became Prosecutor General of the USSR.

5. During the time that citizen Rudenko has been Prosecutor General of the USSR, a series of pogrom-like measures have been applied to a number of Jewish intellectuals. On June 29, 1961, G. R. Pyachersky, the elder of the Judaic religious community in Leningrad, was arrested and sentenced to twelve years on charges of espionage. Twenty-four times (24!) Pyachersky applied to the Prosecutor General for a review of this fabricated case, and twenty-four times Rudenko rejected his request. Only in December, 1964, was it admitted that Pyachersky was not guilty of espionage, but was guilty of agitation. This "case" of Pyachersky is simply one of the manifestations of Jew baiting personally inspired by Nikita Khrushchev. Pyachersky is not even guilty of "agitation"; investigators found at his home one single anecdote he had recorded about Khrushchev. Should a man be given seven years for this?

The handling of Pyachersky's case resembles a pogrom. The authorities in Moscow and Leningrad arrested the Jews Kachinov, Dymkin, [and] Rishal, Jews who had no connection at all with Pyachersky. Here one can plainly see the outline of a pogrom, an action against the Jews. Engineer Rishal is still illegally kept in prison (a nine-year term), only because he expressed sympathy for the State of Israel. Should one really be made to rot seven years in a camp for this? Citizen Rudenko has transformed the courts and the prosecutor's office into a means of suppressing the national intelligentsia of the peoples of the USSR (Jews, Ukrainians, and other nationalities).

6. While holding the position of Prosecutor General of the

USSR, Rudenko transformed the courts into an appendage of the Committee of State Security (KGB) of the Council of Ministers of the USSR. The KGB recruit their agents from among the prisoners sentenced to twenty-five years, or try to persuade them to renounce their political views and condemn their past activities. When some agree to such a compromise, suitable juridical reasons are found to release them. Thus in 1960, Karavans'ky was released from prison, after he had condemned his past activity and had written a statement to that effect. The existence of such a statement, which could be used to advantage in the press, enabled the KGB to release Karavans'ky, although this was formally illegal; Karavans'ky had not completed his term and was not eligible for amnesty. But this did not deter the KGB or the Prosecutor of the USSR from releasing him. In this way the courts (at the behest of the KGB) by-pass the laws, justifying the old saying, "The law is like the tongue of a wagon — it goes wherever it is turned." However, five years after his release Karavans'ky forwarded a complaint to the communists of the other socialist countries (a dreadful threat to the security of the USSR!); after a request from the KGB, the Prosecutor of the USSR straightened out Karavans'ky's "erroneous" release, and he was arrested once more. Thus the Prosecutor General transformed the judicial body of the USSR into an arm of the KGB, and the KGB developed a brisk trade in the places of imprisonment — they exchange the liberty of prisoners for services they require. These acts of citizen Rudenko are indictable according to Article 177 of the c.c. [Criminal Code] of the RSFSR.

7. Being aware that prisoners are retained in prisons and camps without sufficient legal grounds, Prosecutor General Rudenko saw to it that they would not send complaints to the state, judicial, and public organs in the USSR. In accordance with an unpublished secret circular, which is effective in the camp system, the agents of the KGB confiscate from the prisoners all letters and complaints addressed to the higher authorities, and do not forward them. In Dubravlag camp detachment 11, for example, the plenipotentiary of the KGB, Captain Harashchenko, confiscated the complaint addressed to Wolf Messing from the prisoner Pyachersky and refused to give any explana-

tion. Gapichev, the Prosecutor of Dubravlag, has taken no action. Is this not a return to Beria's time, when people were persecuted and even executed by firing squads (as was I. H. Palamarchuk at Vorkuta) for writing complaints from the camps. Nevertheless, Rudenko sanctions this practice.

8. As the Prosecutor of the USSR, citizen Rudenko must see that the governmental agencies of the USSR adhere to the laws and regulations of the Soviet system. But he did not protest against the introduction of dreadful starvation conditions into the USSR camp system. Having acted in 1945 as state prosecutor at the Nuremberg trials, Rudenko knows only too well what crimes against humanity are. Yet he persists in sanctioning the inhuman standards of the camps, which were drawn up by the MMPO[1] of the union republics. The application of these rules to political prisoners can only be regarded as crimes against humanity.

All these facts compel me to apply to the Supreme Court of the USSR with the request that you re-examine Citizen Rudenko's appointment as Prosecutor General of the USSR, and arraign him on criminal charges in accordance with the articles of the Criminal Code of the RSFSR which provide punishment for such acts as: 1. The murder of two or more people. 2. Institution of criminal proceedings against a person known to be innocent. 3. Negligence in carrying out his duties. 4. Suppression of national minorities. 5. Violations of socialist legality in releasing prisoners. 6. The cruel treatment of prisoners, as one of the manifestations of crimes against humanity. 7. The suppression of criticism and repressions against prisoners who send complaints to higher authorities.

(June 7, 1966)

FROM THE LETTERS OF S. KARAVANS'KY TO HIS WIFE

. . . I'll compensate for my short letters with a long translation which will give you a great deal of trouble. It should be retyped and then forwarded to me for final revision. At the moment two chapters are ready. Today I'll complete the third.

---

[1] Ministries for the Protection of Public Order (transl. note).

Finishing writing in the evening. I translated another chapter today (Sunday — V. Ch.) . . .

(February 27, 1966, Yavas)

*

Let's make it a rule to write a letter every week. And to number them. Agreed? Letters are disappearing, so send only registered letters. I'm particularly interested in the fate of the letters, because in the first one (May 23) I sent you a list of books I'd like to have. Send it to book-lovers, they'll find them. Besides this, forward any literature on the etymology of words and on questions related to dictionaries of rhymes which philologists would suggest to you. Send me also *Kilyadky i shchedrivky* [Ukrainian carols] and any other publications in the field of folklore. Since my departure for the north, a lot of interesting things must have been published . . .

(June 2, 1966, Yavas)

*

In your New Year's greetings you are fairly optimistic about 1967. I share your optimism, although if we live, we shall see. I know that to rest great hopes on something is always wrong, for on the other side of the coin of such expectations is disappointment. So I always add a considerable dose of skepticism to optimism. And as a rule it always worked to my advantage.

I've already written to you that I received many congratulations [on his birthday], and I can't reply to them all, although I'll try. I wrote you whom to thank, but if the letter didn't arrive, tell me and I'll write again.[1]

I have started the third notebook on the *Biographies of Words*. By the way, I still don't know whether the first two notebooks have arrived. I also impatiently await the review of the dictionary . . .

(January 22, 1967, Yavas)

*

---

1 The letter was not passed by the camp censorship.

I can't work on the *Biographies of Words*, for all my papers have been again taken away to be carefully examined. But I'm not wasting time, and I work every day. You know how hard I've worked over the translations of Shakespeare. Serious work demands serious application to the work. I don't know whether my work with poetry will be successful. I'm thinking of the poems, *The Telegram*, *The 31st of January*, and *150,000*. Because I have no reviews I have discontinued my scholarly work for the time being.

The written interview with the reply to *Perets'* is wonderful . . .[1]

(February 15, 1967, Yavas)

> *To Citizen Korol'kov*
> *Chief of the Camp P/Ya 385/11*
> *Copy:*
> *To Comrade L. I. Brezhnev,*
> *First Secretary of the CC CPSU*
> *Copy: To the editors of the newspaper Humanité.*
> *From citizen Nina Antonovna Strokataya, residing in the city of Odessa, Chernomorskaya Doroga 56-a, Apartment 12.*

PETITION

For eighteen years the camp administration has been unable to exert an influence upon prisoner S. I. Karavans'ky, and the Karavans'ky family is deprived of the opportunity to maintain the contact with him permitted by law. Therefore I, the wife of S. I. Karavans'ky, ask you to *execute him by a firing squad* to terminate his long torture and his continuous conflicts with the administration.

I write this petition while sober and being fully aware of its gravity.

(N. Strokataya)
December 27, 1966

---

[1] Apparently this is a reference to an interview with I. Dzyuba in the Ukrainian newspaper, *Nove zhyttya*.

Supplement

IVAN DZYUBA'S SPEECH IN BABYN YAR[1] ON SEPTEMBER 29, 1966
(ON THE TWENTY-FIFTH ANNIVERSARY OF THE EXECUTION
AT BABYN YAR)

There are occurrences, there are tragedies, whose enormity defies words, about which more can be said by silence — the great silence of thousands of people. So perhaps it would be more fitting for all of us here to dispense with words and silently contemplate the tragedy at this site. However, silence has value only when all that can be said has been said. When far from everything has been said, when nothing has yet been said, silence becomes an accomplice to injustice and servility. That is why we must speak, whether or not it is allowed, taking advantage of any opportunities, which occur so seldom.

I, too, would like to say a few words, a thousandth of what I am thinking today and of what I would like to say here. I want to address you as men, as fellow humans. I want to address you, the Jews, as a Ukrainian, as a member of the Ukrainian nation to which I proudly belong.

Babyn Yar is a tragedy of all mankind, but it happened on Ukrainian soil. And that is why a Ukrainian, not only a Jew, has no right to forget it. Babyn Yar is our common tragedy; a tragedy, first and foremost of the Jewish and Ukrainian peoples.

This tragedy was brought to our peoples by fascism.

But one must not forget that fascism did not begin at Babyn Yar, nor did it end here. Fascism begins with disrespect to the human being and ends with the annihilation of man, the annihilation of entire peoples, but not necessarily only with the kind of annihilation as that of Babyn Yar.

Let us imagine for a moment that Hitler had been victorious, that German fascism had triumphed. There is no doubt that they would have created a brilliant and "flourishing" society which would have reached a high level of economic and technological development, which would have

---

[1] The site of the mass execution of the Jews of Kiev by the Nazis on September 29, 1941 (transl. note).

attained all those achievements that we have attained. And certainly, the silent slaves of fascism would subsequently have "conquered" the cosmos, would have flown to other planets to represent mankind and the earthly civilization. This regime would have done everything to affirm its "truth" so that people would forget the price with which such "progress" was bought, so that history would justify or even forget the immeasurable crimes, so that an inhuman society would appear to men as a normal one, even the best in the world. And it would not be on the ruins of the Bastilles, but on the defiled places of national tragedies, levelled with a thick layer of sand and oblivion, that an official sign would stand: "Dancing ground".

That is why we should judge any society, not by its external technological achievements, but by the place and worth of the individual in it, by the value it places on human dignity and human conscience.

Today in Babyn Yar we are commemorating not only those who perished here. We are remembering the millions of Soviet soldiers — our fathers — who gave their lives in the struggle against fascism. We are recalling the sacrifices and efforts of millions of Soviet men of all nationalities who unselfishly worked for victory over fascism. We should endeavour to be worthy of their memory, worthy of the obligation placed on us by that memory of countless human sacrifices, hopes, and strivings.

Are we worthy of this memory? Apparently not, if till the present day various forms of hatred are still found among us, including one that is referred to by the overused, banal, but terrible word — anti-semitism. Anti-semitism is an international phenomenon; it existed and still exists in all societies. Unfortunately, our society, too, is not free from it. Perhaps this should not seem strange, because anti-semitism — an offspring and companion of age-old barbarism and subjugation — is the first and unavoidable result of political despotism, and it is not readily overcome. But it is something else that astonishes us: that, in fact, there was no effective struggle against it during the post-war decades, and furthermore, that periodically it was artificially nurtured. It seems that Lenin's directives on the struggle against anti-semitism are being forgotten, like the Leninist directives on the national development of Ukraine.

And in the times of Stalin there were clear and obvious attempts to play on the mutual prejudices of Ukrainians and Jews — attempts to destroy the Jewish culture under the pretext of combating Jewish bourgeois nationalism, Zionism, and so on; attempts to destroy the Ukrainian national culture and language under the pretext of combating Ukrainian bourgeois nationalism. These cunningly devised campaigns brought harm to both peoples and did not facilitate their friendship; they only added one more unpleasant memory to the difficult history of both peoples and to the complicated history of their relations.

We must recall these memories not in order to irritate old wounds, but to heal them completely.

As a Ukrainian, I am ashamed that in my nation, as among other nations, there is this shameful phenomenon, unworthy of humanity, called anti-semitism.

We, the Ukrainians, should combat in our midst any manifestations of anti-semitism, or disrespect to a Jew, and the incomprehension of the Jewish problem.

You, the Jews, should struggle against those in your midst who do not respect Ukrainians, the Ukrainian culture, and the Ukrainian language, those who unjustly perceive in every Ukrainian a disguised anti-semite.

We should drive out all kinds of hatred among men, overpower all misunderstanding, and dedicate all our lives to attain genuine brotherhood.

Who, if not we, should understand one another? Who, if not we, should offer to humanity an example of fraternal co-existence? The histories of our peoples are so similar in their tragic features that in the biblical motifs of his *Moses*, Ivan Franko recreated the path of the Ukrainian people in the form of the Jewish legend, and Lesya Ukrainka began one of her most powerful poems on the tragedy of Ukraine with the words, "And thou once struggled, like Israel . . ."

Great sons of both peoples bequeathed us mutual understanding and friendship. Tied to the Ukrainian soil are the lives of the three greatest Jewish writers — Sholom Aleichem,

Itskhok Perets, and Mendele Moikher Sforim — who loved this land. A brilliant Jewish publicist, Volodymyr Zhabotyns'ky, sided with the Ukrainian people in their battle against Russian tsarism and appealed to the Jewish intelligentsia to support the Ukrainian national liberation movement and the Ukrainian culture.

One of the last public acts of Taras Shevchenko was his well-known protest against the anti-semitic policy of the tsarist government. Lesya Ukrainka, Ivan Franko, Borys Hrinchenko, Stepan Vasyl'chenko, and other prominent Ukrainian writers well knew and highly esteemed the grandeur of the Jewish history and the Jewish spirit, and wrote with sincere compassion about the sufferings of the Jewish poor.

In the past, there was much blind hostility and harsh misunderstanding between us. But there were also examples of courageous solidarity and mutual aid in the struggle for our common ideals of freedom and justice, for a better lot for our nations.

We, the present generation, are obliged to continue this tradition, and oppose the evil one of distrust and insincerity.

Unfortunately, there are a number of factors detrimental to the strengthening and further development of this noble tradition of solidarity.

Among them is the absence of genuine publicity, of openness in matters affecting nationalities, as a result of which a peculiar "conspiracy of silence" develops around painful questions. We would do well to follow the example of Poland in our treatment of this matter. It is well known how complicated the relations between Poles and Jews were in the past. Now not a trace of the former animosity has survived. What is the secret of such success? First, a common misfortune in World War II united Poles and Jews. But such a common misfortune also happened to us. Second, in socialist Poland, relations between nationalities are the subject of scholarly sociological research and of open public discussion, of continual attention and intervention in the press, literature, and so on — and all this creates an atmosphere of good and successful national and international education; unfortunately, this does not exist here.

We, too, should care and strive with all our strength for such effective education — and not only with words. We cannot disregard the facts of anti-semitism, chauvinism, lack of respect for any nationality, discrimination against any national culture and national language. These attitudes are common among us, and with many it begins with the renunciation of their own national identity, culture, history, language (although such renunciation is not always voluntary, and the individual should not always bear the blame for it).

The road to genuine brotherhood consists of self-knowledge, not of self-oblivion. We must not renounce ourselves, adapt ourselves to suit others, but be ourselves and respect others. Jews have the right to be Jews, Ukrainians the right to be Ukrainians, in the most complete and profound sense of these words. Let the Jews learn Jewish history, culture, and language and be proud of them. Let the Ukrainians learn their own history, culture, and language and be proud of them. Let both peoples know each other's history and culture and the history and culture of other peoples. Let them know how to esteem themselves and others — as their brothers.

It is hard to achieve this, but it is better to aspire toward it than to indifferently give up hope and drift with the wave of assimilation and opportunism that will result only in bigotry, blasphemy, and the hidden hatred of humanity.

All our lives we must deny hatred and bigotry. There is nothing more important for us right now, for otherwise all social ideals lose their meaning.

This is our duty towards millions of victims of despotism, our obligation before the best men and women of the Ukrainian and Jewish peoples, who appealed for mutual understanding and friendship, our duty towards the Ukrainian land, on which our both peoples have to live together. This is our obligation before humanity.

Appendix

Partial
List
of
Published Works
of the
"Criminals"

1. *Artist's Anniversary* (dedicated to the 85th anniversary of A. Monastyrs'ky), *Komsomol's'ke Plemya* [The Komsomol Tribe] (Vinnytsya), November 15, 1963.

2. *The Kobzar*[1] *Was Enchanted by Our Songs, Vil'ne Zhytta* [Free Life] (Ternopil'), February 9, 1964.

3. *The Lights of Dawn* (dedicated to the 100th anniversary of the first Ukrainian professional theatre in Galicia), *Komsomol's'ke Plemya*, April 1, 1964.

4. *The Collector of Pearls* (a review of the book by M. Yatsenko, *Volodymyr Hnatyuk* [Scientific Thought], 1964) in *Komsomol's'ke Plemya*, November 13, 1964.

5. *Return the Sun to Us!* (about the poet Y. Kondra), *Komsomol's'ke Plemya*, December 16, 1964.

6. *When the Ancient Writings Are Silent* (about the archaelogical discoveries in the Region of Ternopil'), *Komsomol's'ke Plemya*, January 6, 1965.

7. *Along the Path of the Zbruch Country* (Shevchenko in the Region of Ternopil'), *Komsomol's'ke Plemya*, March 10, 1965.

8. *In the Footsteps of Iskra, Sil's'ki Visti* [Village News], April 2, 1965.

BOHDAN HORYN'

1. *I. Franko on Nature and the Role of Fantasy in Literature, Zhovten* [October], No. 5, 1960.

2. *The Art of Creative Searching* (review of an exhibition of the sculptor, F. Bryzh), *Lenins'ka Molod'* [The Leninist Youth], L'viv, August 7, 1960.

---

1 Poet Taras Shevchenko (transl. note).

3. *Young Artists' Exhibit* (on the exhibition of paintings and drawings by young artists from L'viv), *Lenins'ka Molod'*, December 11, 1960.

4. *"Natalka-Poltavka" in the Worker's Theatre*, newspaper *L'vovskaya pravda* [The L'viv Truth], January 3, 1960.

5. *Talent, Creativity, Work, Lenins'ka Molod'*, November 10, 1960.

6. *Yes, This Is Innovation* (on the works of young Ukrainian poets I. Drach, M. Vinhranovs'ky, and others), *Lenins'ka Molod'*, May 9, 1962.

7. *The Main Thing — Problematics, Lenins'ka Molod'*, June 8, 1962.

8. *The Poetry of Great Humanism, Zhovten'*, No. 6, 1962.

9. *In Search of One's Voice* (review of the exhibition of engravings by A. Zubko), *Lenins'ka Molod'*, July 22, 1962.

10. *Polyphonism of Talent, Molod' Ukrainy* [The Youth of Ukraine], September 8, 1962.

11. *Versatile Talent* (on the occasion of the 85th birthday of Olena Kul'chyts'ka), *Lenins'ka Molod'*, September 19, 1962.

12. *The Interrupted Song, Vil'na Ukraina* [The Free Ukraine], (L'viv), October 7, 1962.

13. *Let us have more good and diverse poets, Molod' Ukrainy*, November 27 and 28, 1962.

14. *A Start into the Unexplored, Molod' Ukrainy*, April 28, 1963.

15. *From Conception to Realization, Molod' Ukrainy.*

16. *From the Source of Folk Traditions, Lenins'ka Molod'*, June 14, 1963.

17. *The Vivid Colours of Life*, (an exhibition by painters of the Moldavian SSR), *Vil'na Ukraina*, November 24, 1963.

18. *The Bard of Hutsul'shchyna* (in honour of the 70th anniversary of H. S. Smol'sky), *L'vovs'kaya Pravda*, November 1, 1963.

19. *An Exhibition Dedicated to Chemistry, Vil'na Ukraina*, November 27, 1963.

20. *In Search of Greatness, Chervony Prapor* [The Red Banner], February 1, 1964.

21. *The Search for Greatness* (works of the sculptor F. Bryzh), *Zhovten'*, No. 2, 1964.

22. *Shevchenko in Graphic Art by Sofiya Karaffi-Korbut, Vil'na Ukraina,* March 3, 1964.

23. *S. Karaffi-Korbut on Shevchenko, Zmina* [The Change], No. 3, 1964.

24. *The Art of the Ukrainian Ex-libris, Zhovten',* No. 8, 1964.

25. *Through the Language of Drawings, Zhovten',* No. 11, 1964.

26. *In Love with Nature, L'vovs'kaya Pravda,* 1964.

27. *Contemporary Sculpture of L'viv, Vil'na Ukraina,* December 23, 1964.

28. *From Likeness to Image* (on the works of sculptor E. Mys'ko), *Zmina,* No. 1, 1965.

29. *Legends in Ceramics* (on the works of painter H. Sevruk), *Zmina,* No. 2, 1965.

30. *Notes on the Works of Evhen Lysyk, Zmina,* No. 3, 1965.

31. *The Beauty of Artistic Discoveries, Literaturna Ukraina,* August 20, 1965.

32. *Untiring Searches* (on the works of S. Karaffi-Korbut), newspaper *Ukrains'ke Zhyttya* [Ukrainian Life], Toronto, Canada, March 17, 1965.

One large work remained unfinished — *The History of Art in Western Ukraine in the Second and Third Decades of the Twentieth Century.*

MYKHAYLO HORYN'

1. *The Study of I. Y. Franko's Poetry in Grade 9 of Secondary School,* in symposium *Ivan Franko in School,* Drohobych, 1957.

2. *The Study of the Theme "Specifics of Literature" in Grade 8,* symposium *The Experience of Teaching Ukrainian Literature in School,* Kiev, 1959.

3. *On Some Popular Publications, Vitchyzna* [Fatherland], No. 8, 1959.

4. *Control of Memory by Instruments, L'vovskaya Pravda,* January 27, 1960.

5. *The Development of the Imagination of Pupils in Senior Grades, Ukrains'ka mova i literature v shkoli* [The Ukrainian language and literature in school], No. 12, 1963.

6. *Psychological Demands on the Place of Work, Sotsialistichesky Trud* [Socialist Toil], No. 8, 1965.

Besides those, nine more articles about the psychology of work and the culture of production appeared in the L'viv truck factory paper, *Zatekhnichny prohres* [For technical progress], *(Mood? Very Important, Colour in Industry, Music in Industry,* etc.)

The regional press, as well as *Izvestiya (A Psychologist Came to the Factory,* 1965), wrote about the work of the experimental laboratory, and in particular about M. Horyn'. A page in the motion picture magazine, *Nauka i Zhyttya* [Science and Life], of the Kiev documentary film studio was also dedicated to the same subject.

MYKOLA HRYN'

1. *On the problem of determining the vector of rock magnetization, Uchenye zapiski L'vovskogo politekhnicheskogo instituta* [Scientific Papers of the L'viv Polytechnical Institute], No. 53, 1959.

2. *Spectra of a single class of impulses, Dopovidi AN URSR* [Papers of the Academy of Sciences of the Ukr. ssr], No. 9, 1959.

3. *Determination of time of wave displacement in the zone of interference by means of spectral analysis, Uchenye zapiski L'vovskogo politekhnicheskogo instituta,* No. 7, 1960.

4. *A monograph on the deciphering of interference zones. Ibid.* No. 75, 1960.

5. *The spectrum of coefficient reflection from a rider of layers, Dopovidi AN URSR,* No. 12, 1961.

6. *Current spectrum of seismic waves, Uchenye zapiski L'vovskogo politekhnicheskogo instituta,* No. 80, No. 2, 1962.

7. *On errors connected with the temporary limitation of an impulse during frequency analysis, Geofizicheskiy sbornik Instituta geofiziki AN USSR* [Geophysical symposium of the

Geophysical Institute, Academy of Sciences of the Ukr. ssr],
No. 3 (5), 1962.

8. *On the spectra of interference waves and ways of utilizing
them, Tezisy dokladev AN USSR* [Abstracts, Academy of
Sciences of the Ukr. ssr], 1962.

9. *About the problem of spectra of waves reflected from a
protruding layer, Geofizicheskiy sbornik Instituta geofiziki
AN USSR* [Geophysical symposium of the Geophysical Institute, Academy of Sciences of the Ukr. ssr], No. 7.

10. *The interference and spectra of waves in seismic investigation.* Kiev: "Scientific Thought", 1965. 127 p.

MYKHAYLO MASYUTKO

1. *The Strength of Stefanyk's Novel,* journal *Radyans'ky
L'viv* [Soviet L'viv], No. 12, 1950.

2. *Taras Shevchenko, Bard of the Friendship of Peoples,*
newspaper *Radyan's'ky poligrafist* [Soviet polygraphist], 1951.

3. *Ivan Franko, Champion of the Liberty and Unity of the
Ukrainian People,* journal *Dnipro,* No. 9, 1964.

4. An article in the column, "Around the World", newspaper *Literaturna Ukraina,* September, 1965.

VALENTYN MOROZ

1. *The Luts'k Trial of 1934,* in the symposium *Theses of
lectures at the scientific conference of the Ivano-Frankivs'ke
Pedagogical Institute, December 27-28, 1964.*

2. *Participation of West-Ukrainian Peasants in the Strike
Campaign of 1936-1937 in Poland,* the same publication.

3. *Solidarity of Ukrainian and Polish Workers in Their
Fight against Fascism in Spain (1936-1939),* in the symposium
*Theses of lectures at the scientific conference of the Ivano-
Frankivs'ke Pedagogical Institute, June 26-27, 1965.*

MYKHAYLO OSADCHY

(a) Articles in literary criticism, theory of journalism, and
reviews.

1. *Some of the problems of informational genres in television*, Yuvileyna naukova sesiya, tezy dopovidey [Jubilee scientific session, theses of papers], L'viv, 1961.

2. *Reporting from the Human Soul*, scenario for a telecast of the L'viv TV studio about the creative work of the young prose writer Yu. Koval', 1961.

3. *Ostap Vyshnya — Journalist*, Bulletin of the Central Committee of the Communist Party of Ukraine, *Na dopomohu redaktorovi hazety* [In aid of the newspaper editor], No. 11, 1961.

4. *A Book about Pravda* (a review of the book *50 years of the Leninist 'Pravda'*), newspaper *Lenins'ka Molod'* L'viv, May 6, 1962.

5. *A Word on Television*, newspaper of the L'viv State University *Za radyans'kunauku* [For Soviet Science], April 24, 1963.

6. *The Land, Glorified by Lesya*, newspaper *Vil'na Ukraina*, L'viv, May 15, 1963.

7. *What is Ostap Vyshyna Really Like?*, Journal *Zhovten'*, No. 10, 1963.

8. *The Vyshnya Smile of the People*, scenario for a telecast of the L'viv TV studio about the creativity of Ostap Vyshnya, 1963.

9. *The Achilles' Heel of Conscience* (review of the book by S. Rudyk, *Akhillesova pyata* [The heel of Achilles]), *Vil'na Ukraina*, 1963.

10. *In Search of the Land of Poetry* (review of the collection of poems by B. Necherda, *Materyk* [Mainland]), *Lenins'ka Molod'*, 1963.

11. *From the creative practice of feuilleton writer Ostap Vyshnya in the newspaper Visti* [News], *Visnyk* [Courier] of the L'viv State University, philological series, the L'viv University Press, No. 1, 1963.

12. *A Funny God* (anti-religious works of Ostap Vyshnya), newspaper *L'vovskaya Pravda*, March 18, 1964.

13. *And how not to love it, that village?* (about *Vyshnya's Village Smiles* by Ostap Vyshnya), *Vil'na Ukraina*, May 18, 1964.

14. *So that the Worker Would Smile* (about the works of

Ostap Vyshnya on workers' subjects), *L'vovskaya Pravda*, June 7, 1964.

15. *Ostap Vyshnya and Western Ukraine, Naukova konferentsiya, prysvyachena 25-richchyu vozz'yednannya, tezy dopovidey* [Scientific conference dedicated to the 25th anniversary of the reunification (of Western Ukraine with central and Eastern Ukraine), Theses of lectures], L'viv University Press, L'viv, 1964.

16. *The Sorcerer of the Word* (on the occasion of the 75th birthday of Ostap Vyshnya), *L'vovskaya Pravda*, November 14, 1964.

17. *The Vyshnya Smile of the People* (on the occasion of the 75th birthday of Ostap Vyshnya), newspaper of the L'viv State University, *Za radyans'ku nauku*, November 14, 1964.

18. *Seven Colours of the Spectrum* (on the occasion of the 75th birthday of Ostap Vyshnya), *Zhovten'*. No. 11, 1964.

19. *The Ukrainian Soviet Village Ladantsi* (publication of an unknown work of Ostap Vyshnya with an annotation), *Zhovten'*, No. 11, 1964.

20. *Taras in the Space of Time* (review of the motion picture, *Taras Shevchenko*), *Lenins'ka Molod'*. November 20, 1964.

21. A problematic article about television, newspaper *Literaturna Ukraina* [Literary Ukraine], 1965.

22. *The Diversity of Philological Variations* (review of the book by A. Pastushenko), *Literaturna Ukraina*, June 11, 1965.

23. *The Journalistic Activities of Ostap Vyshnya (1919-1933)*, Abstract of the dissertation in fulfillment of requirements for the learned degree of a candidate of philology, L'viv, 1965.

(b) Literary works.

1. Selection of Poems *Thoughts, Feelings* (including *The Philosopher and Disciple, Doubt, Outcry, Gift of the Sun, My Beauty*), newspaper *Zorya komunizmu* [The star of communism], Radekhiv, L'viv region, December 29, 1960.

2. *Growth* (an essay in the book *Zhyvemo, pratsyuyerno po-komunistychnomu* [We live and work in communist style], Kamenyar publishing house, 1961.

3. Poem *Poetry*, newspaper *Komsomol'sky Prapor* [Komsomol Banner], Ivano-Frankivs'ke, March 17, 1963.

4. *What Were They Talking About* (short story), newspaper of the L'viv University, *Za radyans'ku nauku*, June 17, 1963.

5. *Blisters* (poem), newspaper *Vil'na Ukraina*, August 18, 1963.

6. *Young Girl, And Hold It Thus* (two short stories), newspaper *Lenins'ka Molod'*, January 10, 1964.

7. *Starlit Nocturne, Moonlit Lullaby* (two poems), newspaper *Lenins'ka Molod'*, March 22, 1964.

8. *To Father, To a Friend* (poems), newspaper *L'vovskaya Pravda*, March 22, 1964.

9. *Wealth, Superstition* (two poems), newspaper *L'vovskaya Pravda*, May 1, 1964.

10. *I Will Not* (etude), newspaper *Vil'na Ukraina*, June 7, 1964.

11. *Smiles* (selection of humorous poems), newspaper *L'vovskaya Pravda*, July 14, 1964.

12. Selection of poems, *When Lilies are Gathered* including *Oranges, The Forest of Churl'onis, Ballad of a Mermaid, Lukewarm, I Will Come to You through the Galaxy on Foot . . .* , newspaper *Lenins'ka Molod'* (L'viv), August 15, 1964.

13. *Elegy* (poem), in the book, *Estafetta pisni* [The Estafette of Song], Kamenyar, L'viv, 1964.

14. *Lance* (poem), journal *Zmina*, No. 2 for 1964.

15. From the cycle *Carpathian Intermezzo* (four poems), newspaper *Vil'na Ukraina*, January 24, 1965.

*

Osadchy's arrest has forestalled the publication of his lectures delivered at scientific conferences of the L'viv State University on *The beginning of Ostap Vyshnya's journalistic efforts* and *Maksym Ryl's'ky and Ostap Vyshnya*. The printing of the book of poetry *Misyachne pole* [Moonlit field], put out by the Kamenyar Publishing House, was destroyed. The textbook for students of the faculty of journalism, *Soviet Tele-*

vision, on which Osadchy was working before the arrest, remained unfinished.

*

COMMENTS ON M. H. OSADCHY'S THESIS

Excerpts from the minutes of the meeting of the Department of Journalism on March 1, 1965.

The meeting heard: the discussion of M. H. Osadchy's thesis on the subject *Journalistic activities of Ostap Vyshnya (1919-1933)*.

The meeting decided: to approve the following evaluation of M. H. Osadchy's thesis. The thesis of M. H. Osadchy, *Journalistic activities of Ostap Vyshnya (1919-1933)*, is a valuable scholarly work of research which reveals new, hitherto unknown, or little known, and insufficiently explored pages of the biography and journalistic activities of Ostap Vyshnya.

The Department of Journalism recommends that M. H. Osadchy's thesis be defended.

Head of the Department of Journalism: Docent I. T. Ts'okh.

*

An analogous decision was reached by the Department of Ukrainian literature of the L'viv State University on April 28, 1965 (Head of the Department: Docent F. M. Neboryachok).

*

"By comparison with the efforts of his predecessors, the research of M. H. Osadchy represents a considerable step forward. And, considering the actuality of questions raised in the work of M. H. Osadchy, it merits immediate publication . . .

The work of M. H. Osadchy fully meets the requirements of a dissertation submitted for the purpose of obtaining a learned degree and, consequently, the Learned Council of the Faculty

236

Partial List of

of Philology of the LSU [L'viv State University] deems it possible to bestow on the author of this dissertation the degree of candidate of philology."

(From the review by Doctor of Philology, M. F. Matviychuk.)

*

"The Department points out that comrade M. H. Osadchy's dissertation . . . has been prepared with laudable scholarly conscientiousness, with knowledge of the concrete material and of the literary and journalistic process in Ukraine during the 'twenties and 'thirties.

. . . The dissertation of comrade M. H. Osadchy has been prepared with the researcher's undisguised reverence and love of the subject of study. It adds new, little known facts to the study of Vyshnya's works and attests to the author's preparedness for scholarly research. His work fully meets the requirements expected of a candidate's dissertation . . ."

(From the comments of the Department of Ukrainian Literature at the L'viv State University.)

*

A completely positive comment was also expressed by the Department of Journalism at the L'viv State University.

*

". . . M. H. Osadchy's candidate's dissertation is the result of many years of long, persistent and purposeful work on the creative legacy of Ostap Vyshnya.

". . . The shortcomings, which will be discussed a bit further down, are, in our opinion, not important. We will speak of them merely because we consider it necessary to recommend M. H. Osadchy's dissertation for publication and, while it is being prepared for printing, the author could take these remarks into consideration and, provided he agrees with us, make the appropriate amendments.

"M. H. Osadchy deserves to be awarded the learned degree of a candidate of philology."
(From comments by F. M. Neboryachko, the Head of the Department of Ukrainian Literature at the L'viv State University.)

*

"Members of the Department of the History of Ukrainian Literature at the Order of Lenin T. H. Shevchenko State University in Kiev have familiarized themselves with the research findings of M. H. Osadchy and have arrived at the unanimous opinion that his work is a worthy contribution to Soviet literary criticism.

". . . The author of the dissertation . . . expresses his attitude towards all that has been written about Ostap Vyshnya. We share this attitude and are in agreement with the author.

"The first chapter is of great scholarly value because of its factuality. This is the first attempt in our study of literature to relate in such a detail the creative biography of Ostap Vyshnya. This one chapter by itself could pass for a whole dissertation.

"We are of the opinion that this work should be published as a separate book. It will be read with the same interest, the same rapture, as the works of Ostap Vyshnya are read."
(From comments of the Department of the History of Ukrainian Literature at the Kiev State University signed by the Head of the Department, professor A. O. Ishchuk.)

*

"The author is a professionally well trained and meticulous researcher; he deserves the learned degree of candidate of philology."
(From the comments of the Docent of the Department of Russian Literature at the Chernivtsi State University, A. R. Volkov.)

*

"Mykhaylo Osadchy is well known in Ukrainian literary criticism and in journalistic circles as an inquisitive researcher of the creative work and contributions to the periodical press of the immortal Pavlo Mykhaylovych Hubenko — Ostap Vyshnya. The articles, publications and papers of the researcher are characterized by his untiring searching, his sober and well-argumented evaluation, his polemical ardour and his bellicose fervour. In his articles, he has raised a string of hitherto unstudied problems, has dotted many of those 'i's' that used to remain a riddle.

"His work is an incontestable and valuable contribution to the study of Soviet Ukrainian literature. It merits high praise, and we are convinced that its author, Mykhaylo Osadchy, fully deserves the learned degree of a candidate of philology to be bestowed on him."

(From the comments of I. M. Duz', Docent in the Department of Ukrainian Literature at the Odessa State University.)

*

POEMS FROM THE DESTROYED BOOK

Mykhaylo Osadchy, *Misyachne pole* [Moonlit field], Poems, Kamenyar Publishing House, L'viv, 1965, 30 pages; price 3 kopecks; printing 2,300 copies (Editor[1] M. Petrenko, editor V. Kolodiy, illustrator I. Ostafiychuk; approved for printing on May 3, 1965, censorship permit No. BH 08321).

Contents of the Book: *The Flare, Wealth, Superstition, Starlit Nocturne, Trees, Shevchenko and Shakespeare, Small Ears of Grain, Faust's Moment, Maternity Home, The World Breathes "Aurora", Vocation, The Death of Ostap Vyshnya, But Ordinary Money Was Given in Payment, Two Ships; Carpathian Intermezzo* (cycle): *And I stood amidst the Carpathians . . . , Laments in minor key on the piano . . . , And tender strings began to sound . . . , As a cloak bags, the mountains in autumn . . . , The Harvest of the Green Fir Trees, There lived the Grandpa Amvrosiy, In the Illusion of a*

---

[1] In the original, "editor on a public basis", i.e. unpaid editor (transl. note).

Strange Dream, In winter, the mountains are like silvery cotton ..., *The fog crept up in a sky-blue haze* ..., *The rococo of shimmering beech trees* ..., *Dreamy Carpathians, Placid Dnipro, And who am I without you, oh cradle song?* ..., *I Am a Communist*. Biographical information.

ANATOLIY SHEVCHUK

In the newspaper *Radyans'ka Zhytomyrshchyna* [The Soviet Zhytomyr Region] (1963-1964):
1. *In the Teteriv River area*
2. *Firebird*
3. *A Generous and Joyful Day*
4. *The Picturesque River Huyva*

Newspaper *Literaturna Ukraina* (1962):
1. *The Small Spruce*
2. *He will not be able to write about it.* Journal *Prapor* [The Banner] (1962), *Ira, Stop Reading*; Journal *Zmina* (1963), *Vanya Escaped to freedom*; Journal *Zhovten', And Evening, and Music, and Stars*; Journal *Dnipro* (1962), selection of poems. Etude, *Your Thoughts Will Not Perish* in the book *A Wreath to Kobzar* (Zhytomyr regional publishing house, 1961).

O. I. ZALYVAKHA

A considerable number of his paintings could not be located after his arrest, among them those that were in his room during the search and arrest. There is additional difficulty in compiling a full catalogue of his works because the artist, as a rule, put neither dates nor names on his paintings. Therefore, in most instances, we are giving tentative names to his paintings and the presumable dates of their completion.

THE LENINGRAD PERIOD (TO 1960)

I. Works of known whereabouts

1. (Market in Kosiv), 1957.
2. (Sophia of Novhorod), 1958-59 (?), 18 x 20

3. (Fresco from Sophia of Novhorod), 1958-59, 20 x 10
4. (At the Leningrad cemetery), ?, 22 x 12
5. *Enbankment of Neva*, étude, ?
6. *Bokorashi,* — 1957 (?)
7. *Street in Kosiv*, study, 1957 (?)

II. Works of unknown whereabouts

1. *The call*, Kosiv, 1957, 61 x 88, exhibited at an individual exhibition of his works in April of 1962 in Ivano-Frankivs'ke.
2. *Portrait of Olena*, 1967.
3. *Portrait of an artist*, 1959, 84 x 63, exhibited in April of 1962.
4. *After work* (graduation work), 1960 (?)
5. *Small courtyard in Leningrad*, 1960, 71.5 x 45, exhibited in April of 1962.

THE SIBERIAN PERIOD (SUMMER OF 1960 — END OF 1961)

I.

1. *Nocturnal still life*, 1961, 82 x 51.5, exhibited in April of 1962.
2. *Portrait of Olena*, 1961, 92 x 62, exhibited in 1963.
3. *Portrait of artist Shrub's wife*, 1961, 67.5 x 47, exhibited in April of 1962.
4. *Girl in blue*, 1961, 117 x 60, exhibited in April of 1962.
5. *Portrait of a woman against yellow background*, 1961, 38.5 x 64.5, exhibited in April of 1964.
6. *Portrait of a girl student*, 1961, 45 x 33.5, exhibited in April of 1964.
7. (The grave of P. Hrabovs'ky in Tobol'sk), 19 x 13.5, 1960-61 (?)

II.

1. *Republic Street in Tyumen'*, 1961, 165 x 95, exhibited in Tyumen' and in Ivano-Frankivs'ke in April of 1962.

2. *Railway workers*, 1961, 118 x 204, exhibited in Tyumen' and in Ivano-Frankivs'ke in April of 1962.
3. *Noontime*, 1961, 94.5 x 65, exhibited in April of 1962.
4. *River Tura in Tyumen'*, 1961, 47 x 67, exhibited in April of 1962.
5. *The nurse*, 1961, 126 x 89, exhibited in April of 1962.
6. *Nina*, 1961, 67.5 x 47.5, exhibited in April of 1962.
7. *Portrait of the artist Sosnovs'ka*, 1961, 60 x 80, exhibited in April of 1964.
8. *By the window*, 1961, 67.5 x 33, exhibited in April of 1962.
9. *A portrait*, 1961, 66.5 x 115, exhibited in April of 1962.
10. *Landscape with a church*, 1961, 27 x 69, exhibited in April of 1962.
11. *Landscape with birches*, 1961, 27 x 69, exhibited in April of 1962.
12. *A ballad*, 1960, 67.5 x 47.5, exhibited in April of 1962.
13. *Etude*, 1961, 47.5 x 33, exhibited in April of 1962.
14. *At the seashore*, 1960, 23 x 70, exhibited in April of 1962.
15. *Monastery in Tyumen'*, 1961, 50 x 70, exhibited in April of 1962.
16. *Portrait of a girl*, 1961, 70 x 50, exhibited in April of 1962.
17. *Girl with a book*, 1961, 60 x 79.5, exhibited in April of 1962.
18. *Portrait of a woman journalist*, 1961, 60 x 37.5, exhibited in April of 1962.
19. *Etude*, 1961, exhibited in 1962.
20. *An architectural motif*, 1961, 54.5 x 37.5, exhibited in 1962.

THE IVANO-FRANKIVS'KE PERIOD
(1962 — August of 1965)

I.

1. (The poppies), 1961-62 (?), exhibited in April of 1962.
2. *Portrait of a lumberjack*, Vorokhta, started in 1962, exhibited in April of 1962, 96 x 65.
3. *The Carpathians*, 1962, 110 x 68, exhibited in April of 1962.

Partial List of

4. *Vorokhta*, 1962, 110 x 68, exhibited in April of 1962.
5. *Still life with books*, 1962, 68.5 x 51, exhibited in April, 1962.
6. *On the street*, 1962, has been exhibited.
7. (Spring in the city), 1962 (?)
8. (Bushy trees in the suburb), 1963.
9. (An abstract composition), 1962 (?)
10. (The sunflowers).
11. (Boy in an embroidered shirt).
12. (A Ukrainian woman, 1963-64 (?)
13. (Street at night).
14. (Youth with a tie).
15. (An abstract composition).
16. (A locomotive).
17. (Girl in a red kerchief), 1962-64 (?)
18. (Room with a gas lamp).
19. *Portrait of artist Figol'*, 1963.
20. *Self-portrait in the studio*, 1963.
21. (Portrait of Tetyana).
22. (Peasant woman in a field), Kharkiv region, 1962.
23. (Outside the village), Kharkiv region, 45 x 78, 1963.
24. (The field), a study, 1963.
25. (Field at night), 1963 (?)
26. (Wheatfield).
27. *Portrait of the artist Karaffa-Korbut*, 1964.
28. (Portrait of a photographer), 1962.
29. *Portrait of the sculptor Balyuk*, after 1962.
30. (Nude woman in a veil).
31. (Tetyana in a sport dress), 1962.
32. (Tetynana on the bed).
33. (Woman with a star on her body, 1964-65 (?)
34. (Woman's face).
35. *Portrait of Ivan Drach*, 1964.
36. (Woman's body). Composition.
37. (Portrait of an elderly woman).
38. (A dream).
39. *Fight and you shall conquer*, 1963-64 (?)
40. (Rook's nests).
41. (A woman). Composition.

42. (Bushy trees).
43. (A Ukrainian woman), 1963-64 (?)
44. (An abstract composition with tinfoil).
45. (Adam and Eve with an apple), 1964-65 (?)
46. *Cossack Mamay.*
47. *An industrial landscape.*
48. *Portrait of the mother of artist Danylo Narbut.*
49. *Portrait of the son of Danylo Narbut.*
50. *Girl from Poltava region,* 1964. Reproduced in magazines *Ranok* [Morning], No. 5, 1965, and in *Mystetstvo* [Art], No. 10, 1965.
51. *Fight and you shall conquer* (mosaic), 1964.
52. *The Prophet ("Will there be judgment . . .")* (mosaic), 1964-1965.
53. *Portrait of T. H. Shevchenko.*

II.

1. *Sunday in Vorokhta,* 1962, 130 x 170, exhibited in April 1962.
2. *Still life,* 1962, 71 x 55, exhibited in April 1962.
3. *Skiers in Vorokhta,* 1962, 80 x 50.5, exhibited in April 1962.
4. *Sunny day,* 1962, 50 x 47, exhibited in April 1962.
5. *Bright day.* Vorokhta, 1962, 50 x 47, exhibited in April 1962.
6. *In Vorokhta,* 1962, 51 x 36, exhibited in April 1962.
7. *Self-portrait,* 1962, 34.5 x 30, exhibited in April 1962.
8. *Meditation,* 1962, 50 x 71, exhibited in April 1962.
9. *By the gate,* 1962, 132 x 52, exhibited in April 1962.
10. *Still life with an apple,* 1962, 40 x 60, exhibited in April 1962.
11. *Etude,* 1962, 36 x 28, exhibited in April 1962.
12. *Apple tree in spring,* 1962, 32.5 x 49, exhibited in April 1962.
13. *Portrait of an old man,* 50.5 x 35, exhibited in April 1962.
14. *To Lenin,* 1961-1962, 182 x 425, exhibited in April 1962.
15. *In the Carpathians,* 1962, 35 x 50.5, exhibited in April 1962.

16. *Houses in Vorokhta*, 1962, 47 x 37, exhibited in April 1962.
17. *Grey day*, 1962, 35 x 50.5, exhibited in April 1962.
18. *Still life with a towel*, 1962, 51 x 57.5, exhibited in 1962.
19. *Portrait of a carpenter*, 1962, 48 x 33.5, exhibited in April 1962.
20. *In a hotel*, 1962, 35.5 x 46.5, exhibited in April of 1962.
21. (Portrait of Olena in black), autumn of 1962.
22. *Winter landscape*, was reproduced in the magazine *Zmina* No. 1, 1964.
23. (Secretary of the District Committee).
24. (Portrait of a Chekist).
25. *Portrait of artist Turets'ky.*
26. (Lenin with children).
27. *Re-united Ukraine*, triptych, exhibited at a zonal exhibition in L'viv.
28. *The weeders*, 1961-62, exhibited at a zonal exhibition in L'viv.
29. Shevchenko stained-glass panel in the Kiev State University (in collaboration with A. Hors'ka, L. Semykina, and H. Sevruk), which were destroyed in the spring of 1964. The sketch was reproduced in the *Ukrainian Calendar* for 1965 (Warsaw).
30. (The last chief of the Zaporozhian Sich, Kalnyshevsky).

*

Panas Zalyvakha, jointly with artist Figol', completed a number of works for the monumental decoration of Ivano-Frankivs'ke, namely mosaics in a store on Moscow Street, interior decorations in the restaurant "Kiev", foyer in the "Cosmos" theatre.

DRAWINGS

1. *Railway workers*, 1961, 40 x 72, lino-engraving, exhibited in April of 1962.
2. *In a dining room*, 1961, 40 x 72, lino-engraving, exhibited in April of 1962.

3. *Evening*, 1961, 57 x 41, lino-engraving, exhibited in April of 1962.
4. *Ivan Gonta.*[1]
5. *Guarding peace.*
6. (Shevchenko with a candlestick).
7. *The Prophet* (three versions, the last one in collaboration with A. Hors'ka). The first version was reproduced in the magazines *Vitchyzna* and *Zhovten'*, and in the newspaper *Moloda gvardiya* [The Young Guard].

*

P. Zalyvakha illustrated several books, especially for the Veselka Publishing House. The last work of this type was his illustration of the book, *Orphan's Fate* by Boleslaw Prus (Veselka, 1965).

---

[1] 18th century Cossack chieftain.